Climate Economics

Climate economics is in a state of flux. Older analyses, which often minimized the climate crisis and called for gradualism, have not vanished – but they increasingly share the stage with very different new approaches. The Stern Review led to an important but incomplete rethinking of climate economics, demonstrating that the benefits of rapid emission reduction could greatly outweigh the costs. Newer work at the frontiers of economic research continues to broaden and deepen our understanding of the dangers of inaction.

This book reviews the state of the art in climate economics, and in the science on which it rests. It covers the estimation of climate damages, an area where economic models lag far behind current empirical research. Recent work on uncertainty and catastrophic risk has challenged past approaches to climate policy, offering new decision rules for extreme uncertainty, and alternative weightings of worst-case scenarios. Longstanding debates on discount rates and intergenerational obligations have been transformed by perspectives from finance, ethics, and other fields. The applied policy debate rests on surprisingly subtle assumptions about mitigation costs and technologies, and on the largely unexplored economics of adaptation.

Important new research findings highlighted in *Climate Economics* include (among many others): projections that temperatures will not decline for centuries after CO_2 concentrations start to drop; new evidence on crop losses and temperature thresholds; Weitzman's "dismal theorem," paradoxically implying infinite benefits from emission reduction; arguments from finance theory calling for very low discount rates; the hidden role of oil price projections; and the limited extent of the much-discussed "rebound" effect. This book is an indispensible guide to recent developments in climate science and economics, and their effects on our understanding of climate risks and the necessary responses.

Frank Ackerman and **Elizabeth A. Stanton** are Senior Economists at Synapse Energy Economics in Cambridge, Massachusetts. At the time when this book was written, they worked at the Stockholm Environment Institute's U.S. Center.

Routledge studies in ecological economics

Climate Economics

The state of the art

**Frank Ackerman and
Elizabeth A. Stanton**

 Routledge
Taylor & Francis Group

LONDON AND NEW YORK

First published 2013
by Routledge
2 Park Square, Milton Park, Abingdon, Oxfordshire OX14 4RN

Simultaneously published in the USA and Canada
by Routledge
711 Third Avenue, New York, NY 10017

First issued in paperback 2014

Routledge is an imprint of the Taylor and Francis Group, an informa business

© 2013 Frank Ackerman and Elizabeth A. Stanton

The right of Frank Ackerman and Elizabeth A. Stanton to be identified as authors of this work has been asserted by them in accordance with the Copyright, Designs and Patent Act 1988.

All rights reserved. No part of this book may be reprinted or reproduced or utilized in any form or by any electronic, mechanical, or other means, now known or hereafter invented, including photocopying and recording, or in any information storage or retrieval system, without permission in writing from the publishers.

Trademark notice: Product or corporate names may be trademarks or registered trademarks, and are used only for identification and explanation without intent to infringe.

British Library Cataloguing in Publication Data
A catalogue record for this book is available from the British Library

Library of Congress Cataloging in Publication Data
Ackerman, Frank.
Climate economics : the state of the art / Frank Ackerman and Elizabeth A. Stanton.
    pages cm
    1. Climatic changes–Economic aspects. 2. Greenhouse gas mitigation–Economic aspects. I. Stanton, Elizabeth A. II. Title.
    QC903.A145 2013
    363.738'74–dc23   2012032409

ISBN 978-0-415-63718-3 (hbk)
ISBN 978-1-138-90143-8 (pbk)
ISBN 978-0-203-06631-7 (ebk)

Typeset in Times New Roman
by Wearset Ltd, Boldon, Tyne and Wear

Contents

Acknowledgments

In 2010, Pablo Gutman and David Reed, of the World Wildlife Fund (WWF), asked us to write a review of new developments in climate economics since the Stern Review. That request led to our report, released by World Wildlife Fund-U.S. and the Stockholm Environment Institute, covering the literature through the beginning of 2011. After the report appeared, Robert Langham at Routledge invited us to turn it into a book.

This book is an updated, expanded and reorganized outgrowth of the WWF report, now covering the relevant literature through mid-2012. We would like to thank the many people who helped us get to this point. Thanks to Alejandro Reuss, Aaron Strong, and Matthew Taylor for research and literature reviews, to Donna Au, Jeffry Cagan, and Ellen Fitzgerald for fact-checking, and to Marion Davis for copy-editing. Thanks also to the peer reviewers of the WWF report, William Cline, Steve DeCanio, Richard Howarth, Robert Litterman, and Rachel Warren. Thanks above all to Pablo Gutman and David Reed at WWF, and to Robert Langham at Routledge, for making it all possible.

Introduction

Climate science paints a bleak picture: the continued growth of greenhouse gas emissions is increasingly likely to cause irreversible and catastrophic effects. Urgent action is needed to prepare for the initial rounds of climatic change, which are already unstoppable. While the opportunity to avert all climate damage has now passed, well-designed mitigation and adaptation policies, if adopted quickly, could still greatly reduce the likelihood of the most tragic and far-reaching impacts of climate change.

Skeptics of this inconvenient truth have mounted incessant, well-funded attacks on the integrity of climate science – and have found only the occasional typographical errors in the research papers and reports that describe the threat of global warming. The challenge, therefore, is to align our understanding of the world, our priorities, and our recommendations for public policy with the disturbing state of the art in climate science.

Climate economics is the bridge between science and policy, translating scientific predictions about physical systems into projections about economic growth and human welfare that decision makers can most readily use. Regrettably, climate economics tends to lag behind climate science, especially in the slow-paced, peer-reviewed economics literature. The analyses rarely build on the most recent advances in climate science; instead, they often incorporate simplified representations of scientific knowledge that is out of date by several years, if not decades. Moreover, climate economics has often been hampered by its uncritical adoption of a traditional cost–benefit framework, minimizing or overlooking the deep theoretical problems posed by uncertainty, intergenerational impacts, and long-term technological change.

In late 2006, the Stern Review broke new ground by synthesizing the current knowledge in climate science and setting a new standard for climate-economics analysis, using up-to-date inputs from climate science, introducing a near-zero rate of pure time preference (thus increasing the importance of future generations' welfare in today's climate decisions), and going beyond the costs and benefits of best-guess climate impacts to look at lower-probability catastrophic outcomes. Then, in 2007, the Intergovernmental Panel on Climate Change (IPCC) published its Fourth Assessment Report (AR4), which provided an authoritative and detailed update on the state of climate science. Since these two landmark publications, some climate-economics models have taken Stern's work as a new benchmark. Others, however, still use outdated estimates of physical impacts, trivialize economic damages from climate change, and oversimplify the climate problem. As a result, these models – some of which have proven influential in the policy arena – continue to call for very gradual emissions mitigation.

Since 2007, both climate science and climate economics have advanced dramatically, partly in response to the well-publicized Stern Review. Scientific predictions have grown ever more ominous, with mounting evidence of near-term thresholds for irreversible catastrophes. The most likely outcomes are grave, even under scenarios of very ambitious emissions abatement. Limiting warming to 2°C, a widely embraced but challenging target, would still result in serious damages and require significant adaptation expenditures – and the much-discussed "2°C" scenarios, which strain the limits of political feasibility, offer only a high probability, not a guarantee, of meeting that temperature limit. In "business-as-usual" scenarios of future emissions without planned mitigation, the likely temperature increases would reach 4°C by the year 2100 if not sooner, and would continue to increase thereafter.

As climate science has matured, it has revealed a slew of complex, nonlinear interactions in the physical system that make it difficult to describe a complete set of consequences with certainty. Under business-as-usual emissions scenarios, catastrophic climate outcomes are all too possible, and they become ever more likely as temperatures rise. Even under rapid mitigation scenarios that offer a high probability of staying below 2°C, there is a chance of worse-than-expected temperature increases and outcomes; climate change is an enormous one-time gamble, a global science experiment that cannot be redone if we dislike the results. A precautionary approach to limiting climate damages would require that emissions be reduced as quickly as possible and that efforts be made to accelerate the rate at which greenhouse gases are removed from the atmosphere. As this review demonstrates, such a precautionary approach is entirely consistent with the latest developments in both the science and the economics of climate change.

Continuing improvement in climate economics is important, above all, because such great credence is given to economic analysis in the public arena. Quantitative analysis is often taken as proof of expertise. "Bottom line" conclusions from cost–benefit analyses are widely cited in policy debates – especially in the United States but in other countries as well. Traditional climate-economics analyses that are far behind the research frontier are thus used as arguments against the urgent warnings from climate science.

Climate economics must be aligned with climate science. The latest science shows that climate outcomes are intrinsically uncertain in detail but that catastrophic worst-case possibilities cannot be ruled out. It is not reasonable for an economic analysis of the same phenomenon to yield a single, definite, modest prediction of overall impacts. Rather, climate economics should have the same qualitative contours as climate science, with a range of irreducible economic uncertainty, including real risks of catastrophic losses.

Fortunately, as this book demonstrates, the latest developments in climate economics are moving in the right direction, presenting new insights into the unique theoretical and practical challenges posed by the problem of climate change.

The structure of this book: a preview

This book provides a synthesis of the current state of the art in climate economics (as of the middle of 2012). Its four parts address key findings from climate science as they affect economic analyses, new research on climate damages, recent developments in economic theory and modeling, and finally the economics of mitigation and adaptation.

Part I, "The science of climate change," reviews the current science of the physical processes of climate change. It places special emphasis on findings that are qualitatively different from those presented in the 2007 IPCC report – and puts these findings in the context of their importance in climate-economic analysis.

The single chapter in Part I – Chapter 1, "Climate science for economists" – begins by reviewing the latest forecasts for business-as-usual emission scenarios, and then turns to the scientific implications of such emissions. It covers areas in which there have been significant new findings since AR4, including the pace of emissions growth and temperature increases; the rate at which ice sheets, glaciers, ice caps, and sea ice are disappearing; current and future sea-level-rise rates; and "tipping points," or thresholds for irreversible change to climate and ecological systems. It also examines climate interactions and feedback loops, and the growing body of literature on regional heterogeneity in climate impacts. One finding from our review of the science literature is of particular importance to climate-economics modeling: new research demonstrates that in "overshoot" scenarios, where atmospheric CO_2 concentrations first exceed the long-run target and then decline, temperatures will remain close to their peak for centuries or even millennia.

Part II, "Climate damages," examines the analysis and modeling of the economic damages resulting from climate change. This is an area in which many economic models are notably inadequate, and where new research provides the basis for a much richer understanding of the problem.

Chapter 2, "Damage functions and climate impacts," reviews the treatment of climate damages in some of the well-known integrated assessment models (IAMs) of climate economics. Relatively aggregated damage estimates, often based on limited and dated empirical information, are frequently expressed in reduced form as a "damage function." For example, damages as a share of GDP are often expressed as a simple function of temperature, such as a polynomial fraction involving the square of the temperature increase. While the empirical information used to calibrate these functions is limited, the functional form is typically completely arbitrary. As some recent studies have shown, alternative functional forms would have very different implications.

Chapter 3, "Climate change impacts on natural systems," looks at new research on climate impacts to forests and fisheries, both of which are complex and not easily quantifiable. Climate change will have both negative and positive effects on forest growth, which, in turn, will have mixed effects on the climate. Recent studies suggest that tropical forest growth will slow warming, but boreal forest growth will accelerate it by reducing the albedo effect. New research also shows how great the ecosystem impacts of ocean warming and acidification will be, with the extinction of many coral and other species possible within this century. Marine species will also be moving toward the poles, reducing the fish catch in all but the highest latitudes.

Chapter 4, "Climate change impacts on human systems," begins with agriculture. New research on CO_2 fertilization and on the relationship between temperature and crop yields supports a much less optimistic outlook for global food production than was previously assumed. The chapter also looks at new models of sea-level rise, which predict serious impacts and permanent inundation of some coastal areas within this century, and important differences across regions. Projections of climate effects on human health and welfare have also become more negative, with higher temperatures, precipitation changes, and more intense weather patterns taking a heavy toll.

Part III, "Economic theories and models," details several transformative advances in the field. Climate change poses unique challenges to economic theory, requiring economists to delve into unfamiliar territory. Earlier analyses, some of which continue to influence public policy, often relied on traditional economic frameworks, leading to results that did not reflect the unique challenges of the climate crisis. Newer research uses different analytical approaches, especially related to the economics of uncertainty, discounting, and equity.

Chapter 5, "Climate economics before and after the Stern Review," looks at the treatment of uncertainty and discounting in climate economics before the Stern Review and at the innovations introduced by Stern. Previous economic models of climate change were typically framed as cost–benefit analyses, evaluating known or expected outcomes; in some cases, predictable, bounded variation was included via Monte Carlo analysis. Stern argued that economists must take the risk of catastrophic damages seriously, although he did not completely break with past modeling approaches. In discounting, the conventional wisdom implied that discount rates should be relatively high; Stern argued for a low discount rate, for ethical reasons, with a near-zero rate of pure time preference.

Chapter 6, "Uncertainty," takes an in-depth look at the economic implications of several dimensions of uncertainty. The probability distribution of potential climate outcomes is still an area of unsettled science; there are small but nontrivial probabilities of irreversible, catastrophic changes, with greater likelihood of these outcomes as temperatures rise. Long-term catastrophic risk is the subject of some of the most important recent developments in climate economics. The chapter looks at Weitzman's argument about unbounded risk arising from irreducible uncertainty about the pace of climate change, and at new frameworks for analyzing decision-making under uncertainty. It concludes with new interpretations of risk aversion and parallels to similar topics in finance.

Chapter 7, "Public goods and public policy," addresses the many reasons why climate policy choices should be made on a different basis from private investment decisions, including the intergenerational implications of climate policy, the "global public good" nature of the problem, and questions of equity within and between countries. These considerations have important implications for discounting and could lead to alternative decision-making criteria and policy frameworks. As an alternative to utility maximization, some economists have advocated a focus on avoiding the risks of possible climate catastrophes, an approach analogous to insurance against catastrophe. This approach starts by setting a threshold (e.g., a maximum temperature increase) necessary to avoid certain catastrophic damages (or keep their likelihood below a certain level) and then looks for the most cost-effective way to meet the standard.

The chapter ends by looking at different burden-sharing approaches that have been proposed to address equity issues in global climate negotiations, and then evaluating the prospects for international climate negotiations, which some economists have analyzed in terms of game theory and strategic interaction.

Part IV, "Mitigation and adaptation," reviews the principal policy responses to climate change, examining the technologies and the economics of mitigation and adaptation. There can be no solution to the climate crisis without rapid worldwide reduction of emissions, but debate continues about both the appropriate choice of technologies and the economic framework within which mitigation should be understood. Even with rapid mitigation, however, significant climate damages can no longer be avoided; adaptation to the early stages of climate change is a necessary complement to mitigation, although not a substitute for emission reduction.

Chapter 8, "Economics and the climate policy debate," explores the latest research and proposals on climate thresholds – drawing on the standards-based, or cost-effectiveness, approach. It describes a number of emissions scenarios consistent with a 50 percent or better chance of staying below the "2°C guard-rail." All of these scenarios require much more rapid abatement than is contemplated in current climate policies and agreements.

Chapter 9, "Technologies for mitigation," looks at recently proposed strategies for reducing emissions and even achieving negative net emissions by removing greenhouse gases from the atmosphere: from well-understood approaches such as improved energy efficiency, tree planting, and painting roofs and roadways white, to new ideas such as fertilizing the oceans so that they grow more carbon-sequestering algae, and larger-scale "geoengineering." The chapter also looks at the technology choices made in specific mitigation scenarios including those developed by the International Energy Agency and McKinsey & Company.

Chapter 10, "Economics of mitigation," reviews new approaches to mitigation in climate economics. Older models often overestimated the cost of mitigation, basing estimates on current costs of mitigation technology, or assumed that costs would decrease automatically over time, requiring no investments in innovation now to reap productivity gains in the future. New models are exploring ways to endogenize technological change, including important effects for "learning by doing." The chapter also looks at the impact of widely divergent assumptions about future oil prices, one of the leading determinants of abatement costs, and at controversies over the accuracy of negative abatement cost projections and over assumptions about the "rebound effect" in energy efficiency.

Even if the world acts promptly to reduce carbon emissions, it is expected that by 2100, temperatures will rise by another 0.1°C to 0.6°C, and sea levels by another 0.1 m to 0.3 m, with substantial impacts on vulnerable regions around the world. Chapter 11, "Adaptation," discusses different approaches to adaptation, which vary considerably across regions. We examine the interconnections among adaptation, mitigation, and development and their implications for economic modeling. This chapter also reviews recent modeling exercises in this relatively new field and concludes with an overview of estimates of the costs of climate adaptation. Despite the obvious importance of the topic, the extreme heterogeneity and site-specific nature of adaptation measures has thus far inhibited systematic economic analysis.

Finally, the brief "Conclusion" summarizes and draws out major implications of the book.

Part I

The science of climate change

1   Climate science for economists

Climate analysis requires an understanding of both economics and science. Climate science is a rapidly evolving field, rich with new areas of research, important advances that refine our understanding of well-established facts, and an increasing reliance on interdisciplinary approaches to complex research questions. Every few years, this body of knowledge is pulled together, subjected to additional layers of peer review, and published in Assessment Reports by the Intergovernmental Panel on Climate Change (IPCC). The latest of these – the *Fourth Assessment Report* (AR4) – was released in 2007 (IPCC 2007b), reflecting the peer-reviewed research literature through 2006. The next IPCC Assessment is expected in 2013–14.

The process of predicting future economic impacts from climate change and deciding how best to react to those impacts begins with estimates of the baseline, or business-as-usual, future world economy and the quantity of greenhouse gas emissions that it is likely to release. Climate scientists build on these economic projections, combining them with records of past climatic changes and the most up-to-date knowledge about the climate system, to predict future atmospheric concentrations of greenhouse gases, temperature increases, and other climatic changes. These projections of the future climate system are used to estimate the type and magnitude of impacts expected in terms of physical and biological processes, such as changes to water availability, sea levels, or ecosystem viability. Economic modeling places monetary values both on measures that would reduce greenhouse gas emissions and thereby avoid climate damages (the costs of mitigation) and on the physical damages that are avoided (the benefits of mitigation). Comparisons of climate costs and benefits are offered to policy makers to support recommendations of the best actions to take.

Each step in this process – from baseline economic projections to climate policy recommendations – adds more uncertainty, which is a central theme of this book. We begin with a review of the current state of the art in climate science as it relates to economic modeling. After a brief discussion of forecasts for business-as-usual (no mitigation) emissions, we review the latest projections of the future climate and the expected impacts to natural and human systems. We summarize climate system projections and impacts both in terms of the most likely, "best guess" prediction, and less probable, but still possible, worst case (at times, catastrophic) predictions. Later chapters of this book discuss techniques for economic impact assessment, as well as the estimation of costs of mitigation and adaptation under conditions of uncertainty.

Business-as-usual emissions

Baseline, or business-as-usual, emission scenarios do not plan for greenhouse gas mitigation. These projections are sensitive to assumptions about population and economic growth, innovation and investment in energy technologies, and fuel supply and choice. Projections of baseline emissions for future years vary widely. The most optimistic business-as-usual scenarios assume significant reductions over time in carbon emissions per unit of energy and in energy use per dollar of output, together with slow population growth and slow economic development. These scenarios project atmospheric concentrations of CO_2 as low as 500–600 ppm in 2100 – up from just above 390 ppm CO_2 today.[1] Pessimistic business-as-usual scenarios project much more rapid growth of global emissions over time, with CO_2 concentrations reaching 900–1,100 ppm by 2100. Recent research, however, suggests that parameters commonly used to link concentrations to emissions may be mis-specified; the fraction of CO_2 emissions sequestered in land and ocean sinks may be shrinking in response to climate change, suggesting that atmospheric concentrations would be higher at every level of emissions.

In this book, we will refer to a range of business-as-usual scenarios projecting from 540 to 940 ppm in 2100; these endpoints are chosen to match two of the Representative Concentration Pathways, RCP 8.5 and RCP 4.5, that will be used as part of a set of central emissions scenarios in AR5, the next IPCC Assessment Report.[2] These scenarios may be compared to those presented in the IPCC's *Special Report on Emissions Scenarios* (SRES; Nakicenovic *et al.* 2000).

- RCP 8.5 was developed using the MESSAGE model. This scenario reaches 540 ppm CO_2 in 2050 and 936 ppm CO_2 in 2100 (or 1,231 ppm CO_2-equivalent [CO_2-e] in 2100, including measures of all climate "forcing" agents). By 2060, it exceeds 560 ppm CO_2, or double the preindustrial concentration – a much-discussed milestone related to the rate of temperature change. Emissions in RCP 8.5 are similar to those of the SRES A1FI scenario, used in previous IPCC Assessment Reports. In the RCP 8.5 scenario, CO_2 emissions grow from 37 Gt CO_2 in 2010 to 107 Gt CO_2 in 2100.
- RCP 4.5 was developed using the MiniCAM model. It reaches 487 ppm CO_2 in 2050 and 538 ppm CO_2 in 2100 (or 580 ppm CO_2-e in 2100); in this scenario, concentrations stabilize before exceeding 560 ppm CO_2. Emissions in RCP 4.5 are similar to those of the SRES B1 scenario, with emissions peaking between 2040 and 2050 and falling to 16 Gt CO_2 in 2100 – a 43 percent decrease from 1990 emissions (a common benchmark). The RCP 4.5 scenario requires substantial use of carbon capture and storage technology (see Chapter 9) and energy efficiency measures; coal use falls significantly,

while biomass, natural gas, and nuclear energy grow in importance.[3] Clearly, this scenario involves investments that have the effect of reducing emissions, but it does not necessarily involve *planned* mitigation with the purpose of reducing greenhouse gas emissions.

Table 1.1 compares the RCP concentration projections to those of SRES, as well as to business-as-usual projections from a recent Energy Modeling Forum (EMF) meta-analysis[4] and from *Energy Technology Perspectives 2008*, published by the International Energy Agency (IEA).[5] RCP 8.5 falls in the upper half of EMF baseline scenarios, while RCP 3-PD is more optimistic than any EMF projection. IEA projections extend only to 2050 and exceed those of RCP 8.5 for that year.

Climate projections and uncertainty

AR4 found unequivocal evidence of global warming and rising sea levels (IPCC 2007c, *Synthesis Report*) and reported a very high confidence that these changes are the result of anthropogenic greenhouse gas emissions. The report also found it likely (with a probability greater than 66 percent) that heat waves and severe precipitation events have become more frequent over the past 50 years. Even if further emissions were halted, great inertia in the climate system would mean that the earth was "locked in" to several centuries of warming and several millennia of sea-level rise (although at a far slower pace and less extreme endpoints than would occur with additional emissions). Continuing the current trend of emissions could lead to abrupt or irreversible changes to the climate system.

Table 1.1 Business-as-usual emissions scenarios

Scenario	CO_2 concentration (ppm)		Year exceeding 560 ppm CO_2
	2050	*2100*	
RCP 8.5	540	936	2060
RCP 6.0	478	670	2080
RCP 4.5	487	538	NA
RCP 3-PD	443	421	NA
SRES A1FI	561	964	2050
SRES A2	527	846	2060
SRES A1B	527	710	2060
SRES B2	476	616	2090
SRES A1T	499	579	2080
SRES B1	485	545	NA
EMF baseline: highest	571	1,030	2050
EMF baseline: mean	522	782	2060
EMF baseline: lowest	499	612	2080
IEA 2008 baseline	550	NA	NA

Sources: see text.

Although it lags behind the most current research, AR4 is the standard reference for the field. In 2009, the University of New South Wales Climate Change Research Centre (CCRC) published a comprehensive review of the literature released since the close-off for material included in AR4 (Allison, Bindoff, *et al.* 2009).[6] CCRC emphasizes several areas of research in which there have been significant new findings:

- Greenhouse gas emissions and global temperatures are following the highest scenarios (A1F1) considered in AR4. Recent CO_2 emissions have been growing three times faster than they were in the 1990s.[7]
- The rate at which ice sheets, glaciers, ice caps, and sea ice are disappearing has accelerated.
- The current rate of sea-level rise was underestimated in AR4, as were projections of future sea-level rise.
- Critical thresholds for irreversible change to climate and ecological systems are both imminent and difficult to predict with accuracy. There is a risk of crossing these tipping points before they are recognized.
- A two-thirds chance of avoiding a 2°C increase in global temperatures above preindustrial levels – the now-ubiquitous benchmark for avoiding dangerous climate change, found in both the science and policy literatures – will require that by 2050, emissions be reduced by 80 to 100 percent from their 2005 levels, depending on the year in which emissions peak.

The remaining sections of this chapter focus on several areas where advances since AR4 seem especially salient, including literature published through mid-2012. Of course, new research has been published in all areas of science over the past five years, but not all scientific findings overturn or qualitatively change previous results; many advance their field by making small improvements in accuracy or precision, confirming earlier findings, or ruling out counterfactuals. In our assessment, areas in which new findings represent a change to older research or an otherwise significant advance in our understanding of the climate system include:

- albedo changes and carbon-cycle feedbacks involving clouds, aerosols, and black carbon;
- sensitivity of temperature to the atmospheric concentration of greenhouse gases;
- the frequency and intensity of severe weather;
- downscaling of precipitation forecasts;
- alternatives to AR4's sea-level-rise projections;
- the unforeseen pace of sea ice loss.

To CCRC's assessment of the most important themes in contemporary climate science we add three more, discussed in detail below:

1   The climate system is complex and nonlinear. Interactions and feedback loops abound, and newer work demonstrates that studies of isolated effects can lead to missteps, confusing a single action in a greater process with the complete, global result.

2   "Overshooting" of global average temperatures is now thought to be irreversible on a timescale of several millennia. Once temperature reaches a peak, it is likely to remain at that level for millennia, even if atmospheric concentrations of greenhouse gases are reduced.

3   Climate impacts will not be globally uniform. Regional heterogeneity is a strong theme in the new literature, shifting findings and research methods in every subfield of climate science.

A complex truth

Many areas of the science of our climate system are well understood. Increased concentrations of greenhouse gases in the atmosphere are amplifying the sun's ability to warm the earth, changing precipitation levels and other weather patterns, causing sea levels to rise, and decreasing pH levels in the oceans. A strong scientific foundation, however, does not always lead to precise forecasts of climate outcomes. While the larger relationship among greenhouse gas emissions, global temperatures, and sea levels is clear, the field is challenged by the call from economists and policy makers for greater precision in modeling future climate impacts. Climate dynamics are rarely simple or linear, and long temporal lags complicate both modeling efforts and popular perceptions of the humans role in causing – and stopping – climate change. In many regions around the world, the present-day effects of CO_2 and other greenhouse gas emissions are unobservable, and year-to-year variability in weather obscures longer-term climatic shifts. Feedback mechanisms, both physical and biological, are of great importance in the work of reducing uncertainty in climate projections.

Evidence has grown, in recent literature, of tipping points, or critical thresholds, for important components of the earth's physical and ecological systems. Once these thresholds have been passed, the effects on global systems may not be instantaneous, but they will be world-changing and irreversible on a timescale of many centuries or millennia. A threshold of a 0.5 to 2°C global average temperature increase above 1990 levels (a range beginning well below the commonly cited but imprecise 2°C target for avoiding dangerous climate damages) will likely signal an end to Arctic summer sea ice and an eventual collapse of the Greenland Ice Sheet. At 3 to 4°C, the Amazon rainforest could begin a permanent dieback. At 3 to 5°C, West African monsoon circulation could be interrupted, the West Antarctic ice sheet could start a gradual collapse, and the Atlantic thermohaline circulation could be significantly disrupted. At 3 to 6°C, the El Niño-Southern Oscillation effects could become more severe. Many of these impacts would have important feedback effects on the climate system (Lenton *et al.* 2008).

It is also widely recognized that some level of climate change is now irreversible. Even if all greenhouse gas emissions were halted today, by 2100 global mean temperatures would rise by another 0.1°C to 0.6°C (above year 2000 levels), and sea levels would rise (above 1990 levels) by another 0.1 to 0.3 m from the slow, implacable process of thermal ocean expansion, plus an uncertain additional amount up to 0.1 m in this century, as land ice continues to melt in response to the global temperature increase that has already taken place (Wigley 2005).

As emissions continue, further temperature increases are now thought, likewise, to be irreversible. Global average temperatures over the next millennia will be strongly determined by peak atmospheric CO_2 concentrations; that is, temperatures will plateau even as greenhouse gas concentrations fall (Solomon, Plattner *et al.* 2009; Gillett *et al.* 2011; Matthews and Caldeira 2008).[8] This important new finding suggests that under emissions scenarios that involve "overshoot" (exceeding target concentrations with the goal of soon dropping back to lower levels), the climate will "remember" the overshoot rather than the eventual target for centuries to come.[9] Using a common assumption about climate sensitivity (the relationship between concentration and temperature, discussed below), if concentrations peak at 450 ppm CO_2, temperature will plateau having increased by about 0.9°C; for a 650 ppm peak, 1.8°C; for 850 ppm, 2.7°C; and for 1,200 ppm, 4.2°C.[10]

Finally, since the publication of AR4 (2007b), great strides have been made in improving climatic projections. A central theme in this new literature is the heterogeneity of regional impacts. Global average temperature change and sea-level rise are still good shorthand indicators for the overall sign and scale of the problem, but they do not reflect the regional magnitude of temperature and sea-level changes, nor do they comprise the full extent of expected climate change. Physical and biological feedback processes will translate global warming into regionally specific changes in precipitation and in storm frequency and/or intensity, and far-reaching changes to ecological systems.

This chapter describes several dynamic areas of research that are pushing climate science toward a more complex assessment of future impacts, with greater regional specificity and an enhanced appreciation of both global and regional interdependency of climate, atmosphere, ocean, terrestrial, and ecological systems. We discuss recent advances in the study of clouds, aerosols, and black carbon; carbon-cycle feedbacks; climate sensitivity; storm patterns; precipitation; sea-level rise; and sea ice. Throughout, our review of key advances in climate science underscores the essential role that the incorporation of uncertainty plays in research efforts throughout the field. Thus we summarize advances in climate system research in terms of both the most likely impacts of continued business-as-usual emissions, and the catastrophes that could occur with low but still important probabilities.

Clouds, aerosols, and black carbon

The impact of anthropogenic emissions on global temperatures is often discussed in terms of "radiative forcing" – the changes that greenhouse gases make to the global balance of energy, measured in incoming solar energy per unit of surface area as watts per square meter (W/m^2). On the whole, the relationship between greenhouse gases (CO_2, methane, nitrous oxide, and a host of gases with smaller effects) and global average temperature increase is well established, but several ancillary effects introduce uncertainty, among them feedback from cloud albedo, reflectivity of aerosols and their role in cloud formation, and radiation absorbed by black carbon.[11]

Cloud albedo

Clouds reflect some solar radiation away from the earth's atmosphere. Compared to many other surfaces, clouds have a relatively high albedo, defined as the fraction of incoming solar energy reflected back into space. Rising temperatures have two opposite feedback effects on cloud cover, and hence on additional warming. Higher sea-surface temperatures result in more evaporation and more clouds, increasing the albedo effect and reducing warming, as radiation reflects off the light-colored surface of clouds. At the same time, warmer temperatures can increase the likelihood of precipitation and cloud dissipation, revealing darker (lower-albedo) land and water below and increasing the absorption of solar radiation.

Current models differ regarding the net impact of cloud feedbacks on radiative forcing. A recent review of the literature found that the general circulation models that best predict the seasonality of Arctic cloud cover over the last half-century project that rising greenhouse gas emissions and global temperatures will increase the region's cloud cover (Vavrus *et al.* 2008). Another study using a different methodology, however, suggests the opposite effect: that rising temperatures will lead to reduced cloud cover (Clement *et al.* 2009). New research reveals the heterogeneity of cloud albedo impacts both regionally and seasonally, dynamics that will have important effects on the design of future studies (Balachandran and Rajeevan 2007; Vavrus *et al.* 2008; Clement *et al.* 2009).

Aerosols

Small particles in the atmosphere called aerosols (some of which result from the burning of fossil fuels and biomass) have two effects on radiative forcing. Aerosols, like clouds, reflect solar radiation away from the earth's atmosphere. They also can act as cloud condensation nuclei that encourage the formation of clouds. Recent studies show these effects to be highly regionalized, because local atmospheric pollution is an important predictor of cloud formation and precipitation (Solomon, Daniel *et al.* 2011; Sorooshian *et al.* 2009), and suggest flaws in previous research techniques that inaccurately modeled radiative forcing from partly cloudy conditions as the average of clear and overcast conditions (Charlson *et al.* 2007).[12]

AR4 estimates current anthropogenic radiative forcing at +1.6 (90 percent confidence interval: +0.6, –2.4) W/m^2, including $-0.5 \pm 0.4\,W/m^2$ from the direct (that is, excluding cloud-formation) effects of aerosols (IPCC 2007e, *Working Group I*, Chapter 2).[13] A study by Myhre (2009) updates aerosols' direct effect to -0.3 ± 0.2 W/m^2, a decrease in their expected cooling that drives up overall radiative forcing to $+1.8$ W/m^2.

Black carbon

The direct impacts of aerosols on radiative forcing include both negative and positive effects. Most atmospheric aerosols reflect solar energy, but a few, most importantly black carbon (soot), absorb it. Aerosols' direct effect of -0.50 ± 0.40 W/m^2, as reported by AR4, included $+0.20 \pm 0.15$ W/m^2 from atmospheric black carbon. In addition, total anthropogenic radiative forcing was estimated to include an additional $+0.10 \pm 0.10$ W/m^2 from the reduction in albedo caused by soot deposited on snow and ice surfaces (IPCC 2007e, *Working Group I*, Chapter 2).

Ramanathan and Carmichael (2008) review updated estimates of atmospheric black carbon's impact on radiative forcing, presenting a new central value of $+0.9$ (-0.5, $+0.3$) W/m^2, more than half of total anthropogenic effects. With the exception of CO_2, black carbon has a larger radiative forcing than any greenhouse gas, aerosol, or albedo effect, although its persistence in the atmosphere is measured in weeks, as compared to decades or centuries for many greenhouse gases (Ramanathan and Carmichael 2008).[14] The range of possible impacts from soot is wide, due to the regionalized effects of weather and the presence of other pollutants (Moffet and Prather 2009; Ramana *et al.* 2010), as well as the vertical distribution of black carbon in the atmosphere (Zarzycki and Bond 2010). Black carbon deposited on Himalayan glaciers is accelerating the rate at which the glaciers melt, reducing long-run water availability (Xu *et al.* 2009).

New research is investigating the impact of black carbon on precipitation (Pendergrass and Hartmann 2012; Frieler *et al.* 2011), and the relationship between the altitude of black carbon and its effect on radiative forcing and precipitation (Ban-Weiss *et al.* 2011). Updated values for black carbon's snow albedo effect reduce AR4 estimates to $+0.05$ (90 percent confidence interval: $+0.01$, -0.12) W/m^2, with some variation related to the extent of boreal forest fires in a given year (Flanner *et al.* 2007). Some researchers trace black carbon on snow to fossil fuels burned in eastern North America and in Asia over time (McConnell *et al.* 2007). Others report that nine-tenths of Arctic black carbon on snow results from combined natural and anthropogenic biomass burning (Hegg *et al.* 2009).[15]

Carbon-cycle feedbacks

Some of the least-understood feedback effects to the climate system may have large and far-reaching results. Among these are complex biological interactions among soil, vegetation, and climate systems. Warming temperatures will release greenhouse gases now locked away in frozen sediments below the oceans and in the permafrost soils of the tundra and boreal forest ecosystems. Forest systems sequester carbon, reducing atmospheric concentrations, but this storage is both sped up by carbon fertilization and disrupted by wildfires and forest dieback. Forest albedo is an additional countervailing force – carbon fertilization results in more carbon sequestration but also more dark surface areas that absorb more radiation; the net effect of forest feedbacks varies by latitude, as explained in Chapter 3. One study reports that negative carbon-cycle feedback – the uptake of carbon by land and ocean – is four times greater than is positive feedback but far more uncertain (Gregory *et al.* 2009).

Oceanic sedimentary deposits

Deep-sea sediments hold between 1,600 and 2,000 Gt of carbon in methane hydrates, hundreds of times the annual mass of anthropogenic carbon released into the atmosphere each year (net emissions amount to 4.1 Gt C per year[16]). With 3°C of warming, 35 to 940 Gt C are expected to be slowly released from this reserve as methane, depending on the behavior of the gas bubbles as they pass through additional layers of sediment on their way to the surface. Shallow ocean deposits are particularly unstable; even a 1.0°C change in ocean temperature could trigger a significant release of deposits (Moridis and Reagan 2009). Here there is an unfortunate positive feedback: while warming leads to potential releases of methane hydrates, those releases lead to even more warming. Models project that 450–600 Gt C releases of methane hydrate deposits would lead to an additional 0.4–0.5°C of warming (Archer *et al.* 2009).

Approximately 540 Gt of carbon lying under a layer of permafrost beneath the Arctic Ocean was thought, until recently, to be extremely stable. New research shows that the Arctic Ocean floor is currently venting methane hydrates and finds an abrupt release of as much as 50 Gt C highly possible – an amount twelve times greater than the current annual emissions of all greenhouse gases (Shakhova *et al.* 2010; Shakhova *et al.* 2008).

Methane released from soils

Still more carbon is stored in terrestrial soil, although the net effects of climate change on these deposits is uncertain. Climate change may facilitate removal of carbon from the atmosphere by some types of plants and sequestration in soil; conversely, decomposition of organic matter is accelerated by warming, thereby releasing greenhouse gases back into the air (Davidson and Janssens 2006; Khvorostyanov, Krinner, *et al.* 2008; Khvorostyanov, Ciais, *et al.* 2008). The northern permafrost region accounts for 16 percent of the world's soil area and contains 50 percent of the world's below-ground carbon (Tarnocai *et al.* 2009). In a recent paper, O'Donnell *et al.* (2010) discuss the complex interactions among temperature, precipitation, snow cover, and wildfire in determining the rate of release of carbon from frozen soils in the boreal region. Schuur *et al.* (2009) find that in the long run, thawing permafrost releases more carbon than plant growth absorbs, suggesting that this source may generate significant carbon emissions with climate change, perhaps as much as the current release of carbon from land-use changes (1.5 ± 0.5 Gt C per year).

Small temperature increases also have a much larger effect on CO_2 emissions from Arctic peatlands than previously thought. Under experimental conditions, annual CO_2 emissions accelerated by 50 to 60 percent with just 1°C of warming due to enhanced respiration of peat deposits – results that are consistent with annual emissions of 38–100 Mt of carbon (Dorrepaal *et al.* 2009). Nitrous oxide emissions from permafrost are an additional source of global warming potential that is still under study (Repo *et al.* 2009). Studies also show that methane is released from wetlands with warming. Predictions for methane emissions increase by 30 to 40 percent when feedback from warming is included in model assumptions (Eliseev *et al.* 2008; Volodin 2008).

Forest feedback effects

Positive and negative feedbacks of climate change on forests, and of forests on climate change, are discussed in detail in Chapter 3. As explained there, increased CO_2 concentrations accelerate tree growth, especially in young trees, but the higher temperatures and changes in precipitation projected with climate change are expected to increase tree mortality in many regions as a result of more frequent wildfires, among other effects. In the Amazon, negative impacts from climate change are expected to dwarf positive effects; a recent study suggests that the threshold temperature for permanent loss of the Amazon forest may be as low as 2°C. Forests impact climate change via carbon sequestration, changes in the evaporative cooling caused by forests, and variations in albedo (where deforestation leads to higher albedo and afforestation leads to lower). Net forest feedback is expected to be negative (reducing warming) for tropical afforestation, neutral for temperate forests, and positive (increasing warming) for boreal forests.

Climate sensitivity

The strength of the basic "greenhouse effect," together with the feedback effects of clouds, aerosols, and other factors, can be expressed in terms of the "climate sensitivity parameter," defined as the equilibrium global average temperature increase caused by a doubling of the atmospheric concentration of CO_2. The climate sensitivity parameter, essentially a gauge of the expected severity of climate change, plays a central role in the economic analysis of climate uncertainty, as seen in Chapter 6.

An important recent paper shows that uncertainty about climate sensitivity is an unavoidable consequence of the nature of the climate system itself, suggesting that further research might not be able to significantly narrow the distribution of climate sensitivity estimates (Roe and Baker 2007; see also Roe and Armour 2011). The direct effect of greenhouse gases, with no feedback effects, would lead to climate sensitivity of about 1.2°C. Temperature increases, however, cause positive feedback, amplifying the direct effect.

If a temperature increase of ΔT causes positive feedback of $f\Delta T$, where $0 < f < 1$, then there is a secondary positive feedback of $f^2 \Delta T$, and so on; the ultimate temperature effect is the direct effect ΔT multiplied by $1/(1-f)$. Thus $1/(1-f)$ is the climate sensitivity parameter. As f approaches 1, small uncertainties in f translate into large uncertainties in $1/(1-f)$ and hence into climate sensitivity. A similar logic implies irreducible uncertainty in complex, positive-feedback systems in general; the earth's climate may be the most important example (Roe 2009).[17] Climate sensitivity estimates may therefore be inescapably uncertain, implying a probability distribution with "fat tails" – i.e., with relatively large chances of extreme values.

Since AR4, some studies have widened the distribution of climate sensitivity estimates, and almost all studies have pushed the estimated distribution to the right, toward higher climate sensitivities. AR4 gave a likely (two-thirds probability) range of climate sensitivity as 2.0 to 4.5°C, with a most likely value of 3.0°C (IPCC 2007e, *Working Group I*, Chapter 10.2).[18] Newer studies show a range (90 percent probability) of climate sensitivity of 1.5 to 6.2°C (Hegerl *et al.* 2006; Royer *et al.* 2007) and suggest that climate sensitivity may vary over time (Williams *et al.* 2008).

One analysis of the paleoclimatic record supports a long-run climate sensitivity of 6°C, doubling the most likely estimate presented in AR4. According to this study, slow climate feedbacks related to ice loss, changes in vegetation, and greenhouse gases released from soil and ocean sediments, which are not included in most general circulation models, could have important temperature effects on a timescale of centuries or less (Hansen *et al.* 2008). Other paleoclimatic research has found that the data support both higher (Pagani *et al.* 2009) and lower (Schmittner *et al.* 2011) estimates of long-run climate sensitivity.[19]

Our review of this literature suggests that at present there is no single distribution of climate sensitivities that can be identified as the new norm; climate sensitivity research is still in flux, and markedly different distributions are being employed by different researchers. Two analyses of the climate sensitivity distribution warrant special mention:

- The Murphy *et al.* (2004) distribution has a median value of 3.5°C and a 5th to 95th percentile range of 2.4 to 5.4°C. This distribution does not incorporate the latest findings on the probability of very low and very high climate sensitivities, but it is the distribution used – in combination with uncertainty distributions for ocean vertical diffusivity and temperature/carbon-cycle feedback amplification – in Bernie's (2010) analysis of the temperature implications of the AR5 RCP emission scenarios discussed above.
- Roe and Baker (2007) explore a range of recently published climate sensitivity distributions – including Murphy *et al.* (2004) – and offer a generalized function with two free parameters that can be chosen to provide a good fit to most recent distributions.[20] Roe and Baker incorporate evidence from

newer studies of the climate sensitivity distribution, suggesting a greater probability of higher values.

Climate sensitivity is the key link between greenhouse gas emissions and most climate damages. Current CO_2 concentrations are above 390 ppm, up from 280 ppm in preindustrial times.[21] Business-as-usual emission scenarios vary greatly: projected baseline CO_2 concentrations for the year 2100 range from 540 ppm under the RCP 4.5 scenario to 940 ppm under RCP 8.5. (When a full suite of radiative forcing agents is included, these levels correspond to 580 and 1,230 ppm of CO_2-e in 2100.) The temperature increases caused by these concentrations depend on the unknown – and perhaps unknowable – level of climate sensitivity, several other less-studied and uncertain parameters (including ocean vertical diffusivity and temperature/carbon-cycle feedback amplification), and the time lag before temperatures approach the equilibrium level associated with changes in atmospheric CO_2.[22]

According to Bernie (2010), the array of temperature increases consistent with this range of business-as-usual concentration projections is 2.3 to 7.1°C (from the 10th to the 90th percentile of combined probabilities across three uncertain parameters). At the 50th percentile of the uncertainty distribution, the mean temperature change across these two scenarios is 4.2°C. At the high end of business-as-usual emissions scenarios, there is a near-zero chance of staying below an increase of 3°C and a 6 percent chance of staying below 4°C; using the lowest baseline scenario, with a 43 percent decrease from 1990 CO_2 emissions by 2100, there is a 4 percent chance of staying below an increase of 2°C, a 53 percent chance of staying below 3°C, and an 88 percent chance of staying below 4°C. And the peak temperatures, once reached, might not fall for millennia, even with dramatic decreases in CO_2 concentrations (Solomon *et al.* 2009; Gillett *et al.* 2011).

Storm patterns

Another ongoing debate in climate science regards the projected effects of greenhouse gas emissions on hurricanes (tropical cyclones). AR4 found it likely (with a two-thirds probability) that there would be an increase in the lifetime and intensity of hurricanes with climate change, and that it is possible that their frequency would decrease (IPCC 2007e, *Working Group I*, Technical Summary and Chapter 3.8).[23] Some studies find that hurricane frequency, too, will increase as sea-surface temperatures rise (Nigam and Guan 2010; Mann and Emanuel 2006; Knutson *et al.* 2008; Elsner *et al.* 2008; Wang and Lee 2009; Yu and Wang 2009; Mann *et al.* 2009). Others find that hurricane frequency may diminish or remain unchanged, even as hurricane wind speed becomes more intense (Wang and Lee 2008; Emanuel *et al.* 2008; Barsugli 2009).[24]

A clear anthropogenic signal has been identified in the factors influencing changes in precipitation extremes (Min *et al.* 2008), but research continues on the causes of and regional variations in tropical cyclone formation in the Atlantic,

Pacific, and Indian oceans. Some studies find sea-surface temperatures to be the best predictor of hurricane formation (Zhang and Delworth 2009), while others point to vertical shear from increased radiative forcing (Kim *et al.* 2009). The mechanisms causing increased hurricane intensity are also a source of some dispute. Climate-change-induced shifts in the location of hurricane formation may increase the length of storms tracks over the open ocean and allow more time for storms to absorb energy before striking land (Wu and Wang 2008). Changing sea-surface temperatures also have the potential to shift the historical tracks of typhoons (Colbert and Soden 2012; Wang *et al.* 2011).

Like hurricanes, South Asian monsoons are likely to increase in intensity with climate change. Monsoon weather has become less predictable over the past few decades (Kumar *et al.* 2010; Mani *et al.* 2009; Turner and Slingo 2009); warmer sea-surface temperatures have been linked to the increased intensity and reduced predictability of the monsoon in the Indian Ocean near Australia (Taschetto *et al.* 2009). A thermal gradient caused by seasonal effects of black carbon – the "Asian brown cloud" – causes stronger precipitation, an additional source of changes to monsoon weather (Meehl *et al.* 2008; Wang *et al.* 2009). The ongoing departure of monsoons from their past pattern could reach the point of an abrupt transition from weak seasonal rainfall to episodic violent storms as a result of a threshold effect in radiative forcing (Levermann *et al.* 2009).

Precipitation

New "downscaled" models couple global general circulation models together with regional climate models to produce climate projections at a finer geographic resolution. Refinements to regional downscaling techniques now make it possible to approximate future climate impacts on a smaller geographic scale. Since AR4, the trend toward regional downscaling of global climate models has accelerated, especially with regard to hydrological cycles and interactions between human and natural systems. Climate forecasts remain more reliable for larger areas; nonetheless, temperature and precipitation predictions are now presented at ever-finer levels of spatial resolution. This literature is extensive, and the review presented here is therefore illustrative rather than comprehensive.

Overall, warming is increasing the atmosphere's capacity to hold water, resulting in increases in extreme precipitation events (Min *et al.* 2011). Recent regionalized findings support and extend a more general finding of AR4: both observational data and modeling projections show that with climate change, wet regions will generally (but not universally) become wetter, and dry regions will become drier (Sanderson *et al.* 2011; John *et al.* 2009). Perceptible changes in annual precipitation are likely to appear in many areas later in this century (Mahlstein *et al.* 2012). The first regions expected to undergo significant precipitation changes, in the next few decades, are the Arctic, the Mediterranean, and eastern Africa. Important changes to average annual precipitation may next appear in eastern and southern Asia and the Caribbean, followed, in the later decades of the twenty-first century, by southern Africa, the western United

States, the Amazon Basin, southern Australia, and Central America (Giorgi and Bi 2009). By 2099, hydrological effects, coupled with albedo effects of changes in vegetation, are projected to increase the global area of "warm desert" by 34 percent above 1901 levels, mostly through expansion of the Sahara and other existing deserts (Zeng and Yoon 2009).

With 2°C of warming, dry-season precipitation is expected to decrease by 20 percent in northern Africa, southern Europe, and western Australia, and by 10 percent in the southwestern United States and Mexico, eastern South America, and northern Africa, by 2100 (Giorgi and Bi 2009).[25] In the Sahel area of Africa, the timing of critical rains will shift, shortening the growing season (Biasutti and Sobel 2009), and more extensive periods of drought may result as temperatures rise (Lu 2009).[26] In the Haihe River basin of northern China, projections call for less total rainfall but more extreme weather events (Chu *et al.* 2009). In the United States, there is a strong relationship between higher temperatures and lower precipitation levels, especially in the South (Portmann *et al.* 2009). Recent research on the United States highlights another key finding related to regional downscaling: Land-use changes – affecting vegetation and soil moisture, along with a concurrent release of aerosols – impact both precipitation levels and the incidence of extreme weather events (Portmann *et al.* 2009; Diffenbaugh 2009; Leung and Qian 2009).

Sea-level rise

For most areas of research, AR4 represented the best in scientific knowledge as of 2006, but sea-level-rise projections are an exception. The AR4 projections of 0.18 to 0.38 m of sea-level rise in the twenty-first century under B1, the lowest-emission SRES scenario, and 0.26 to 0.59 m under the highest-emission A1FI scenario are widely viewed as too conservative (Rahmstorf 2007; Overpeck and Weiss 2009; Allison, Bindoff, *et al.* 2009).[27] In making these projections, the IPCC chose to leave out feedback processes related to ice melt, citing uncertainty of values in the published literature – a decision that essentially negates the contribution of melting ice sheets to future sea-level rise. The net contribution of the polar ice sheets is near zero in AR4, with Greenland melting balanced out by greater snowfall in Antarctica (IPCC 2007e, *Working Group I*, Chapter 10.6). The AR4 sea-level-rise projections are consistent with the assumption that the aggregate mass of ice sheets will not change as global temperatures grow warmer.

Research since the publication of AR4 indicates that the rate of sea-level rise over the past four decades has been faster than was formerly assumed and that an improved understanding of melting ice has an essential role in informing sea-level-rise projections. New, more refined estimates show that global average sea levels rose at a rate of 1.5±0.4 mm per year from 1961 to 2003 (Domingues *et al.* 2008), including a greater contribution of melting land ice than in previous estimates.[28] Four-fifths of current annual sea-level rise is a result of melting ice sheets and glaciers (Cazenave *et al.* 2009).[29] In addition, a recent study reports that even with far more rapid reductions in greenhouse gas emissions than thought possible – including measures to remove CO_2 from the atmosphere – sea-level rise will still exceed 0.3 m over the next century (Moore *et al.* 2010). At current temperatures, glacial and small ice cap melt alone will result in 0.18 m of sea-level rise over the next century, while a continuation of current warming trends will result in 0.37 m from non-ice-sheet melting (Bahr *et al.* 2009). Committed sea-level rise from changes in the Greenland ice sheet in the last decade alone will amount to 4 to 8 mm (Price *et al.* 2011).

Newer studies of future sea-level rise have included systemic feedback related to melting ice, but only partially incorporate the latest revised empirical evidence. Of these, the best known is Rahmstorf's (2007) response to AR4, which projected 0.5 to 1.4 m of sea-level rise by 2100 across all six SRES scenarios. Other models, each using slightly different techniques, project 0.54 to 0.89 m (Horton *et al.* 2008), 0.72 to 1.60 m (Grinsted *et al.* 2009), 0.75 to 1.90 m (Vermeer and Rahmstorf 2009), and 0.6 to 1.6 m (Jevrejeva *et al.* 2010).[30] For higher-emission scenarios with temperatures rising by 4°C, a range of 0.5 to 2.0 m by 2100 has been estimated (Nicholls *et al.* 2011). UK government climate projections place an upper limit on global mean sea-level rise in the twenty-first century at 2.5 m, based on the estimates of average rates of change during the last interglacial period (Jenkins *et al.* 2010; Rohling *et al.* 2008). Emissions mitigation may have the potential to reduce expected sea-level rise by about one-third over the twenty-first century (Pardaens *et al.* 2011).

The latest empirical research highlights the unexpectedly fast pace of ice melt, including observations of ice sheets that are not only shrinking in expanse but also thinning (Pritchard *et al.* 2009; Velicogna 2009; Chen, Wilson *et al.* 2009; Van Den Broeke *et al.* 2009). Another study demonstrates that – far from the gain in ice mass projected in AR4 – rapid ice loss on the Antarctic Peninsula is responsible for 28 percent of recent sea-level rise (Hock *et al.* 2009).[31] The Antarctic as a whole has warmed significantly over the past half-century (Steig *et al.* 2009), and paleoclimatic evidence indicates a clear relationship between Antarctic temperatures and global sea levels. Prehistoric rates of sea-level rise are thought to have reached 5 m per century at the ends of ice ages, and as much as 2.5 m per century in some other periods (Rohling *et al.* 2009). Uncertainty about the likelihood of collapse of the Greenland or Antarctic ice sheet is a key unknown in sea-level-rise modeling (Allison, Alley, *et al.* 2009).

The complete collapse of the West Antarctic Ice Sheet (WAIS) alone would add 3.26 m to long-term global average sea levels, including up to 0.81 m in the first century after collapse. A detailed study modeling the gravitational pull of the ice, together with improved topographical data, reveals regional variation in sea-level changes unrelated to local subsidence and uplift. Peak sea-level increases from WAIS melt are forecast to be approximately 4 m and follow a latitudinal band around the earth centered at 40°N, which includes the United States' Pacific and Atlantic coasts, among many other densely populated regions (Bamber *et al.* 2009). Other studies support this finding: due to a relaxation of the gravitational attraction of ocean waters toward the current locations of ice sheets, sea-level rise from WAIS collapse would be substantially higher in North America and the Indian Ocean, and lower in South America and some parts of Europe and Asia. The highest values of sea-level rise from WAIS, more than 30 percent higher than the global average, are projected for the Pacific Coast of North America and the U.S. Atlantic seaboard (Mitrovica *et al.* 2009; Gomez *et al.* 2010; Han *et al.* 2010). In one study, local levels of sea-level rise projections (after adjusting for subsidence and uplift) for the twenty-first century range from –3.91 to 0.79 m, with a global mean of 0.47 m (Slangen *et al.* 2012).

In addition, new evidence indicates that the climate models may overestimate the stability of the Atlantic Meridional Overturning Circulation (AMOC) (Hofmann and Rahmstorf 2009), although little agreement exists among experts regarding processes determining the strength of the AMOC (Zickfeld *et al.* 2007). The expected slowdown of the AMOC due to decreased salinity will likely cause additional regional variation in sea-level rise, particularly during the twenty-second century. As lower salinity levels gradually disrupt the AMOC, higher-than-average sea-level rise is projected for the Atlantic Coast of North America (Körper *et al.* 2009).[32]

Sea ice

The loss of sea ice due to warming is a critical positive feedback mechanism in climate dynamics; as light-colored, reflective ice is replaced by darker, radiation-absorbing waters, surface albedo decreases and radiative forcing is enhanced (see Stroeve *et al.* 2011 for a detailed review of the mechanisms involved). AR4 predicted a decline in Arctic ice cover, and new research shows that sea ice loss is advancing much more rapidly than expected. According to observational data from 1953–2006, annual summer sea ice coverage has fallen 7.8 percent each decade, three times faster than projected by the models used in AR4. The current minimum annual ice coverage now corresponds to the extent projected for 30 years in the future (Stroeve *et al.* 2007, 2011). Seasonal ice (melting and reforming each year) now covers a larger share of the Arctic than does perennial ice, and the remaining sea ice grows thinner with each passing year (Kwok and Rothrock 2009; Kwok *et al.* 2009). The fraction of total Arctic sea ice composed of multi-year ice shrank from 75 percent in the mid 1980s to 45 percent in 2011 (Maslanik *et al.* 2011), but several studies suggest that ice-free summer conditions are reversible (Armour *et al.* 2011; Serreze 2011).

Summer sea ice extent has decreased by nearly 25 percent over the last quarter-century. If current trends in greenhouse gas emissions continue (modeling under the A1B scenario), projections show an ice-free Arctic by 2100 (Boé *et al.* 2009). The potential for an ice-albedo feedback effect (where albedo loss speeds ocean warming and, thus, more ice melts) is increased by climate change, paving the way for a year-round, ice-free Arctic. Unlike ice-free summers, which are thought to be reversible, the transition to year-round ice-free conditions could represent an abrupt and irreversible threshold (Eisenman and Wettlaufer 2008). Loss of sea ice is already adding to radiative forcing, reducing Arctic cloud cover (an additional decrease in albedo) and changing Arctic weather patterns (Seierstad and Bader 2008; Liu *et al.* 2009; Simmonds and Keay 2009; Deser *et al.* 2010).

The indirect effects of sea ice melting will also cause a modest increase in sea levels. (Like an ice cube melting in a glass of water, melting of sea ice does not increase the total quantity of frozen plus liquid water in the ocean.) While melting sea ice chills ocean water, causing thermal contraction (and sea-level decrease), it also freshens water, which reduces its density, causing sea levels to rise. The latter effect slightly outweighs the former, and a total loss of sea ice would cause a net addition of 3.5 to 5.2 mm to current global average sea levels (see Table 1 in Jenkins and Holland 2007). Sea-ice melt added 0.05 mm to the annual rate of sea-level rise from 1994 to 2004 (Shepherd, Wingham *et al.* 2010).

Likely impacts and catastrophes

The most likely, best-guess effects of business-as-usual trends in greenhouse gas emissions are about 4.2°C of warming (averaging the RCP 8.5 and RCP 4.5 scenarios) and 1.2 m of sea-level rise by 2100, compared to 0.3°C and 0.15 m by 2100 if all emissions were to come to a halt today. If global greenhouse gas emissions are not sharply curtailed in the near future, the best guess shows the world exceeding 2°C of warming well before the end of this century. The exact effects of exceeding 2°C are uncertain; among the possible effects are several thresholds for irreversible processes, including the collapse of the Greenland and West Antarctic ice sheets and the permanent loss of the Amazon rainforest (Lenton *et al.* 2008). As noted above, if we overshoot the concentration level that will trigger 2°C of warming and then later reduce emissions, temperatures are not expected to fall with concentrations; the temperature overshoot will last for millennia. Moreover, the (probably inescapable) uncertainty about climate sensitivity means that the safe levels of emissions and atmospheric concentration of greenhouse gases are also uncertain.

Of course, as discussed below in Chapter 6, people rarely make important decisions based solely on the most likely effects of our actions. Instead, it is normal to include consideration of unlikely but very dangerous risks; the existence of the insurance industry is proof that worst-case scenarios are often taken seriously. Today's projections of climate change impacts include low-probability events that could, with some understatement, be described as world-changing. If the high end of business-as-usual emissions scenarios comes to pass, there is about a one-in-ten chance of adding 7.1°C or more by 2100; even under the lowest credible emissions scenarios for little or no planned mitigation, there is a one-in-ten chance of exceeding 2.3°C. In addition, if ice sheets collapse sooner than expected, sea-level rise in this century could reach or exceed 2 m, the high end of current estimates. At these rates of temperature change, still more irreversible thresholds could be crossed, including large-scale release of methane hydrates, disruption of the Atlantic thermohaline circulation, and disruption of important climate patterns such as the El Niño-Southern Oscillation.

In examining the potential for catastrophe, two fundamental characteristics of the climate system have been repeatedly confirmed. First, the climate system is not linear. Greenhouse gas emissions increase radiative forcing, which increases temperatures, but these emissions also set off a host of feedback effects that are difficult to quantify and in many cases are expected to accelerate warming and other climate damages: changes in cloud cover and aerosols, including black carbon; precipitation's effect on vegetative albedo; warmer oceans; and various carbon-cycle effects. The uncertainty that these feedback effects imply for climate sensitivity is thought to be irreducible. The nonlinear nature of the climate system creates the potential for threshold effects, complex or chaotic dynamics, and sensitive dependence on initial conditions – all of which undermine hopes for precise prediction. In view of this nonlinearity, it is important for climate-economics models to investigate – and report results across – a range of different climate sensitivities and scenarios, including some drawn from the low-probability, high-sensitivity (i.e., high-damages) right tail of the distribution.

The second key characteristic of the climate system is regional diversity in climate impacts. Temperature changes, sea-level rise, and above all the changes in precipitation patterns will vary widely from place to place; a neutral or even (at first) slightly beneficial change in one region can coexist with very harmful changes or even ecological collapse in other areas. This diversity should shape our understanding of what climate change and climate damages will mean to communities around the world. Important new findings in this area include a wealth of temperature and precipitation change predictions from downscaled general circulation models, as well as expected geographic disparities in sea-level rise. As the geographic coverage of regionalized climate projections becomes more complete, more specificity in damage function parameters may be expected in integrated assessment models that include regional disaggregation.

Part II
Climate damages

2   Damage functions and climate impacts

The uncertainties about the climate sensitivity parameter, and about the physical processes of climate change in general, are not the only unknowns that climate economics must confront. Additional uncertainty surrounds the economic damages that result from a given temperature, or other physical manifestations of climate change such as sea-level rise. Such damages are often represented in integrated assessment models by a "damage function" expressing economic losses as a function of temperature. Simple algebraic expressions are often used, as a reduced-form estimate of damages as a whole. It is not surprising to find that model estimates are strongly dependent on the unknown, hypothesized form of the damage function. For a review of a wide range of functional forms that have appeared in recent literature and their effects on estimates of damages, see Kopp *et al.* (2012).

While uncertainty about climate sensitivity is starting to be incorporated into economic analysis, uncertainty in damage functions remains a relatively unexplored frontier. For example, the U.S. government's Interagency Working Group met in 2009 to estimate the "social cost of carbon" (the marginal economic damages per ton of CO_2 emissions) for use in cost–benefit analysis of regulations. It performed a careful Monte Carlo analysis of uncertainty in climate sensitivity, but accepted without question the default assumptions about damages in its three selected models: the Dynamic Integrated Climate-Economy model (DICE), the Policy Analysis of the Greenhouse Effect model (PAGE), and the Framework of Uncertainty, Negotiation and Distribution model (FUND) (Interagency Working Group 2010). Initial uses of that estimate of the social cost of carbon, and areas for potential improvement in its calculation, are described by Kopp and Mignone (2012).

An examination of those three models shows that current economic modeling of climate damages is often based on very limited and dated research, and is not remotely consistent with recent research on climate impacts. This is an area where significant additional research effort is clearly needed.

The FUND model performs a detailed, disaggregated calculation of 15 categories of costs and benefits, with an extensive Monte Carlo analysis of uncertainty.[1] Yet it projects net economic benefits to the world from the first several degrees of warming. One recent study has shown that FUND's damage calculations, in the

aggregate, can be closely approximated with a polynomial function of temperature (Marten 2011). Another analysis of FUND's damage calculations found that
they include large net benefits in agriculture, balanced against modest expected
costs in other areas (Ackerman and Munitz 2012). That analysis found that
FUND's agriculture calculations are calibrated to research published from 1992
to 1996, a time when the understanding of climate and agriculture was primitive
by today's standards; FUND embodies physically implausible estimates of the
optimum temperature for agriculture. Moreover, the agriculture calculations in
FUND 3.5 and earlier versions contain a mathematical error that could cause division by zero for a relatively likely value of one of the Monte Carlo variables.[2]

DICE relies on a single, aggregated damage function calibrated to estimates
of losses at 2.5°C and assumes a simple quadratic relationship between temperature and climate losses.[3] The net output ratio R, or output net of climate damages,
can be expressed as a fraction of the output that would have been produced in
the absence of climate change:

$$R = \frac{1}{1 + \left(\dfrac{T}{18.8}\right)^2} \tag{2.1}$$

Here T is the global average temperature increase in °C above the level of the
year 1900.

The DICE damage function is calibrated to estimates of six categories of
climate impacts at 2.5°C of warming that sum to a loss of less than 2 percent of
world output (Nordhaus 2008; Nordhaus and Boyer 2000). One of the categories
is unique to DICE: the estimated monetary value of the subjective benefit of
warmer weather. Based on a survey of U.S. attitudes toward outdoor recreation
at varying temperatures, DICE assumes a (global) preference for average annual
temperatures of 20°C (68°F).[4] In DICE-1999, the subjective benefit of warmer
weather outweighed all damages at low temperatures, leading to a net benefit
from the early stages of warming (Ackerman and Finlayson 2006). In DICE-
2007, net damages are constrained to be positive at all stages, but the subjective
benefit of warming is still included, lowering net global damages at 2.5°C.

A recent study of climate and happiness provides an updated look at this
question, finding that happiness is maximized by monthly average temperatures
close to 18.3°C (65°F); by this criterion, Guatemala, Rwanda, and Colombia are
among the countries with the best current climates[5] (Maddison and Rehdanz
2011). Modeling the welfare changes due to expected temperatures between
2070 and 2099 under the A2 climate scenario, the study projected large losses in
tropical countries, and gains in northern countries. The projected welfare
changes were worth less than 2 percent of current GDP in the USA, Japan, Italy,
and Argentina.

In a review and critique of the DICE damage estimates as applied to the
United States, Michael Hanemann develops alternative estimates for damages at
2.5°C, which are, in total, 2.4 times the DICE-2007 default values (Hanemann

2008).[6] The Hanemann recalculation, extrapolating to the world as a whole, can be written as:

$$R = \frac{1}{1 + \left(\dfrac{T}{9.1}\right)^2} \qquad (2.2)$$

Another analysis, exploring mathematical properties of the feedbacks between climate change and economic growth, assumes (without discussion) ten times the DICE level of damages – and consequently finds severe negative feedbacks and possibilities for instability (Kellie-Smith and Cox 2011).

The PAGE model, from its outset through PAGE2002, has calibrated its damage estimates to other models such as DICE. Thus it is not surprising that its estimates of the social cost of carbon have often resembled those from DICE. PAGE calculates three categories of damages: market impacts, nonmarket (non-catastrophic) impacts, and catastrophic losses. The major innovation in early PAGE damage calculations was the treatment of catastrophic risk; when combined with very low discount rates, as it was in the Stern Review, this yields a substantially increased present value of expected damages. PAGE09, the latest version of PAGE, includes a separate treatment of sea-level rise; initial results show that PAGE09 includes much higher estimates of climate damages and may represent a departure from past modeling practice in this area (Hope 2011).

One approach to modeling uncertainty in damages would involve a long march through the many categories of disaggregated damages – for example, revising each of FUND's 15 categories based on the latest research. (The next two chapters introduce parts of that literature.) Another approach is to modify a simple, aggregated damage function to reflect catastrophic risks at high temperatures (the damage functions reviewed in Kopp *et al.* 2012 include several possible specifications). For instance, Weitzman (2010a) suggests a damage function that matches the DICE model's estimates for low temperatures but rises rapidly above it at higher temperatures. Weitzman assumes, as a round-number representation of catastrophic risks, that 50 percent of world output would be lost to climate damages at 6°C of warming and 99 percent at 12°C. To motivate the latter estimate, effectively assuming that the world economy would be destroyed by 12°C of warming, Weitzman cites the finding, discussed in Chapter 4, that at 12°C, large parts of the world would, at least once a year, exceed the temperatures that human physiology can survive (Sherwood and Huber 2010).

DICE provides little basis for projecting damages at much higher temperatures.[7] It has become conventional to extrapolate the quadratic relationship (equation 2.1) to higher temperatures, but there is no economic or scientific basis for that convention. The extrapolation implies that damages grow at a leisurely pace: from equations (2.1) and (2.2), it is apparent that half of the world output is not lost to climate damages until temperature increases reach 18.8°C, according to DICE, or 9.1°C, according to the Hanemann variant.

To reach his catastrophic estimates for 6°C and 12°C while keeping the DICE low-temperature damages unchanged, Weitzman suggests adding an additional temperature-related term, yielding roughly (with numerical estimates rounded):[8]

$$R = \cfrac{1}{1+\left(\cfrac{T}{20.2}\right)^2 + \left(\cfrac{T}{6.08}\right)^{6.76}} \tag{2.3}$$

Equation (2.3) matches (2.1) at $T=2.5$, but diverges thereafter. When the temperature increase is well below 6°C, the last term in the denominator of (2.3) is very small and can almost be ignored. On the other hand, as the temperature climbs above 6°C, the last term grows very rapidly; it is more than 100 times as large at 12°C as at 6°C.

It is essentially impossible to distinguish between equations (2.1) and (2.3) on the basis of low-temperature empirical evidence. Yet they have very different implications. The first leads to the gradual "climate policy ramp" discussed by Nordhaus (2008), while the second, as Weitzman (2010a) demonstrates, can lead to more substantial, vigorous initiatives to reduce emissions, even at a discount rate as high as 6 percent. For a demonstration of the impact of a switch from damage function (2.1) to (2.3) – holding all other assumptions constant, a switch multiplies the social cost of carbon by a factor of three to four – see Ackerman and Stanton (2012). A similar analysis appears in Botzen and van den Bergh (2012).

Equations such as (2.1) or (2.2), relying on the arbitrary convention of quadratic damage functions and assuming that temperatures can increase by 18°C or even 9°C before damages reach half of global output, are difficult to reconcile with the results of scientific climate impact assessments. Quadratic damage functions are an arbitrary convention, not based on anything in the science reviewed in this book. Moreover, the estimate that 2.5°C of warming would cause losses of less than 2 percent seems incompatible with the projections of serious climate impacts that are expected at that temperature or even lower. The potential climate losses reflected in a much steeper damage function, as in equation (2.3), bring the possibility of catastrophic damages into the realm of modeling results. This introduces a broader range of uncertainty into the seemingly precise and often surprisingly low monetary estimates of climate damages found in the economics literature.

Reduced-form damage functions can be useful for modeling purposes, especially in relatively simple and transparent models – at the level of complexity of DICE, for example – that are often employed in policy analyses. Yet simple damage functions can tell a wide range of stories, as the contrast between equations (2.1) and (2.3) makes clear. The choice of a functional form and calibration of damage function parameters should be informed by an in-depth understanding of climate impacts on specific sectors. Research on climate impacts has progressed far beyond the level that is reflected in the last generation of integrated assessment models.

Climate impacts

The next two chapters examine recent research on key areas of climate damages. While complex interactions can make specific regional outcomes difficult to predict, the latest climate science tells us that the likely effect of continued greenhouse gas emissions is a warmer climate with rising sea levels and more intense storms, and that there is a chance that business-as-usual emissions could lead to climatic changes that would result in a largely unrecognizable earth in the future. Economic analysis of climate change impacts takes as its starting point detailed scientific assessments of the effects of continued greenhouse gas emissions on human communities: How will climate change impact our sources of food and other materials? Will there be damages to buildings and infrastructure? How do emissions impact human health and water availability? Economists' projections of costs and benefits can be only as good as the scientific assessments upon which those projections are based, and development of integrated assessment models must begin by synthesizing the scientific literature on climate impacts.

This literature, as it stood in 2006, was well represented in AR4 (IPCC 2007a, *Working Group II*, Technical Summary, TS4.1), and many of these findings have been confirmed by more recent studies. With climate change resulting from business-as-usual (SRES A2) emissions:

- The number of people exposed to water stress will triple by 2050. Precipitation effects will vary regionally. In areas where precipitation is projected to increase, its variability will likely grow, as will the risk of floods. Many regions that are arid today will have less precipitation in the future, with the expected consequence of an increased demand for irrigation water.
- By 2100, many ecosystems will no longer be able to adapt naturally to climate change. The structure and functioning of both terrestrial and marine ecosystems will undergo substantial changes, and 20 to 30 percent of species will be at risk of extinction.
- Human health will be impacted by malnutrition, water stress, injury in extreme weather events, exposure to ground-level ozone, and increased incidence of certain diseases. Decreased mortality from cold exposure will be outweighed by increased mortality related to rising temperatures. Today, climate change is already increasing the incidence of disease and premature deaths.
- The communities at greatest risk of the worst climate-related damages are those that live in coastal lowlands, river deltas, or low-lying islands; that rely on climate-sensitive resources; that are in the midst of rapid urbanization; or that have low-income populations.

The AR4 findings still represent the best knowledge regarding these impacts. Post-2007 studies refine these projections, but new research does not overturn or otherwise qualitatively change these findings. On the whole, the latest science confirms that the expected impacts of climate change are severe and takes important steps toward accurate and precise prediction of these impacts. There are several key research areas, however, where the newest studies offer findings that are qualitatively different from AR4. These impact areas are the focus of Chapters 3 and 4.

Chapter 3, "Climate change impacts on natural systems," focuses on new research regarding climate change impacts to forests and fisheries. Forests' interaction with the changing climate system is complex; forests will undergo both negative and positive effects from climate change, and the climate system will undergo both increases and decreases to overall warming from forest growth. New research suggests that warming will be slowed by tropical forest growth and accelerated by boreal forest growth; temperate forest growth will have little effect. Other recent studies have clarified the ecosystem effects of ocean warming and decreased ocean pH. Coral reef ecosystems – important habitats and breeding grounds for many marine organisms – are expected to face widespread extinction of many species in the coming decades. The geographic distribution of marine species around the world will shift as sea-surface temperatures grow warmer, resulting in decreased fish catch everywhere but in the highest latitudes.

Chapter 4, "Climate change impacts on human systems," examines the latest research on climate change impacts to agriculture, coastal infrastructure, and human health. A better understanding of CO_2 fertilization – and of the relationship between temperature and agricultural productivity – calls into question older projections of increasing global food production with climate change. Newer, more accurate modeling of a full range of influences on sea-level rise now shows much more serious impacts, including some coastal communities facing permanent inundation in this century, even in scenarios with lower greenhouse gas emissions. Newer modeling also demonstrates important regional differences in the rate of sea-level rise. Higher temperatures and sea-levels, as well as new, less predictable and more intense weather patterns, will have costly impacts on the health of human communities around the world.

These climate impacts are the key inputs to assessments of the economic damages from climate change. In almost all cases, estimation of monetary damages lags far behind estimation of physical damages – there exists very little literature connecting the physical impacts to their expected monetary costs. Instead, climate-economics models employ generalized damage functions that assume a simple, often quadratic relationship between temperature and losses in global economic output, in a rule-of-thumb effort to assign an order of magnitude to monetary losses. This near-universal disconnect between the science and the economics of climate change is nothing less than astounding.

3 Climate change impacts on natural systems

The impacts of climate change are often popularized in terms of photogenic species such as coral and polar bears. The expected effects on natural systems, however, extend well beyond the best-known images. If business-as-usual emissions continue, the most likely late-21st-century temperature increase is more than 4°C (with a one-in-ten chance of exceeding 7°C; see Chapter 1). With 2 to 3°C of warming, AR4 projected that 20 to 30 percent of plant and animal species are likely to be at high risk of extinction and that substantial changes in the structure and functioning of terrestrial and aquatic ecosystems are very likely. With 1.7°C warming, all coral reefs will be bleached, and by 2.5°C they will be extinct; at 2.8°C there is high risk of extinction for polar bears and other Arctic mammals. At 4°C of warming, AR4 projects major extinctions around the world (IPCC 2007a, *Working Group II*, Chapter 4).

Evidence of the impacts of anthropogenic climate change on ecosystems is compiled in a wide-ranging review article that identifies all significant, temperature-related changes in physical and biological systems reported in peer-reviewed literature, in cases where 20 or more years of temperature data are available (Rosenzweig *et al.* 2008). The review encompasses a massive European database of more than 28,000 biological indicators and more than 1,000 other biological and physical indicators worldwide. More than 90 percent of the biological indicators and more than 95 percent of the physical indicators are consistent with the response expected from anthropogenic climate change; the pattern of results is very unlikely to be caused by natural variability in climate. An evaluation of possible publication bias, using the extensive European data, shows that a similar conclusion is reached when the larger number of data series showing no temperature-related changes is included.

Another review article analyzes 71 studies that identify a specific temperature or CO_2 concentration for the onset of climate impacts on species or ecosystems and summarizes their findings on a consistent scale, relative to preindustrial global average temperature (Warren *et al.* 2010). Some ecosystem thresholds are reached as low as 1.7°C above preindustrial temperatures. Beyond 2°C, projections of ecosystem impacts become widespread; critical aspects of ecosystem functioning begin to collapse at 2.5°C.

Many species migrate in an attempt to follow their preferred climate niches. A meta-analysis found that terrestrial species are now moving an average of 11 meters per decade toward higher elevations, and 17 kilometers per decade toward higher latitudes, several times the rates previously estimated (Chen *et al.* 2011). Rates of movement vary widely from one species to another, however, and there are cases in which species have moved toward lower elevations in response to changes in water availability (Crimmins *et al.* 2011). Climate change interacts with other threats to biodiversity; for instance, many amphibian species are at risk from the combination of climate change, land use change, and disease (Hof *et al.* 2011).

Climate change threatens to overwhelm the resilience of many ecosystems, as changes in temperature, precipitation, atmospheric CO_2 concentrations, ocean acidification, and other conditions move beyond the ranges to which many species can adapt. Although often studied at the individual species level, the response to climate change also affects ecosystem interactions. Species that currently interact may respond to warming and other climatic conditions at differential rates, disrupting the timing of food requirements and availability, the synchronization of pollinators and flowering plants, and other interdependencies. Likewise, complex ecological communities may undergo different changes in geographical range, moving to higher altitudes or latitudes at differential rates. In either case, the result is the disruption of existing ecosystems (Walther 2010).

Global warming may do the most harm to natural systems in tropical regions, even though temperature changes there will be smaller than the global average: Tropical species normally undergo little seasonal variation in temperature, so they may not be resilient to small changes, and in many cases they are already close to their optimal temperatures (Deutsch *et al.* 2008; Tewksbury *et al.* 2008). By 2100, 75 percent of current tropical forest regions will be too hot for closed-canopy forest, which could lead temperature-sensitive species to seek refuge in areas that still provide their historical temperature ranges. The nearest such cool refuges, however, will be more than 1,000 km away for more than 20 percent of the tropical mammals with small ranges (Wright *et al.* 2009).

Post-AR4 research has extended the understanding of climate impacts, providing greater detail in many areas. Here we focus on two kinds of natural systems in which new research provides a qualitative change from that presented in AR4: forestry and fisheries. In forestry, contributions of afforestation and deforestation to climate change can now be differentiated by tropical, temperate, and boreal forests. In fisheries, a serious decline in the viability of coral reefs and the far-reaching ecosystems that rely on these reefs may already be inevitable, and these impacts are expected earlier in the century than previously thought.

Both forests and marine ecosystems are of great economic importance both directly and indirectly. The economic role of natural systems in general may be less obvious but is also of paramount importance. The diverse range of economic benefits produced by ecosystems and biodiversity is documented in the recent reports of the United Nations-sponsored The Economics of Ecosystems and Biodiversity (TEEB) project.[1] While noting the difficulty of monetizing the "priceless" benefits of natural ecosystems, TEEB presents numerous arguments and methods for valuing ecosystem services. One summary estimate of the costs of climate policy inaction suggests that the ongoing loss of biodiversity in land eco-systems already has a global welfare cost equal to $68 billion per year and that these welfare losses will grow rapidly over time.[2] Taking the order of magnitude of this estimate together with the importance of both market and subsidence for-estry and fisheries activities, it seems clear that natural systems are an important component of a comprehensive climate-economics analysis.

Forestry

Vast amounts of carbon are stored in forests, both in vegetation and in the soil. Atmospheric carbon continues to be absorbed by forests in large quantities (Pan *et al.* 2011); changes in this process are of great importance for climate dynam-ics. Land clearing and deforestation, often for agriculture, continue to be major threats; for example, there are large carbon emissions from forest clearing for palm oil plantations in Indonesia (Carlson *et al.* 2012). Mangroves are a surpris-ingly important part of the picture, with a high density of carbon storage; man-grove deforestation could account for ten percent of global deforestation emissions (Donato *et al.* 2011). On the other hand, the fate of wood cleared from forests varies by country. Thirty years after forest clearing, more than one-third of forest carbon is stored in long-lived wood products in Europe and North America; the proportion is much lower in the rest of the world (Earles *et al.* 2012).

Forests have other important interactions with the earth's climate. There is a complex cyclical pattern of feedbacks: Climate change affects forests, and forests affect climate change, and there are positive and negative effects in both directions. Recent research has clarified many of the individual effects, but the net result varies regionally and, for many areas, remains uncertain.

Positive effects of climate change on forests

Plants grow by photosynthesis, a process that absorbs CO_2 from the atmosphere. For many plants, including trees, the availability of CO_2 is the limiting factor on their growth, so an increase in atmospheric CO_2 will cause acceleration of plant growth and of the resulting removal of carbon from the atmosphere. This process, known as "carbon fertilization," is discussed further in the review of agricultural research in Chapter 4. Other positive effects of climate change on forests include increased temperatures and longer growing seasons at high lati-tudes or high elevations.

There is empirical evidence of benefits to forests from carbon fertilization. Free-Air CO_2 Enrichment (FACE) experiments, which allow plants to be grown outdoors simulating conditions in nature, show an average 23 percent increase in net primary production (i.e., growth in biomass) at 550 ppm CO_2 (compared to today's 394 ppm[3]) in young forest stands but little or no impact in older forest stands (Norby *et al.* 2005; Kirilenko and Sedjo 2007; Lenihan *et al.* 2008). A study of temperate forests finds faster-than-expected growth over the past two decades and offers six possible explanations, three of which – increased temperatures, longer growing seasons, and carbon fertilization – are consequences of climate change (McMahon *et al.* 2010). Modeling of forest growth in California projects that climate change will increase the size of pine trees and the yields of managed pine forests, with greater growth in warmer and wetter climate scenarios (Battles *et al.* 2009). Global estimates project worldwide increases in timber output due to climate change over the next 50 years (Seppälä *et al.* 2009).

Forest carbon sequestration, particularly in tropical countries, is often identified as one of the lowest-cost options for reducing net global emissions. Carbon accumulation in forests slows down as trees mature, but recent research finds that old-growth forests, particularly in the tropics, continue to absorb significant amounts of additional carbon over time (Luyssaert *et al.* 2008; Phillips, Lewis *et al.* 2008; Lewis *et al.* 2009). Forest sequestration is a low-cost emission reduction strategy for the European Union, but, if pursued unilaterally, could perversely increase timber production in other areas of the world that already suffer from high deforestation rates (Michetti and Rosa 2012). Realistic afforestation scenarios would lead to only small reductions in future temperatures (Arora and Montenegro 2011), implying that forest sequestration needs to be part of a much broader strategy.

Recent research models the joint dynamics of the carbon and nitrogen cycles; this reduces but does not eliminate the projected effect of carbon fertilization (Zaehle *et al.* 2010; Thornton *et al.* 2009). Both carbon and nitrogen are essential for plant growth; the lack of available nitrogen could cause a large decrease in the long-term effect of carbon fertilization, particularly in boreal and temperate forests. Modeling the nitrogen cycle also reveals a smaller, opposing effect of climate change: As temperatures rise, accelerated decomposition of dead biomass makes more nitrogen available, easing the nitrogen constraint on plant growth. The first effect is much larger, so the net effect of the nitrogen cycle is to decrease forest carbon sequestration. By 2100, under the A2 emissions scenario, the atmospheric concentration of CO_2 is projected to be 48 ppm higher in an integrated carbon-nitrogen model than in a climate model that ignores nitrogen dynamics (Zaehle *et al.* 2010). One study finds that an increased atmospheric concentration of CO_2 will stimulate emissions of N_2O and CH_4 from some soils, negating one-sixth of the estimated terrestrial carbon sink benefits from elevated CO_2 (van Groenigen *et al.* 2011).

Negative effects of climate change on forests

There are a number of effects of climate change that threaten the growth or, in the extreme, the survival of forests.

AR4 found a likely increased risk of forest fire associated with a decrease in summer precipitation (IPCC 2007b). New research refines this global assessment, pointing to regionally heterogeneous impacts. While there is a potential for widespread impacts of climate change on wildfire, regional downscaling reveals both increases and decreases to wildfire incidence. Under a business-as-usual emissions scenario (A2), in the next few decades many areas around the world that do not currently have wildfires will be at an increased risk of suffering these events, including parts of the U.S. Southwest; much of the European and Siberian northern latitudes; a large part of Western China; and some areas of Asia, Africa, and South America. At the same time, the risk of wildfire will decrease in central Canada, southeastern Brazil, northeastern China, and southeastern Siberia (Krawchuk *et al.* 2009).

In northern forests, wildfire has an important influence on net changes in carbon storage. By 2100, wildfire-related carbon emissions from North America's boreal forests are projected to increase by 2.5 to 4.4 times, depending on climate change scenario and assumptions regarding CO_2 fertilization; boreal wildfires release 13 to 26 percent of the carbon stored aboveground in the forest and 5 to 38 percent of the ground layer of carbon storage (Balshi *et al.* 2009).[4] Wildfires also form charcoal, which sequesters carbon when stored in soil, a countervailing effect. Boreal soils store 1 Gt of carbon as a result of past forest fires, an amount equal to 1 percent of carbon stored in plants in boreal forests (Ohlson *et al.* 2009).

In the United States, the connection between climate and forest fires is becoming increasingly clear. A study of twentieth-century forest fires in the northern Rocky Mountains found that the peak fire years were those with warm springs; low spring snowpack; and warm, dry summers (Morgan *et al.* 2008). A study of large forest fires throughout the western United States from 1970 to 2000 found an abrupt increase in the mid-1980s, closely correlated with increases in spring and summer temperatures, and a shift toward earlier spring snowmelt (Westerling *et al.* 2006).

There is also evidence that more trees are dying as the climate changes. A study of unmanaged forests in the western United States found that "background" (non-catastrophic) mortality rates had increased almost everywhere, across different elevations, tree sizes, species, and past fire histories (van Mantgem *et al.* 2009). The study found a correlation of tree mortality with regional warming and water deficits. Recent African data show that, for the same annual total of precipitation, forest cover is greater with more frequent, less intense rainfall events (Good and Caylor 2011); if, as sometimes projected, climate change leads to the opposite (less frequent but more intense rains), it will impede forest growth.

Tree mortality is difficult to analyze because the precise influence of temperature on mortality appears to be mediated by species-specific traits; thus, predictions for different forest areas will depend on their mix of tree species (Adams *et al.* 2009). The mechanisms linking climate change to tree death are not simple and can include increased vulnerability to disease; increased survival of pests such as bark beetles; decreased moisture availability leading to desiccation; and physiological temperature stress that induces mortality and/or makes other species more competitive, forcing out the weaker species (Kliejunas *et al.* 2009).

Tropospheric (low-level) ozone, a pollutant that results from fossil fuel combustion, inhibits forest growth. Although ozone is not a consequence of climate change, it is a byproduct of the principal source of greenhouse gas emissions. High ozone levels are associated with insect-related disturbances, worsen the negative effects of frost, and affect leaf gas exchange, offsetting some of the forest productivity gains from CO_2 fertilization (Boisvenue and Running 2006).

Insects, especially the mountain pine beetle and other bark beetles, kill trees across millions of acres in the western United States each year. Rising temperatures increase their survival rates, accelerate their life cycle development, facilitate their expansion in range, and reduce their hosts' capacity to resist attack. At lower elevations, it is possible but not certain that the area favorable for mountain pine beetles will shrink; at higher elevations, bark beetles will continue to expand their range (Bentz 2008). Similar insect outbreaks, killing trees and reducing forest sequestration, have occurred in other areas, such as Scandinavia, and may become more common as temperatures rise (Heliasz *et al.* 2011).

A number of climate-related threats are specific to tropical forests. Woody vines, or lianas, respond to carbon fertilization, perhaps more rapidly than do trees; lianas also fare better than trees under drought conditions (Swaine and Grace 2007). The growth of lianas can strangle and kill large trees, leading to a net decrease in forest biomass (Warren *et al.* 2010). In this way, rising CO_2 concentrations, combined with droughts, could lead to carbon fertilization of the "wrong" plants and an overall decrease in forest carbon sequestration.

Researchers have also identified the potential for catastrophic collapse in tropical forests, resulting from deforestation and climate-related changes in temperature and precipitation. One study finds three distinct states – forest, savannah, and treeless areas – separated by abrupt tipping points, which are tied to precipitation levels (Hirota *et al.* 2011). The best-studied example, the Amazon rainforest, may be approaching a threshold beyond which an irreversible dieback will be set in motion.

Over the past few decades, deforestation associated with land-use conversion has dramatically reduced the size of the Amazon forest; this forest loss is altering the hydrological cycle, reducing precipitation, and causing still more forest loss (Brovkin *et al.* 2009). Studies suggest that only large-scale intervention to control deforestation and wildfire can prevent the Amazon from passing a tipping point for its demise and that the dieback could occur during the twenty-first century (Malhi *et al.* 2008; Malhi *et al.* 2009). Recent research suggests that the threshold for eventual Amazon dieback could be less than 2°C (Jones *et al.* 2009), as compared to the more commonly cited 3 to 4°C (Lenton *et al.* 2008).

Even if greenhouse gas levels were eventually reduced and temperatures stabilized, the Amazon – like many other biological systems – would be locked into a particular path by considerable inertia in its response to climatic change (Jones *et al.* 2009). Carbon lost from Amazon vegetation and soil has the potential to cause significant climate feedback effects; a 2005 Amazon drought has been estimated to have caused the loss of 1.6 Gt C in that single year (Phillips *et al.* 2009).

Effects of forests on climate change

While climate change has multiple positive and negative effects on forests, there are also complex effects of forests on climate change; the net impact differs by region (Bonan 2008). Positive effects of forests that reduce the impact of climate change include sequestration of carbon, which lowers atmospheric CO_2 concentrations; and evaporative cooling, which lowers temperatures. On the other hand, forests have lower albedo (they are darker and therefore absorb more solar radiation) than do alternative land uses, which tends to increase radiative forcing and raise temperatures.

In tropical forests, which contain most of the world's forest carbon, the sequestration and evaporative cooling effects are strong, while the decrease in albedo is only moderate, leading to a net reduction in warming. At the other extreme, in boreal forests, the sequestration and evaporative cooling effects are weaker, while the change in albedo – when forests replace snow- or ice-covered surfaces – is large; it is possible, therefore, that boreal forests make a positive net contribution to warming. Temperate forests are intermediate in all these dimensions, with an uncertain net effect on climate change (Bonan 2008).

The possibility that boreal forest growth intensifies climate change may be surprising to many readers but is extensively discussed in the research literature. One study found that boreal forest fires have a long-term net cooling effect, because the increase in surface albedo over the many years before the trees grow back outweighs the loss of carbon storage and the effect of emissions from the fires themselves (Randerson *et al.* 2006). Simulation of large-scale deforestation in a detailed climate model found an increase in long-run equilibrium temperature from tropical deforestation, roughly no change from temperate deforestation, and a decrease in equilibrium temperature from boreal deforestation (Bala *et al.* 2007). Boreal forest expansion leads to increased local summer temperatures, accelerating the process of climate change (Liess *et al.* 2011).

One contrary view argues that the particular places where forests have been cleared for agriculture in the past are the most fertile and least snowy areas – so that reforestation of those areas would have greater sequestration benefits and smaller albedo effects than suggested by regional averages (Pongratz *et al.* 2011). This point aside, there appears to be little dissent from the consensus about boreal forests' impact on climate change.

Forests provide many important ecological and economic services in addition to climate stabilization; thus, the surprising findings described here do not justify advocacy of boreal deforestation or indifference to temperate deforestation. When viewed as a strategy for climate mitigation, however, afforestation and prevention of further deforestation should be focused specifically on tropical forests.

Fisheries

Global fisheries are both an important economic sector and a key source of nutrition. Freshwater fish will be affected by climate change; for example, the habitat for trout in the western United States will decline under the impact of temperature increases and water flow changes (Wenger *et al.* 2011). Our focus here, however, is on the larger and better researched area of marine fisheries. Climate change is expected to have profound effects on marine ecosystems, driving many species of coral to extinction, decreasing crustacean and mollusk populations, and causing large-scale disturbances to the distribution of numerous commercial fish species (Sumaila *et al.* 2011). Changes to ocean pH, driven by high concentrations of CO_2, are expected to cause some of the first serious, irreversible ecosystem damages due to anthropogenic greenhouse gas emissions. It is possible that a tipping point triggering widespread coral extinction has already been passed. Here we discuss two main pathways for climatic disruption of marine biological systems: ocean warming and ocean acidification.

Ocean warming

As the earth's atmosphere warms, so too will the ocean waters nearest to the surface, where most marine flora and fauna live. Ocean warming will shift the distribution of many ocean species poleward, including fish species of utmost importance to commercial fisheries. These changes will vary regionally and by species, depending on complex factors of reproductive biology, shifts elsewhere in the food chain, and the physical oceanography of currents. A model of global shifts in fish production under climate change (using the A1B scenario) projects a large-scale redistribution of potential fisheries catch by 2055; on average, catch potential would increase by 30 to 70 percent in northern subarctic areas and decrease by up to 40 percent in the tropics. Norway, Greenland, Alaska, and Siberia would see the greatest gains to potential marine catch, while Indonesia, the U.S. lower 48 states, Chile, and China would see the greatest losses (Cheung *et al.* 2010).

Biodiversity is likely to be very sensitive to climatic changes, especially in the high northern and southern latitudes. Species everywhere are vulnerable to temperature change. Polar marine species tend to have especially narrow bands of temperature tolerance; tropical species often exist at the top end of their thermal tolerance already. Many species in the subpolar regions, the tropics, and semi-enclosed seas may become locally extinct, even as new species rapidly invade the Arctic and Southern oceans (Cheung *et al.* 2009). Regional studies indicate that distributional shifts due to climate change are species specific. Among the diadromous[5] fish of Europe, North Africa, and the Middle East, for example, the distribution of some species (including shad, herring, and several other commercially important fish) is expected to contract while others expand (Lassalle and Rochard 2009).

New research suggests that "fish recruitment," or growth in a fish population, is the key mechanism driving climate-change-related shifts in the distribution of oceanic species. Distributions shift as more larvae survive (or fail to survive) under the new climatic conditions (Rijnsdorp *et al.* 2009). On the northeast U.S. continental shelf, the distribution of fish species has already shifted with climate change over the past 40 years. Temperatures have become too warm for cod and other larvae at the southern end of their New England range, causing a north-ward shift (Nye *et al.* 2009)

Reef-forming coral are among the organisms most sensitive to ocean warming, and many marine species rely on reefs as a source of food or as shelter for nursery grounds. Coral depend on a symbiotic relationship with photosyn-thetic protozoa for their source of food. This symbiosis is extremely sensitive to temperature: Slight increases in temperature cause the coral to release or expel the algae, triggering the phenomenon known as "coral bleaching." While it is possible for coral to survive bleaching by recruiting new protozoa, this reversal occurs only when the original stressor to the symbiotic relationship is removed. Where the stressor is a continual, gradual increase to ocean temperatures, the most likely outcome is coral mortality, with local and sometimes global extinc-tion of species.

One-third of all coral species are already at risk of extinction as a result of bleaching and disease caused by ocean warming in recent years. Caribbean coral appears to face the greatest and most immediate threat (Buddemeier *et al.* 2011), although coral around the world are at risk (Carpenter *et al.* 2008). A report from the Global Coral Reef Monitoring Network and the Reef and Rainforest Research Centre (Wilkinson and Souter 2008) documents impacts to Caribbean coral reefs and finds that 2005 had the warmest sea-surface temperatures on record and the highest rates of coral bleaching and mortality ever recorded.

Ocean acidification

Greenhouse gas emissions have a second important impact on ocean ecosystems: Marine waters are absorbing CO_2 at higher rates, causing ocean pH to fall. At lower (more acidic) pH levels, concentrations of calcium carbonate decrease, and as a result, calcifying organisms such as coral, mollusks, and crustaceans may have difficulty forming their shells and skeletons, causing populations to decline.

Most of the surface ocean is currently supersaturated with both aragonite and calcite, the two major forms of calcium carbonate. Different calcifying species use one or the other. Supersaturation makes it easy for calcium carbonate shells and skeletons to form and helps maintain their integrity after formation. As calcium carbonate concentrations fall, however, the oceans approach the point at which they become undersaturated and hence potentially corrosive; in undersatu-rated water, calcium carbonate tends to dissolve out of unprotected shells into the water.

Undersaturation does not mean immediate collapse for calcifying organisms, but it is a significant challenge. Lower ocean pH levels and undersaturation of calcium carbonate have the potential to affect a wide range of commercially important species: Mussel, oyster, giant scallop, clam, crab, sea urchin, dogfish, and sea bass populations are all projected to decline in health and/or numbers with higher concentrations of CO_2 in ocean waters. One study finds that 30 percent of U.S. commercial fishing revenues come from mollusks, 19 percent from crustaceans, and another 50 percent from predators that consume calcifiers (or consume the predators of calcifiers). Only 1 percent of revenues is not influenced by changes in ocean pH (Fabry *et al.* 2008; Cooley and Doney 2009). There is also evidence that elevated ocean CO_2 levels may disrupt some coral-reef-dwelling fish larvae's sense of smell and, therefore, their ability to navigate and to select appropriate areas for settlement (Munday *et al.* 2009).

AR4 reported that anthropogenic CO_2 emissions have already caused ocean surface pH to fall by 0.1 (equivalent to a 30 percent increase in hydrogen ion concentrations) and that a further decrease in pH of 0.3–0.4 is predicted for 2100. This was projected to be particularly harmful to cold-water coral ecosystems and to the numerous calcifying species in the Arctic and Southern oceans (IPCC 2007a, *Working Group II*, Chapter 4). IPCC scenarios imply that by 2050, global mean surface pH is likely to be lower than at any time in the last 24 million years (Turley *et al.* 2010).

Detailed modeling of ocean chemistry projects an accelerated timeline for declining concentrations of calcium carbonate. Undersaturation is expected to occur first near the poles, and then spread toward the equator over the course of a few decades. Undersaturation of aragonite, which is used by most mollusks and corals, could take place as early as 2020–30 in the Arctic Ocean and 2050–60 in the Southern Ocean (Feely *et al.* 2009). Indeed, it has already been observed on a seasonal basis in the Bering Sea, along with at least one episode of calcite undersaturation (Mathis *et al.* 2011, 2012).

Research on impacts of acidification on marine life has also expanded, with complex results that differ by species. One study subjected 18 calcifying species to high levels of atmospheric CO_2, inducing low levels of calcium carbonate in water. In ten of the 18 species, calcification slowed down as CO_2 concentrations rose; in six species, there was net dissolution (loss of calcium carbonate) at the highest level of CO_2. In seven species, however, there was an increase in calcification at intermediate and/or high levels of CO_2, perhaps reflecting differences in their ability to regulate pH and protect their shells (Ries *et al.* 2009). Some species can maintain shell stability at low pH and low saturation but at great metabolic cost (Turley *et al.* 2010). Two meta-analyses of the effects of acidification on marine organisms reach opposite conclusions, one suggesting that the likely damages have been exaggerated (Hendriks *et al.* 2010) and the other projecting serious damages to many species (Kroeker *et al.* 2010). Both agree that calcification is expected to decline on average and that impacts on individual species will differ widely.

Coral reefs have been extensively studied, leading to ominous projections of decline. From 1990 through 2005, calcification rates fell by 14 percent among *Porites* coral in the Great Barrier Reef, a phenomenon that researchers refer to as "severe and sudden"; in 400 years of calcification records, there are no similar anomalies. These results indicate that a tipping point for coral mortality may already have been passed in the late twentieth century (De'ath *et al.* 2009). Other studies support this finding and suggest that coral reefs worldwide are already committed to irreversible decline. If atmospheric CO_2 concentrations were to reach 450 ppm (from today's 394 ppm), rapid coral mortality would follow, along with widespread ecosystem effects (Veron *et al.* 2009). Some researchers project that there will be great temporal and spatial heterogeneity in reef degradation – that is, coral reefs will not all die at once (Pandolfi *et al.* 2011).

Likely impacts and catastrophes

There are multiple, interdependent impacts of climate change on the oceans. Warming, acidification, and hypoxia (deoxygenation) exhibit complex interactions, and many of the effects will be essentially irreversible on a time scale of centuries or longer (Gruber 2011; Tyrrell 2011). Note that, with the exception of warming, the major ocean impacts depend on CO_2 levels in specific rather than greenhouse gases in general; reduction in CO_2 emissions is essential for mitigation of these impacts.

Given business-as-usual emissions, the most likely climate outcomes are around 4.2°C of warming (with a one-in-ten chance of temperatures falling below 2.3°C in the most optimistic business-as-usual scenario and exceeding 7.1°C in the most pessimistic) and 1.2 m of sea-level rise by 2100 (see Chapter 1). Even if greenhouse gas emissions ceased today, with 0.5°C of inevitable warming still to come, the least resilient ecosystems would suffer some impacts – indeed, the most vulnerable ecosystems already are feeling the effects of climate change.

If emissions are not greatly reduced from current trends, the expected impacts to vulnerable natural systems are likely to be devastating. By the end of this century, there would be extinctions of vulnerable plants and animals worldwide. For some species, these extinctions are likely to happen much sooner. For many coral species, the stresses of changing temperatures and pH levels may have already been too great; the tipping point for some species' extinction may already have been passed, and the threshold for extinction of all coral ecosystems may be as low as 2.5°C. For the Amazon rainforest ecosystem, the threshold for an irreversible dieback may be as low as 2.0°C, and high risk of the extinction of many Arctic mammals is expected at 2.8°C.

For these especially vulnerable natural systems, the impacts of business-as-usual emissions are enormous, and depend on the uncertain value of climate sensitivity (as discussed in Chapter 1). At higher climate sensitivities, extinctions and other catastrophic ecosystem effects would be more widespread and would occur at an earlier date.

4   Climate change impacts on human systems

As temperatures and sea levels rise and precipitation patterns change, human systems are expected to suffer damages. Like forestry and fisheries, described in Chapter 3, agriculture, coastal settlements, and human health are expected to undergo the most direct impacts from climate change. In the coolest regions, agriculture output may show modest gains from the first few degrees of climate change, but in most temperate and almost all tropical regions, changes to temperature and precipitation are expected to lower yields in the coming century. Low-lying coastal settlements are extremely vulnerable to rising sea levels, from both permanent inundation and greater storm damage. Human health is affected not just by high temperatures but also by climate-induced changes in disease vectors and by decreasing water availability, which is expected to have the biggest impact on already-dry regions.

Agriculture

Climate impacts on agriculture have been studied for at least 20 years and are central to many economic assessments of climate change. At first glance, the emphasis on this small economic sector might seem surprising; agriculture represents 1.2 percent of GDP in the United States, 1.6 percent in the European Union, and 2.9 percent for the world as a whole. In the least developed countries, however, agriculture makes up nearly one-quarter of GDP – a value that still ignores all subsistence agriculture grown and consumed by the same family.[1] Regardless of its contribution to individual countries' GDP, food is an absolute necessity of life. In economic terms, this is reflected in a very low price elasticity of demand, implying a large consumer surplus. Thus agriculture looms much larger in welfare terms if industries are measured by their contribution to consumer surplus rather than to GDP.

Agriculture is unmistakably climate-dependent, more so than many industries. Research in the 1990s (e.g., Mendelsohn *et al.* 1994) often projected net global benefits in agriculture from the early stages of climate change. Such projections were based primarily on the expected effects of carbon fertilization and on longer growing seasons as temperatures rise in cold northern areas. As recently as 2001, the first National Assessment from the U.S. Global Change

Research Program estimated that climate change would on balance be beneficial to U.S. agriculture through the 2090s, causing yield increases, many of them quite large, for most crops (Reilly *et al.* 2001). Beginnings of a shift in the consensus view could be seen in AR4, which found that 1 to 3°C warming in mid-to-high-latitude regions would result in small crop yield increases but that 1 to 2°C warming would reduce yields in low-latitude regions (IPCC 2007a, *Working Group II*, Chapter 5).

Newer work based on older agricultural research continues, nonetheless, to appear. The latest (2007) version of the well-known integrated assessment model, DICE, largely relies on the previous version for damage estimates (Nordhaus 2008, p. 42, note 3). The previous version relied on a 1995 study to estimate total agricultural losses due to CO_2 doubling at a few *thousandths* of one percent of world output (Nordhaus and Boyer 1999; compare Tables 3.1 and 4.4). The nearly undocumented on-line "lab notes" explaining the DICE-2007 data inputs refer to taking a "judgmental average" between these earlier estimates and calculations by Cline (2007), resulting in an estimate of agricultural impacts from 2.5°C of warming at close to zero (a few hundredths of a percent of GDP) in China and all developed countries, losses from 0.32 to 0.67 percent of GDP in developing countries, and a gain of 0.82 percent of GDP in Russia.[2]

The FUND integrated assessment model, one of the three used to develop the U.S. government's 2009 estimate of the social cost of carbon, projects net benefits to the world from the first 3°C of warming (Interagency Working Group 2010). A disaggregated analysis of climate damages in FUND finds that the model's net global benefit comes almost entirely from agriculture, an area where FUND's calculations are benchmarked to studies from the mid-1990s (Ackerman and Munitz 2012).

Recent research has raised new questions that suggest a more complex relationship between climate and agriculture. In a number of cases, this has led to still-lower estimates of the agricultural benefits of warming. It seems clear that new approaches are needed to modeling climate impacts on agriculture; there is not yet an adequate summary analysis that incorporates the latest findings. This review addresses four major areas of research on climate and agriculture, reaching the following conclusions:

- Empirical research on carbon fertilization has reduced earlier estimates of this benefit of rising carbon dioxide concentrations.
- The new "threshold model" of temperature effects on crop yields provides a better explanation of (non-irrigated) U.S. data, and selected international data, than models based on average temperatures – and implies larger losses from warming.
- In some areas of the world, including California, the availability of water for irrigation is more important than anticipated near-term temperature increases; climatic changes that threaten water supplies could pose a threat to these areas.

• To date, Cline (2007) provides the best available aggregate estimates of climate impacts on agriculture. Cline includes current research on carbon fertilization, but not the threshold model of yields; incorporation of that model would be likely to lower his estimates.

Carbon fertilization

Plants grow by photosynthesis, a process that absorbs CO_2 from the air and converts it into organic compounds such as sugars. If the limiting factor in this process is the amount of CO_2 available to the plant, then an increase in the atmospheric concentration of CO_2 could act as a fertilizer, providing additional nutrients and allowing faster growth.

Almost all plants use one of two styles of photosynthesis.[3] In C_3 plants, which include the great majority of food crops and other plants, growth is limited by the availability of CO_2, so that carbon fertilization may be important. In contrast, C_4 plants have evolved a different photosynthetic pathway that uses atmospheric CO_2 more efficiently. C_4 plants, which include maize (corn), sugarcane, sorghum, and millet (as well as switchgrass, a potential biofuel feedstock) do not benefit from increased CO_2 concentrations except in drought conditions (Leakey 2009).

Initial experimental studies conducted in greenhouses or other enclosures found substantial carbon fertilization effects. The 2001 U.S. National Assessment summarized the experimental evidence available at that time as implying yield gains of 30 percent in C_3 crops and 7 percent in C_4 crops from a doubling of CO_2 concentrations (Reilly *et al.* 2001). More recently, Free-Air CO_2 Enrichment (FACE) experiments have allowed crops to be grown in outdoor environments with a greater resemblance to the actual conditions of production. According to a widely cited summary, the effects of CO_2 on yields for major grain crops are roughly 50 percent lower in FACE experiments than in enclosure studies (Long *et al.* 2004).[4] Another literature review reaches similar conclusions, offering "six important lessons from FACE," of which the sixth is that "the [CO_2] 'fertilization' effect in FACE studies on crop plants is less than expected" (Leakey 2009).

One summary of the results of FACE experiments reports that an increase in atmospheric CO_2 from 385 ppm (the actual level a few years ago) to 550 ppm would increase yields of the leading C_3 crops, wheat, soybeans, and rice, by 13 percent and would have no effect on yields of maize (corn) and sorghum, the leading C_4 grains (Ainsworth and McGrath 2010). Cline (2007) uses a similar estimate; because C_4 crops represent about one-fourth of world agricultural output, he projects a weighted average of 9 percent increase in global yields from 550 ppm.

While research on carbon fertilization has advanced in recent years, there are at least three unanswered questions in this area that are important for economic analysis. First, there is little information about the effects of very high CO_2 concentrations; many studies have only examined yields up to 550 ppm, and few have gone above 700 ppm. Long-term projections of business-as-usual emissions scenarios, however, can reach even higher concentrations. Does CO_2 fertilization continue to raise yields indefinitely, or does it reach an upper bound?

Second, most studies to date have focused on the highest-value crops, primarily the leading grains and cotton; other crops may have different responses to CO_2. In at least one case, the response may be negative: Cassava (manioc), a dietary staple for 750 million people in developing countries, shows sharply reduced yields at elevated CO_2 levels, with tuber mass reduced by an order of magnitude when CO_2 concentrations rise from 360 ppm to 710 ppm (Gleadow *et al.* 2009; Ghini *et al.* 2011).

Third, carbon fertilization may interact with other environmental influences. Fossil fuel combustion, the principal source of atmospheric CO_2, also produces tropospheric (ground-level) ozone, which reduces yields of many plants (Ainsworth and McGrath 2010). The net effect of carbon fertilization plus increased ozone is uncertain, but it is very likely to be less than the experimental estimates for carbon fertilization alone.

Temperature and yields

Many studies examine the effects of temperature on crop yields in order to project the expected results of climate scenarios. These studies often omit the effects of carbon fertilization, because CO_2 concentrations were roughly constant throughout the time span of the underlying data (typically the late twentieth century).

Most crops have an optimum temperature, with lower yields when it is either colder or hotter. A common model of this effect assumes that yields are a quadratic function of temperature. A recent worldwide survey of the four leading grain crops, using this model, estimated that from 1980 to 2008, climate change reduced maize yields by an average of 3.8 percent, and wheat yields by 5.5 percent; smaller reductions for rice and soybeans were not statistically significant (Lobell, Schlenker *et al.* 2011). Adding the assumed impact of carbon fertilization, a 3 percent gain for rice, wheat, and soybeans and zero for maize, the likely net effect was a small gain for rice and soybean yields, but losses for maize and wheat.

The quadratic model, however, imposes symmetry around the optimum: One degree too hot and one degree too cold are modeled as having the same effect on yields. A detailed study of temperature effects on corn, soybeans, and cotton in the United States finds strongly asymmetric patterns: Yields increase very slowly as the temperature rises to the optimum and then drop rapidly at higher temperatures (Schlenker and Roberts 2009). The study estimates the optimum temperatures to be 29°C for corn, 30°C for soybeans, and 32°C for cotton.

A very similar pattern was found in a study of temperature effects on maize yields in Africa, with a threshold of 30°C (Lobell, Bänziger, *et al.* 2011). Under ordinary conditions, the effects on yields of temperatures above the threshold were similar to those found in the United States; under drought conditions, yields declined even faster with temperature increases. Limited data on wheat in northern India also suggest that temperature increases above 34°C are more harmful than similar increases at lower levels (Lobell *et al.* 2012).

A key innovation in these studies, and in some other work cited below, is the specification of the temperature variable as degree days above a threshold; this fits the data much better than average temperature.[5] This approach has a solid grounding in plant biology: many crops are known to have temperature thresholds, in some cases at varying temperatures for different stages of development (Luo 2011). The drop in yields as temperatures rise above the threshold can be dramatic: For corn, Schlenker and Roberts (2009) estimate that replacing 24 hours of the growing season at 29°C with 24 hours at 40°C would cause a 7 percent decline in yields. The relationship between temperature and yields is quite similar in the coolest and warmest parts of the country, suggesting that there has been little or no adaptation to long-standing temperature differences. Assuming no change in growing locations, average yields (without carbon fertilization) are projected to decrease by 30 to 46 percent under slow (B1) warming or 63 to 82 percent under fast (A1FI) warming by the end of this century.

A study of five leading food crops in sub-Saharan Africa found strong relationships of yields to temperatures (Schlenker and Lobell 2010). By mid-century, under the A1B climate scenario, yields are projected to drop by 17 to 22 percent for maize, sorghum, millet, and groundnuts (peanuts) and by 8 percent for cassava. These estimates exclude carbon fertilization, but maize, sorghum, and millet are C_4 crops, while cassava has a negative response to increased CO_2, as noted above. Negative impacts are expected for a number of crops in developing countries by 2030. Among the crops most vulnerable to temperature increases are millet, groundnut, and rapeseed in South Asia; sorghum in the Sahel; and maize in Southern Africa (Lobell *et al.* 2008).

Other crops exhibit different patterns of temperature dependence; some perennials require a certain amount of "chill time," or hours below a low temperature threshold such as 7°C (chill thresholds and time requirements vary by crop and variety). In a study of the projected loss of winter chilling conditions in California, Germany, and Oman, fruit and nut trees showed large decreases in yield due to climate change (Luedeling *et al.* 2011). In this case, as with high-temperature yield losses, the relevant temperature variable is measured in terms of threshold effects, not year-round or even seasonal averages. Small changes in averages can imply large changes in the hours above or below thresholds, and hence large agricultural impacts.

Studies of temperatures and yields based on recent experience are limited in their ability to project the extent of adaptation to changing temperatures. Such adaptation has been important in the past: as North American wheat production expanded into colder, drier regions, farmers adapted by selecting different cultivars that could thrive in the new conditions; most of the adaptation occurred before 1930 (Olmstead and Rhode 2010). On the other hand, regions of the United States that are well above the optimum temperatures for maize, soybeans, and other major crops have grown these crops for many years, without any evidence of a large-scale shift to more heat-resistant crops or cultivars; temperature-yield relationships are quite similar in northern and southern states (Schlenker and Roberts 2009). Thus adaptation is an important possibility, but far from automatic.

In cases where adaptation is possible, including a shift in farm locations toward colder areas, the net impacts of 21st-century climate change may be modest. A study of China's rice, wheat, and maize production (Xiong *et al.* 2007), together with a more detailed analysis of the country's rice production (Xiong *et al.* 2009), finds that by the 2080s, yields will decrease without carbon fertilization but will increase if carbon fertilization is taken into account. Rice production, now concentrated in the hotter, southern regions of China, is expected to migrate northward; the development and adoption of heat-resistant cultivars are important to the prospects for grain yields. Slower climate change (the B2 rather than A2 scenario) will lead to greater food production in China.

Not every country has the option of shifting agriculture to colder regions. A study of wheat production in Australia projected that carbon fertilization would offset yield losses due to temperature and precipitation changes through 2050 but by 2070 yields would fall by 6 percent, even with carbon fertilization (Wang *et al.* 2009).

Water supply: precipitation and irrigation

There are multiple impacts of climate change on agriculture. Global rice production is at risk from inundation of coastal rice paddies by sea-level rise, as well as from temperature changes (Chen *et al.* 2011). Projected temperature changes appear to be more important than precipitation to overall uncertainty about climate effects in agriculture (Lobell *et al.* 2008). There are, however, important cases where water availability is the limiting factor, particularly in areas dependent on irrigation. Many irrigated areas are arid or semi-arid, and face the combined effects of reduced overall water supplies, greater variability, and greater salinity (Connor *et al.* 2012).

A study of rain-fed wheat cultivation in India found that yields in the years of lowest rainfall are 33 percent of the baseline (based on moderate rainfall years); a high level of irrigation is required to prevent major losses in the driest years (Pathak and Wassmann 2008). Indian monsoon rainfall has become less frequent but more intense, part of a pattern of climate change that is reducing wet-season rice yields (Auffhammer *et al.* 2011).Thus the most immediate climate risk to crops in India may be changes in rainfall.

In California, by far the leading agricultural state in the United States, the availability of water for irrigation is crucial to yields. One study projects an increase in California farm profits due to climate change, with gains for some crops and losses for others, assuming that current policies and the availability of irrigation are unchanged (Costello, Deschênes, *et al.* 2009). A study of farmland values in California found no significant correlation with temperature or precipitation but a strong relationship with irrigation water per acre (Schlenker *et al.* 2007). Perennial crops such as fruits and nuts are of great importance in California; individual crops differ widely in the impacts of climate on yields (Lobell *et al.* 2007). Among six leading California perennial crops, climate change through 2050 is projected to decrease yields in four cases and to cause no significant change in the other two – again, assuming that irrigation remains unchanged (Lobell *et al.* 2006).

The principal climate risk to California agriculture appears to be the possibility of shortfalls in irrigation. According to one recent study, climate change is increasing irrigation requirements, because crops need more water at warmer temperatures. This makes the already-serious, long-term regional water supply problems even harder to solve (Ackerman and Stanton 2011). A study of climate and California agriculture that focuses on the growing scarcity of water projects a drop in irrigated acreage and a shift toward higher-value, less-water-intensive crops (Howitt *et al.* 2009). An analysis of potential water scarcity in California due to climate change estimates that there will be substantial costs in dry years, in the form of both higher water prices and supply shortfalls, to California's Central Valley agriculture (Hanemann *et al.* 2006).

Other major agricultural areas in the United States, as noted above, generally have sufficient precipitation for rain-fed agriculture. Yet the second-generation bioenergy crops that have been discussed in the United States, such as switchgrass, require much more water than maize production, potentially limiting their use in low-rainfall areas (Le *et al.* 2011).

Aggregate impacts of climate on agriculture

A comprehensive assessment of climate impacts on U.S. agriculture, from the U.S. Climate Change Science Program, projects the effects on major crops of the next 30 years of climate change – interpreted as the combination of a 1.2°C temperature increase and an increase in atmospheric CO_2 from 380 to 440 ppm (Hatfield *et al.* 2008). It concludes that the benefits of CO_2 fertilization and the damages from rising temperatures will roughly offset each other in that time frame, resulting in only small changes in yields. Specifically, it projects yield gains (percentage changes in parentheses after each crop) in soybeans (+9.9 Midwest, +3.9 South), cotton (+3.5), and peanuts (+1.3); roughly no change in wheat (+0.1); and yield losses in dry beans (–2.5), maize (–3.0), rice (–5.6), and sorghum (–8.4). It anticipates that the outlook beyond 30 years will be less favorable, because adverse temperature effects will worsen while CO_2 fertilization benefits will diminish. The study also comments on the relative lack of research on climate impacts on livestock, which accounts for about half the value of U.S. agricultural output. And it notes that CO_2 fertilization appears to promote greater growth in weeds than in cash crops and that the widely used herbicide glyphosate (Roundup) is less effective against weeds at higher CO_2 concentrations. Climate effects on weeds are not included in the study's estimates of changes in crop yields (or in most research on yields).

As an alternative to studies of individual crops, some economists have tried to estimate the aggregate impacts of climate change on agriculture as a whole. One common approach, hedonic, or "Ricardian," analysis takes the value of farmland as an indicator of agricultural productivity and correlates it with climate variables. The name is inspired by David Ricardo's argument that the value of agricultural land depended on its fertility. Here, as with carbon fertilization, the conclusions of studies in the 1990s were more optimistic than newer research about the benefits of near-term warming.[6]

In a worldwide assessment of global warming and agriculture, William Cline projects that by the 2080s, a business-as-usual climate scenario (A2) would reduce world agricultural output by 16 percent without carbon fertilization or by 3 percent with carbon fertilization effects (Cline 2007).[7] Cline finds that the losses from climate change will be disproportionately concentrated in developing countries; for the United States, he projects an agricultural output loss of 6 percent without carbon fertilization or a gain of 8 percent with carbon fertilization.

Two major studies of U.S. agriculture have reached somewhat contradictory conclusions. Deschênes and Greenstone (2007) analyze county-level farm profits per acre[8] as a function of temperature, precipitation, and soil quality. Their model assumes quadratic relationships with temperature and precipitation. They estimate that by the end of the century, climate change will cause a 4 percent increase in agricultural profits nationwide, with considerable diversity among states; California suffers a 15 percent loss in farm profits in this model. A subsequent study of California, however, uses a similar model to project climate-related increases in farm profits for the state, with faster climate change (A2 versus B1) causing larger profits (Costello, Deschênes, *et al.* 2009).

Schlenker *et al.* (2006) analyze farmland values per acre for agricultural counties east of the 100th meridian.[9] They include similar explanatory variables and distinguish between two measures of temperature: growing season degree days in the range of 8 to 32°C (a range in which warmth is beneficial to many crops) and growing season degree days above 34°C (temperatures that are harmful to almost all crops).[10] By the end of the century, assuming there will be no change in growing locations, Schlenker *et al.* project average decreases in farmland value due to climate change ranging from 27 percent under the B1 climate scenario to 69 percent under A1FI. All the climate variables are significant, but more than 90 percent of the losses in every scenario are attributable to the increase in degree days above 34°C. A subsequent study of agriculture in California, the most important agricultural area west of the 100th meridian, found no significant correlation of farmland values and temperature or precipitation but a strong relationship with irrigation water per acre (Schlenker *et al.* 2007).

The differences between the studies of U.S. agriculture could reflect simply the differences in specification; there is no measure of extreme temperatures in the Deschênes and Greenstone (2007) analysis that corresponds to the all-important variable, degree days above 34°C, in the Schlenker *et al.* study. In addition, the latter research group has circulated a technical critique of the Deschênes and Greenstone analysis, alleging that there are significant gaps and errors in its data set and analytical problems in its use of the data (Fisher *et al.* 2010). A draft reply by Deschênes and Greenstone acknowledges the errors.[11]

The current understanding of agriculture

The rapid expansion of research on climate and agriculture has challenged earlier conclusions and broadened our knowledge of many specific aspects of the problem. It has not yet coalesced into a streamlined new synthesis. Based on the research now available, it appears that there is a moderate carbon fertilization benefit to most C_3 plants, with the caveats noted above. The relationship of yield to temperature, at least for several leading crops, is markedly asymmetrical, with a gradual increase as temperatures rise toward the optimum, followed by a rapid decline in proportion to degree days above that threshold. In some parts of the world, risks of change in the supply of water, either from precipitation or irrigation, may be the most important effect of climate on agriculture. In other farming areas, the anticipated increase in extremely hot days rather than the change in average temperature may be the dominant climate effect.

For an analysis of global impacts, Cline (2007) appears to be the newest and best available. Note, however, that Cline's estimate for the United States is much more optimistic than is the more-detailed Schlenker *et al.* (2006) study of climate impacts on U.S. agriculture, and does not include a measure of extremely hot days, or degree days above a threshold. For the 2080s in a business-as-usual emissions scenario, Cline projects a 3 percent net global loss of production due to climate change when carbon fertilization is included, with many northern countries seeing net gains. Net losses are expected for most developing countries and even with carbon fertilization benefits included, Cline projects yield losses greater than 20 percent for 29 countries and regions, primarily in Africa, Latin America, and South Asia; the expected losses are greater than 50 percent in some parts of Africa.[12]

In tropical areas, even small temperature increases are expected to cause a decline in yields for many crops; these impacts could be observable on a regional scale by the 2030s. Even 2 to 3°C of warming in this century would result in devastating losses to agricultural yields in many developing countries. In many temperate areas, new research continues to roll back earlier claims of increased agricultural yields from climate change. The latest research shows very modest net global gains from business-as-usual emissions throughout this century, but these net increases include net losses from many crops and regions.

The potential for adaptation to the early stages of climate change is a major uncertainty, and is likely to be quite site-specific. Changes in temperature, precipitation and other climate conditions provide a powerful incentive for adaptation, but even in high-income countries, agriculture has not always adapted to prevailing temperatures. Development of heat-resistant and drought-resistant crop varieties and farming practices is an important challenge, with unknown prospects for success.

Coastal flooding

With nearly two-fifths of the world population living in coastal zones, there is immense global exposure to a 1-in-100-year coastal flood (Hanson *et al.* 2010). Flooding from sea-level rise and storm surges has the potential to prompt large-scale migration of human populations, together with political instability, and could cause devastating losses of homes, businesses, infrastructure, and coastal shallow-water ecosystems. Recent studies of sea-level-rise impacts improve on older projections by including the best current estimates of the contribution from melting ice sheets (which were left out of AR4's estimates – see Chapter 1) by taking into account more information about regional variation in the rate of sea-level rise and by modeling the combined effects of sea-level rise and storm surge instead of taking each effect in isolation.

Sea-level rise

The combined effects of sea-level rise and storm surges pose a significant risk to coastal populations everywhere. As of 1995 (the latest year for which complete data are available), 39 percent of the world's population lived within 100 kilometers (60 miles) of the coast, with some of the most densely populated coastal areas in East and Southeast Asia, Europe, and the East Coast of the United States.[13] Sea-level rise varies significantly by region. Between 1992 and 2009, the rate of sea-level rise (including local subsidence and uplift) ranged from +20 mm per year in parts of Southeast Asia, Oceania, and northern Australia to –20 mm per year in the Caspian Sea and in isolated parts of the Arctic and Antarctic. Most areas saw sea levels rise at a rate of 2 to 5 mm per year. No standard source for projected sea-level rise currently exists (as discussed in Chapter 1), but a review of recent estimates by Nicholls and Cazenave (2010) gives a range of 0.3 to 1.8 m by 2100 across all SRES emissions scenarios.

Nicholls and Cazenave also review recent literature on populations vulnerable to climate-change-induced sea-level rise and report three areas of particular risk. First, the deltas of South, Southeast, and East Asia have large, rapidly growing coastal populations living at very low elevations. Second, Africa's coastal areas often have very low-income populations with high growth rates; Egypt and Mozambique are especially at risk. Finally, small island states in the Pacific and Indian oceans and the Caribbean face the worst risks, including the submergence of some low-lying islands such as the Maldives or Tuvalu during the twenty-first century. Other research confirms that developing countries are particularly at risk (Dasgupta *et al.* 2010).

In the United States, coastal counties accounted for 29 percent of the 2008 population and contained five of the ten most populous cities. Much of this population lives within a few meters of sea level, and is at risk from storm surges (Strauss *et al.* 2012). Nearly half of the U.S. coastal population (by this definition) lives on the Atlantic Coast – including 15 percent each in New York and Florida and another 15 percent on the Gulf Coast – and 29 percent live in

California (Wilson and Fischetti 2010). Sea-level-rise projections for the U.S. Atlantic and Pacific coasts are considerably higher than global mean changes.

A study of the U.S. coastline from Virginia to Massachusetts using mean global sea-level rise of 0.38 m (under the B2 climate scenario) and 0.45 m (under A2) by 2100 resulted in an increase in modeled sea levels up to 0.74 m, depending on local rates of sea-level rise and subsidence. The largest increases to sea level were projected for Maryland, New Jersey, and Virginia. By far the most populous areas likely to be inundated by 2100 are in New York and New Jersey (Wu *et al.* 2008). Other studies have found greater risks farther south, with the greatest threat to Miami, New Orleans, and Virginia Beach (Weiss *et al.* 2011). Recent research finds that coastal property values are much more sensitive to beach width than previously recognized, emphasizing the costs of sea-level rise and beach erosion (Gopalakrishnan *et al.* 2011).

For New York City, the effect of the expected change in ocean salinity on circulation alone has been projected to reach 0.15 to 0.21 m by 2100 – an additional source of sea-level rise not included in global mean projections (Yin *et al.* 2009). Detailed modeling of expected storm surge impacts shows growing risks to the New York City area (Lin *et al.* 2012).

On the U.S. Gulf Coast, the combined effect of sedimentation lost due to upstream dam construction and climate-change-induced sea-level rise may result in widespread inundation of the Mississippi Delta (Blum and Roberts 2009; Heberger *et al.* 2009). The combined effects of storm surges and sea-level rise are illustrated in a case study of the Corpus Christi, Texas region (Mousavi *et al.* 2010).

Storm surge

In the past, studies of coastal damages from climate change have often focused on a single mechanism, either permanent inundation from sea-level rise or storm-surge flooding from hurricanes and other major storms. The real impact of climate change on coastal regions, however, can be understood only as the confluence of these two effects. Some newer economic analyses of coastal climate damages look at both kinds of flooding: permanent inundation and *additional* storm-surge inundation starting from these new average sea levels.

Several recent studies combine the DINAS-COAST database of coastal social, economic, and ecological attributes with the Dynamic Interactive Vulnerability Assessment (DIVA) modeling tool and include both permanent and storm-surge inundation in their climate change scenarios (Vafeidis *et al.* 2008). Using DIVA, Nicholls *et al.* (2008) rank port cities by their vulnerability to flooding in the absence of adaptation. Assuming 0.5 m of flooding, along with some city-specific assumptions about anthropogenic subsidence, the ten most vulnerable cities with current populations greater than one million are Mumbai, Guangzhou, Shanghai, Miami, Ho Chi Minh City, Kolkata, Greater New York, Osaka-Kobe, Alexandria, and New Orleans. In terms of exposed assets, the most vulnerable cities are Miami, Greater New York, New Orleans, Osaka-Kobe,

Tokyo, Amsterdam, Rotterdam, Nagoya, Tampa-St. Petersburg, and Virginia Beach. All these cities are located in just three countries: the United States, Japan, and the Netherlands. Dasgupta *et al.* (2009) use DIVA to model how storm-surge impacts intensify in developing countries with a 1-meter rise in sea levels. The ten countries at greatest risk in terms of the share of coastal population affected are the Bahamas, Kuwait, Djibouti, United Arab Emirates, Belize, Yemen, Togo, Puerto Rico, El Salvador, and Mozambique.

Countless other studies use detailed Global Information System (GIS) elevation data, local tide, subsidence and uplift observations, and regionalized sea-level-rise projections to fine-tune economic analyses to the best possible current information. For example, one study projects that 1.4 m of sea-level rise would put half a million Californians at risk of storm-surge flooding, many of them in low-income communities. This same study also emphasizes that many areas of the California coast are not directly vulnerable to flooding (because of their steep topography) but are still extremely susceptible to erosion (Heberger *et al.* 2009).

Local studies offer the greatest accuracy but are generally very small in scope, covering a single island, inlet, or coastal region. A study by Stanton *et al.* (2010) applies the techniques used in local sea-level-rise studies to the full length of the Canadian coastline. Combining detailed elevation and sea-level-rise data with national census data, the study finds that the combined effects of permanent and storm-surge flooding will have the greatest economic impacts on British Columbia. Throughout Canada's coastal regions, low-income and racial/ethnic minority populations face elevated vulnerability to climate-change-related flooding.

Projections of future increases in tropical cyclone intensity (see Chapter 1) have been applied in economic analyses. A widely cited recent study projects rapid growth in storm damages (Mendelsohn *et al.* 2012); other researchers have suggested reasons why that study may be an underestimate (Hallegatte 2012). Modeling of worldwide mortality risk from tropical cyclones shows steep increases due to increased storm intensity, demographic pressure and poverty in vulnerable areas, and other factors (Peduzzi *et al.* 2012). A review emphasizing the uncertainties surrounding climate effects on hurricanes concludes that the policy implications – such as the need for increased protection of vulnerable regions – may be independent of the underlying causal relationships (Grossmann and Morgan 2011).

Human health

Likely impacts on human health from climate change documented in AR4 include increased incidence of malnutrition; increased incidence of disease, injury, and death from heat waves, floods, storms, fires, and droughts; and changes in the range of some infectious diseases, including malaria (IPCC 2007a, *Working Group II*, Chapter 8).[14] Climate change exacerbates the spread of diseases attributable to poverty and globalization (Yacoub *et al.* 2011). In historical perspective, it is no surprise that climate change affects health; past episodes of climate change, milder than we face today, have led to destabilization of societies, food shortages, disease outbreaks, and related problems (McMichael 2012). Today, as much as 88 percent of the disease burden from climate change falls on children, compared to the overall pediatric burden of disease – 5 percent in high-income countries and 31 percent in developing countries (Sheffield and Landrigan 2011; Tillett 2011; Bernstein and Myers 2011).

A number of specific diseases and health conditions are worsened by climate change. One study of the change in incidence of diarrheal diseases under a business-as-usual emissions scenario projected a 22 to 29 percent increase by the late twenty-first century (Kolstad and Johansson 2010). In Bangladesh, the incidence of cholera is linked to coupled ocean-atmospheric variability in the Indian Ocean (Hashizume *et al.* 2010), while sea-level rise causes increased salinity of drinking water during the dry season, leading to increases in hypertension during pregnancy (Khan *et al.* 2011).

Temperature is by far the best-studied link between climate and human health.[15] While most experts expect negative health effects from rising temperatures, this opinion is not quite unanimous. One study projects that 1°C of warming will save more than 800,000 lives a year by 2050. This appears to be based on a series of errors that led to mistaken projections of large reductions in cold-related deaths and much smaller increases in heat-related deaths.[16] In the opinion of most other analysts, global warming will be harmful to human health (Huang *et al.* 2011; Anderson and Bell 2010). The real culprit in heat-induced mortality, however, is not gradual warming but rather the greater incidence of life-threatening heat waves.

Heat waves have caused widespread mortality and morbidity, notably in 2003 in Western Europe and in 2010 in Russia, but also in smaller events around the world. The latest research on temperature stress in humans shows that heat waves associated with a 7°C increase in mean global temperatures could make some regions uninhabitable without air conditioning. At an 11 to 12°C increase, regions currently containing a majority of the world population would be rendered uninhabitable – that is, these regions would reach, at least once a year, combinations of temperature and humidity that human beings cannot survive (Sherwood and Huber 2010). Weitzman (2010a) has argued on this basis that 12°C warming would essentially destroy the world economy (see Chapter 2).

Heat waves have important health effects short of mortality. Even with just a few degrees of warming, labor productivity would be affected in many tropical areas (Kjellstrom *et al.* 2009). Extreme heat reduces the gestational age (increases prematurity) of babies (Dadvand *et al.* 2011).

Greenhouse gas mitigation not only is expected to keep temperature increases to a minimum but also holds great potential for providing ancillary benefits in relation to human health. Combustion of fossil fuels and biomass results in the release of particulates, ground-level ozone, and other pollutants, thereby greatly reducing air quality. Climate-change-induced wildfires have similar effects, and the increasing incidence of asthma and other diseases triggered by airborne allergens is also thought by some researchers to be related to climate change. Emission mitigation would have the beneficial side effect of improving air quality

(Haines *et al.* 2010; Markandya *et al.* 2009; Tagaris *et al.* 2009).[17] Measures to reduce black carbon and methane emissions have large health benefits, and increase crop yields; these benefits are worth much more than the likely costs of abatement (Shindell *et al.* 2012; Anenberg *et al.* 2012).

New research that incorporates effects on air quality into general circulation models shows increased ozone and particulate levels, especially in urban areas (Jacob and Winner 2009). Fuel choice is a key predictor of future air pollution levels. A study comparing the life-cycle emissions of biofuels to those of gasoline found health impacts to be higher for corn ethanol, lower for cellulosic ethanols, and especially low for ethanols derived from diverse prairie vegetation (Hill *et al.* 2009). Research from the United Kingdom finds that fuel choices have complex effects on air quality, which may limit the near-term ancillary benefits of mitigation in practice. Since 2001, UK policies to reduce greenhouse gas emissions have been associated with an increase in the market share of diesel cars, and diesel fuel releases pollutants that have more dangerous health effects than those of gasoline (Mazzi and Dowlatabadi 2007).

Undesirable organisms will also be affected by climate change. In North America, warming is already extending the ragweed pollen season (Ziska *et al.* 2011). There is an ongoing debate about the relationship between climate change and malaria: On the one hand, transmission of malaria is optimized at temperatures of 28 to 32°C but is blocked by temperatures below 16°C, implying that warming will increase vulnerability in many areas. On the other hand, there are many other factors that have an equal or greater influence on the spread of malaria, creating uncertainty about the future outlook for the disease (Chaves and Koenraadt 2010; Ermert *et al.* 2011). Dengue fever is transmitted by a particular mosquito whose range is limited by adult and larval cold tolerance, and warming will allow the mosquito, and hence the disease, to expand into areas currently too cold for it (Kearney *et al.* 2009).

A final area of concern human health is water availability. Regional downscaling of climate models suggests that in most cases, wet regions will become wetter and dry regions dryer with climate change, posing a grave problem for areas that are already water stressed. The Sahara, Kalahari, Gobi, and Great Sandy deserts are expected to expand, and 10 to 20 percent decreases in precipitation are projected for already-dry areas around the world (see Chapter 1). Arid regions facing reduced precipitation risk water shortages unless they can make up the difference from groundwater (a finite source and, therefore, a short-term solution), energy-intensive ocean desalination, and conservation and efficiency measures.

Recent advances in modeling water availability, due in part to improved projections of the rate of melting glaciers and other land ice (see Chapter 1), suggest that precipitation changes can only partially predict water stress suffered by human communities. Since AR4, global systems for tracking glaciers have become more complete and more accurate (Cogley 2010), and effects on glaciers can now be represented in regional climate models (Kotlarski *et al.* 2009). As climate change progresses, water availability will decrease in river systems fed by glacier meltwater, including large parts of Southeastern Europe, and Central and Eastern Asia. In a few areas, high dependence on glacial meltwater coincides with high population density. The regions that rely on the Aral Sea, Indus River, and Ganges River stand out in their water supply vulnerability (Kaser *et al.* 2010).

Likely impacts and catastrophes

With continued business-as-usual emissions, the most likely end-of-the-century temperature increase is 4.2°C (with a one-in-ten chance of temperatures falling below 2.3°C in the most optimistic business-as-usual scenario and exceeding 7.1°C in the most pessimistic). At this rate of change in temperatures, agricultural productivity will decline in South Asia and Africa by the 2030s. Without adaptation, by late in the century average global agricultural yields will have fallen by 6 percent, with much larger losses in most of the developing world. In some parts of Africa, more than half of the current agricultural output would be lost to climate change by the 2080s.

Another most likely result of business-as-usual emissions is 1.2 m of sea-level rise by 2100. Low-lying small islands, coastal and delta populations are especially vulnerable to rising sea levels. Without adaptation, serious flooding damage could occur before mid-century. Studies using one-half or less of the most likely 2100 sea-level rise predict large-scale damages. With the likely changes in temperature and sea levels will come an increase in disease, injury, and death associated with heat waves; changes to the range of disease vectors; and reduced access to clean water. Children, especially, will be vulnerable to negative health effects from climate change.

In catastrophic scenarios of climate change, with temperatures and sea levels rising much faster than the most likely rates, the probable impacts on human systems described here would occur closer to mid-century.

Climate-economics models commonly include estimates of damages in terms of GDP losses – losses to economic output from the forestry, fisheries, agriculture, and tourism sectors – and also sometimes include damages to coastal infrastructure or a decrease in labor productivity. Climate damages may, however, include losses that cannot easily be measured in monetary terms: permanent inundation of entire communities and even entire nations; irreversible harm to ecosystems, including the permanent loss of biodiversity; or lives lost to climate-induced disease or injury. Economic models of damages to human systems cannot truly represent these catastrophic losses, and in any case, this is an area where economic analysis currently lags far behind scientific research (see Chapter 2).

Part III

Economic theories and models

5 Climate economics before and after the Stern Review

Recent scientific research has deepened and transformed our knowledge of climate change. As seen in Chapter 1, the earth's climate is a complex, nonlinear system with dynamics that cannot be predicted in detail – including, among other hazards, the possibility of thresholds at which abrupt, irreversible transitions could occur. A range of feedback effects intensify the warming caused by rising concentrations of greenhouse gases, leading to a rapid, though perhaps irreducibly uncertain, pace of climate change. There is also a growing understanding of the numerous harmful impacts that are expected before the end of this century, even at the most likely rate of climate change, and of the additional catastrophic outcomes that could result – with lower but nontrivial probability – if climate change proceeds more rapidly.

These results of climate science have important implications for economic theory. Analyses and models that project modest-sized, precisely known climate impacts, although still seen in the economics literature, now seem quaint and dated. They are based, at best, on hopes and guesses that might have been reasonable to entertain in the 1990s or earlier, before the nature and magnitude of the problem became so painfully clear. New developments in climate science require corresponding new developments in climate economics (Scrieciu *et al.* 2011).

In the most general terms, there should be a qualitative match between the economics of climate change and the pattern of scientific findings on which it rests. Scientific projections of climate outcomes are uncertain, with the range of possibilities including extremely damaging impacts; therefore, the corresponding economic projections should consist of ranges of possibilities, including economic results that reflect the seriousness of worst-case climate outcomes.

There are three fundamental features of climate change that pose unique challenges to economic theory, requiring extensions of economic analysis into unfamiliar territory. In brief, they involve the extent of uncertainty, the spans of time involved, and the global nature of the problem and its solutions. Each of these issues arises, often in a more limited form, in other areas of economics; an extreme form of each of these issues is central to climate economics, potentially requiring new and different approaches. Moreover, as explained later in this chapter, one of the traditional frameworks for climate economics conflates all three issues, leading to paradoxical implications that are only beginning to be resolved in recent economics research.

High-stakes uncertainty

Any analysis involving future outcomes is subject to some uncertainty. The accumulated effect of small unknowns naturally grows over time, with the result that uncertainty is normally greater at a longer horizon. A standard practice in economic theory is to calculate the expected value, or certainty equivalent, of future outcomes over the range of possibilities, but this is of limited help in cases where the future probability distribution is unknown. In the terminology introduced long ago by Frank Knight (1921), expected values can be calculated for risks with known probabilities but not for uncertainties with unknown probability.[1] The dilemmas of decision making under Knightian uncertainty arise in multiple policy arenas, including, among others, toxic chemical hazards (Ackerman 2008), nuclear reactor safety, and nuclear waste management, as well as the threat of terrorism and, perhaps, systemic financial crises (for a thoughtful review, see Farber 2011).

Climate change involves uncertainty on many levels. In the near term, climate change appears to be associated with increased hazards from extreme weather events. Individual extreme events are not predictable on any but the shortest timescale; the global weather system exhibits very complex dynamics that defy long-run prediction. Indeed, a path-breaking early analysis of chaotic dynamics and sensitive dependence on initial conditions emerged from a simple weather model (Lorenz 1963; Gleick 1987). The probability distribution of extreme events is, in part, an area of still-unsettled science but may well be worsening as the world warms (see, for examples, the ongoing debates over hurricane frequency and intensity in Chapter 1). The uncertainty surrounding extreme events is a central concern in the economics of adaptation (see Chapter 11).

In the longer run, much of the science described in Chapter 1 implies that there are nonzero probabilities of irreversible changes that would threaten the prosperity or even survival of human society in its present form. While still reasonably improbable under today's conditions, these dangers will become ever less unlikely as the temperature rises. There may even be tipping points at which fairly abrupt transitions to worse outcomes will occur (Lenton *et al.* 2008). Learning about the risks of tipping points by trial and error is not an option, because climate change is an experiment that we can only do once. The stakes could not be higher, forcing us to consider disastrous risks and to question how unlikely is unlikely enough. In contrast to most other policy problems that involve decision making under uncertainty, the worst-case outcomes from climate change appear to be unbounded, involving arbitrarily large threats to our common future. Long-term catastrophic risk is the subject of some of the most important recent developments in climate economics, discussed in Chapter 6.

Deep time

Comparisons of costs and benefits at different points in time are common in economics; most investments involve consequences that stretch multiple years into the future. In the case of climate change, however, the standard methodology for intertemporal calculations, or the discounting of future values, has resulted in extensive, unresolved controversy. Discount rates used in other areas are often so high that, if applied to climate policy, they imply that the well-being of future generations and the most serious long-term consequences of climate change can be ignored.

The logic of the elementary textbook argument for discounting is unimpeachable once its numerous assumptions are granted. Suppose that an investor is evaluating a private investment that yields a known monetary benefit at a future date within the investor's lifetime and imposes no externalities on anyone else. Assume that future market outcomes, including incomes and rates of return on capital, are known with certainty. Then the future benefit should be discounted at the market rate of return. If the market rate of return is a constant r, and a benefit X occurs T years from now, then its present value is either $X(1+r)^{-T}$ or Xe^{-rT}, depending on whether time is treated as a discrete (annual) or a continuous variable.

Many of the assumptions in this story about discounting are clearly inapplicable to climate economics. Hence the discounting debate can be reframed around two related questions: Which assumptions have to be changed in order to apply discounting to climate change? And how does that affect the discount rate or the discounting process? Each of the three major issues in climate economics addressed in this review has implications for the discounting debate.

Uncertainty pervades the calculations of climate costs and benefits, affecting, among other things, future incomes, market rates of return, and climate outcomes. Much of the discussion of uncertainty in Chapter 6 has a direct effect on the appropriate discount rate. Some aspects of uncertainty imply that a low and/ or declining discount rate should be used. This involves still-unsettled questions at the frontiers of economic research.

The global externalities associated with greenhouse gas emissions, and the view of climate policies as global public goods (discussed below), raise questions about the appropriateness of the private investment framework for decision making. That framework is implicit in the elementary argument for discounting. Here, too, there is ongoing, unresolved debate, often presented in terms of political economy and ethics rather than formal economic theory.

The vast time span of climate processes also affects the discounting framework, requiring it to be applied to events far beyond a single lifetime. Climate science makes it clear that causation stretches across centuries. A significant fraction of CO_2 emissions remains in the atmosphere for more than a century, continuing to warm the earth and change the climate throughout that period of time. As atmospheric temperatures rise, the oceans take centuries to catch up; the thermal expansion of oceans causes sea-level rise, which will continue for centuries after atmospheric temperatures are stabilized. Major ice sheets melt (and hence contribute to sea-level rise) over a multi-century time frame. Even if a tipping point were to occur at which, for instance, complete loss of the Greenland Ice Sheet became inevitable, it would take centuries to finish melting.

As a result, costs and benefits of the same climate policy will typically be spread across multiple centuries. This changes one of the important, usually implicit assumptions in the simple story about discounting: It is impossible for a single individual to experience both the costs and benefits of today's actions. Instead, current costs must be weighed against benefits to be experienced, in significant part, by future people whose lifetimes will not overlap with those of us who are alive today. Is discounting applicable to intergenerational decisions? If so, what discount rate should be used? If not, what other methods should be used for intergenerational decision making?

The problem of decision making across "deep time" arises in other contexts, perhaps most dramatically in the case of nuclear waste. Some of the byproducts of nuclear reactors and nuclear weapons production will remain hazardous for hundreds of thousands of years, raising unique challenges for protection of and communication with our far-future descendants (see, e.g., Benford 1999).

Climate change occurs on a timescale that is modest compared to the many millennia of nuclear waste hazards – but immense compared to almost everything else, and outside the boundaries of familiar methodologies such as single-lifetime discounting. This question is explored further in Chapter 7.

It's a small world

Externalities and public goods are familiar features of economics; free-rider problems and other conflicts over the provision and financing of public goods are endemic. In political economy terms, all public policies are debated and adopted in the context of an unequal world where costs, benefits, incomes, and opportunities are often distributed unfairly. Yet in most cases, externalities and remedies can be addressed at a local, national, or regional level, setting aside the formidable problems of international inequality and the lack of effective global governance.

Climate change is the ultimate global externality. Greenhouse gases emitted anywhere contribute to global warming everywhere. Sea-level rise on all islands and coastal regions is a function of the total volume of water in the world's oceans. Climate solutions are equally universal, requiring virtually complete global cooperation in emission reduction and other policies. Other global externalities have arisen in the past; the frequently cited example of stratospheric ozone depletion provides a success story for international negotiation. The Montreal Protocol for elimination of ozone-depleting substances, however, involved costs that are smaller by orders of magnitude than the likely costs of climate mitigation, as well as technological changes in only a few industries. Climate change appears to be unique in the magnitude of costs and the extent of technological transformation required for a solution. (The expected costs and technology implications of climate policies are discussed in Chapters 8 and 9.)

While the global nature of climate change means that we are all in the same boat, some of us have much nicer cabins than others. There are important inequalities in climate impacts, historical responsibility, and ability to pay for both adaptation and mitigation. Climate damages are expected to vary greatly by location, with tropical, coastal, and arid regions likely to be hardest hit; these are disproportionately lower-income parts of the world. In terms of responsibility, the long-term persistence of greenhouse gases in the atmosphere means that global warming today is driven by emissions over the past century or more; those historical emissions are in large part the result of the economic growth of high-income countries. In terms of ability to pay, climate costs will be felt everywhere, but the need for adaptation funding will be greatest in the hardest-hit, disproportionately low-income countries, and the need for mitigation funding will be most urgent in rapidly industrializing, emerging economies with low-to-medium per capita incomes.

In this small and interdependent world, a climate solution must be accepted as fair by both rich and poor nations in order to succeed. This challenging requirement has been widely discussed in the context of international negotiations but has received less attention in the economics literature. It is explored further in Chapter 7.

Stern and his predecessors

The remainder of this chapter reviews the treatment of two of these fundamental issues, uncertainty and discounting, in climate economics before and in the Stern Review (Stern 2006). (The somewhat separate and more limited literature on global equity issues in climate economics is presented in Chapter 7.) The chapter then closes with a comparison to the economics of financial markets, which has become important in the recent discussion of climate economics. Chapter 6 examines the analysis of uncertainty since the Stern Review, and Chapter 7 turns to developments in discounting and equity – both between generations and within the world today.

Uncertainty before Stern

In the era before the Stern Review, economic models of climate change were typically framed as cost–benefit analyses, evaluating known or expected outcomes. In some cases, predictable, bounded variation was included via Monte Carlo analysis, as in studies by Richard Tol (for example, Tol 2002) using the FUND model. (On the approach to uncertainty in early studies, see Watkiss and Downing 2008.) Two well-known models, DICE and PAGE, took another step: Each included, in a limited fashion, the potential for abrupt, "catastrophic" losses. These losses initially have low or zero probability but become less improbable as temperatures rise.

In DICE, the magnitude of a potential catastrophe was initially based on a survey of expert opinion in the early 1990s (discussed most fully in Roughgarden and Schneider 1999); minor adjustments have been made since then (Nordhaus 2008). Uncertainty is represented by assigning a small, temperature-dependent probability to the average of expert guesses about the magnitude of catastrophe. The certainty-equivalent value (i.e., the product of probability and magnitude) is then included in the DICE damage function. Thus, DICE assigns a value to its interpretation of uncertainty but then treats the expected value as if it were a certain cost of climate change.

PAGE, from its earliest versions through PAGE2002 (the version used by the Stern Review), has calibrated its damage estimates to other studies and models such as DICE (Hope 2006). PAGE includes a potential catastrophe, with its most likely magnitude comparable to the DICE estimate of catastrophe. In PAGE, however, three key parameters – the temperature threshold for catastrophe, the (temperature-dependent) probability of occurrence once that threshold is reached, and the magnitude of catastrophe – are all Monte Carlo variables. While producing average results similar to DICE, PAGE is also able to generate probability distributions, showing extremes such as 95th percentile outcomes, as well as mean outcomes.

Uncertainty in the Stern Review

The Stern Review called for a broad reframing of the economics of climate change. Regarding uncertainty, its starting point was the scientific analyses of potential tipping points, with serious threats of large-scale, irreversible harms from just a few degrees of warming. In later writing as well, Stern has continued to argue that economists need to take such dangers seriously (Stern 2008).

The quantitative calculations in the Stern Review, however, did not represent a complete break with past modeling. The Stern Review used the PAGE2002 model with only limited changes in its inputs and parameters; the assumptions about catastrophes, calibrated to DICE and other earlier studies, remained unchanged. Thus, it could be argued that the narrative of the Stern Review implied a need for upward revision in the estimates of both the magnitude and likelihood of catastrophe (Ackerman *et al.* 2009) – a perspective that is influencing a forthcoming revision of the PAGE model[2] – but the Stern Review's economic calculations only partially reflect Stern's prescription for change in climate economics. Nonetheless, the PAGE2002 model results used in the Stern Review projected larger climate damages than did many other economic analyses, in part because the Stern Review's low discount rate raised the present value of catastrophes, which are more likely to occur in the later years of the multi-century simulations.

Some critics argue that the Stern Review overstates the risk, and therefore the certainty-equivalent value, of future damages. In their view, Stern's damage calculations are biased upward both by the use of damage estimates based on assumptions about risk that are incompatible with the Stern Review's own model and by the assumption that uncertainty is not reduced by learning about the climate system over time (Tol and Yohe 2006). Other critics make the opposite argument, maintaining that the Stern Review underplays the degree of uncertainty in climate science, making excessively confident predictions of severe climate impacts (Carter *et al.* 2006; Byatt *et al.* 2006).

The Stern Review team's response is that, if anything, the Stern Review understates uncertainty and damages; it uses damage estimates based on "best guess" calculations (thus ignoring known sources of uncertainty), and it deliberately includes only modest feedback effects. While future learning about the climate system is possible, this may not diminish uncertainty (e.g., see the discussion of climate sensitivity in Chapter 1). It does not support delayed action, which could be an additional source of risk (Dietz, Hope, *et al.* 2007; Dietz, Anderson, *et al.* 2007).

Discounting before Stern

The early discussion of discounting and intertemporal equity in climate economics was framed by a chapter of the IPCC's Second Assessment Report, written by six prominent economists, including Kenneth Arrow and Joseph Stiglitz (Arrow *et al.* 1996). They introduced the basic distinction between "prescriptive" and "descriptive" approaches to discounting, as well as summarizing leading arguments for and against each approach.[3]

The prescriptive approach, according to Arrow *et al.* (1996), assumes that discounting of future costs and benefits is an ethical issue; the appropriate discount rate, therefore, should be deduced from first principles, focusing on the utility of consumption today versus consumption tomorrow. The foundation of this approach, credited to Ramsey (1928), is an argument demonstrating that along an optimal growth path, the discount rate for consumption equals the productivity of capital. Later mathematical analysis led to the formalization of this principle in what is often referred to as the "Ramsey equation." In the *Stern Review*'s (2006) notation:

$$\rho = \delta + \eta g \tag{5.1}$$

Here, ρ is the discount rate applied to consumption, or to goods and services in general; δ is the rate of pure time preference, i.e., the discount rate that would apply if all generations had equal resources (or equivalently, it is the discount rate for utility); η is the elasticity of the marginal utility of consumption (discussed later in this chapter); and g is the growth rate of per capita consumption.

The descriptive approach, on the other hand, assumes that discounting should be based on the choices that people actually make about present versus future consumption. That is, the discount rate should be inferred from current rates of return on financial assets. In this view, setting the discount rate below market interest rates would allow investments in mitigation to crowd out more valuable, higher-return investments in other activities, thus reducing the overall resources available for future generations.

Another valuable background source is the massive literature review by Frederick *et al.* (2002). It surveys the rich complexity of economic thinking about time and discounting, both before and after the brief paper by Samuelson (1937) that introduced the idea of a constant discount rate. Frederick *et al.* (2002) examine numerous arguments for hyperbolic or declining discount rates, including evidence drawn from experimental or behavioral economics. They do not, however, include the important analysis of Weitzman (1998), which demonstrates that under a descriptive approach to discounting, uncertainty about future interest rates can imply a steadily declining "certainty equivalent" discount rate. The same qualitative conclusion is reached when the analysis is reformulated to account for additional risks and complexities (Weitzman 2010a).

Discounting in the Stern Review

The Stern Review provides an extensive discussion of the ethical issues involved in discounting, advocating a prescriptive approach with a near-zero value for δ, the rate of pure time preference. All people of current and future generations are of equal moral standing and deserve equal treatment, according to the Stern Review. A larger rate of pure time preference would inappropriately devalue future people who are not yet here to speak for themselves. Similar arguments date back at least to Ramsey and have been made by many economists and philosophers; no attempt will be made to review that earlier literature here.

At the same time, a value of exactly zero for pure time preference is problematic for economic theory. With an unbounded time horizon, it would imply that the present value of future utility is infinite and that the welfare of the current generation could be ignored as a vanishingly small part of the intergenerational whole. Stern's solution is to include a small probability that human society will not survive some unspecified cataclysm, arbitrarily set at 0.1 percent per year. This becomes the rate of pure time preference: Because we are only 99.9 percent sure that anyone will be around next year, the certainty-equivalent present value of next year's well-being is 0.999 as great as this year's. There is a strong feeling of *deus ex machina* (or perhaps *diabolus ex machina*) about this solution, but it results in a low discount rate without setting the pure time preference literally to zero.

Stern was not the first economist to advocate low discount rates. Cline (1992) proposed a similarly low discount rate, including the pure time preference of zero, and reached conclusions similar to Stern's about the economic justification for immediate, large-scale mitigation efforts. The high profile of the Stern Review, however, led to renewed debate on the issue. Many critiques, such as Nordhaus (2007), Tol and Yohe (2006), and Yohe (2006), identified the low discount rate – much lower than rates conventionally used by economists or policy makers – as the principal weakness of the Stern Review. Some noted that Stern's near-zero rate of pure time preference, if used by individuals, would imply much higher savings rates than are actually observed (Arrow 2007; Weitzman 2007), so that if discount rates are to be consistent with actual savings behavior, the rate of pure time preference should be higher. In this context, Stern's very low rate of pure time preference has been described as paternalistic (Weitzman 2007; Nordhaus 2007), imposing its own ethical judgment over the revealed preferences of most individuals. Debate continues on these issues, with Baum (2009), for example, defending Stern against the charges of paternalism. It seems safe to conclude that no resolution has been reached, or is in sight, to the fundamental disagreement over the rate of pure time preference.

The Ramsey equation: an unsolved puzzle?

The rate of pure time preference is not the only locus of controversy concerning the discount rate. As seen in equation (5.1), the discount rate also includes a term involving η, the elasticity of marginal utility. Additional, perhaps more esoteric controversy surrounds the choice of η. Both Cline and Stern assumed relatively low values of η (1.5 and 1.0, respectively), contributing to their low discount rates. Other economists have argued that η should be higher, which implies a higher discount rate (as long as per capita consumption is rising, so that $g > 0$ in equation 5.1).

It is common to assume a utility function that exhibits constant relative risk aversion (CRRA), of the form

$$u(c) = \frac{c^{1-\eta} - 1}{1 - \eta} \tag{5.2}$$

Here c is per capita consumption and η is the coefficient of relative risk aversion. (When $\eta = 1$, equation 5.2 is replaced by $u(c) = \ln c$.) The CRRA utility function is mathematically convenient but is not based on empirical evidence about consumer behavior. Even in theoretical terms, CRRA utility is problematic: Although it is useful under a specific set of conventional assumptions about growth and uncertainty, its useful properties are not robust under small changes in these assumptions (Geweke 2001). Indeed, there are problems with the entire analysis of risk aversion in terms of utility maximization with a concave utility function such as CRRA. In general, this approach cannot provide an explanation of risk aversion that applies consistently across risks of widely differing magnitudes (Rabin 2000; Rabin and Thaler 2001).

Despite these problems, the CRRA utility function is almost an industry standard in climate-economics models. When it is used in combination with the Ramsey equation, the same parameter η simultaneously measures risk aversion, "inequality aversion" within the current generation, and inequality aversion over time toward future generations (Atkinson *et al.* 2009). A larger value of η implies greater risk aversion in equation (5.2) and hence greater inequality aversion in the present, i.e., more egalitarian standards. It also implies a higher discount rate in equation (5.1), diminishing the importance attached to future generations. This paradox is highlighted in the response to the Stern Review from Dasgupta (2007), who accepts Stern's low rate of pure time preference but still maintains that Stern's overall discount rate is too low, because a higher value of η is required for equity in public policy decisions today. In this formulation, fairness to the poor in this generation seems to require paying less attention to future generations.

Similar problems have arisen in the economics of finance, which uses some of the same analytical apparatus. It has been known for some time that models based on the CRRA utility function cannot easily explain the "equity premium puzzle," i.e., the relatively high level of the return on equity and the low level of the risk-free rate (Mehra and Prescott 1985). Using a standard growth model, Mehra and Prescott found that values of η less than 10 were not consistent with either a high enough return on equity or a low enough risk-free rate to match the historical data. Despite decades of analysis, there is no universally accepted resolution to the equity premium puzzle (DeLong and Magin 2009).

There are, however, many analyses and rival proposed explanations. Several innovative ideas in climate economics, described in the next chapter, arise as analogs to the equity premium puzzle literature in finance.

New ideas in climate economics

The next two chapters review the new and ongoing developments that are transforming climate economics. Traditional cost–benefit frameworks are not appropriate to the challenges of modeling our uncertain, multigenerational, and uniquely global climate crisis. Chapter 6, "Uncertainty," looks at the latest research incorporating uncertain climate and economic forecasts into integrated assessment models. The likelihood of irreversible, catastrophic damage is small but nontrivial, and irreducible uncertainties in the physical system raise the possibility of unbounded risks and the question of how to model such risks.

Chapter 7, "Public goods and public policy," addresses new innovations in modeling costs and damages over long timescales and disparate populations. Climate change is a global public goods problem that raises modeling challenges unique in the literature of economic analysis. Equity both within and between countries complicates assumptions about the discount rate and calls into question the best way to aggregate the well-being of an economically diverse world population in order to make fair policy decisions.

6 Uncertainty

A core message of the science of climate change is that climate outcomes are uncertain – and the range of possibilities includes very serious threats to human society and existing natural ecosystems. The Stern Review (Stern 2006) took a step forward in recognizing the significance of this deep uncertainty and calling for its incorporation into economics, as described in Chapter 5. Since Stern, there has been an ever-expanding exploration of the economics of climate uncertainty, which is the subject of this chapter. Even in analyses that lead to moderate rates of abatement, the results may be driven more by uncertainty than by expected outcomes (Pindyck 2012).

Uncertainty about the climate sensitivity parameter – the temperature increase resulting from a doubling of the atmospheric concentration of CO_2 – has been widely discussed and is the basis for Weitzman's "dismal theorem," the subject of the first section of this chapter. A second section briefly reviews studies that have incorporated several varieties of uncertainty. The final section examines new work on interpretations of risk aversion and the parallels to similar topics in finance.

The line separating this chapter from the following one is inevitably somewhat blurred. Many issues relating to discounting and intergenerational analysis, decision-making standards, and global equity – subjects covered in Chapter 7 – have implications for uncertainty. Conversely, the discussion of uncertainty in this chapter affects discounting and other topics in the next chapter. The two should be read as a linked pair, treating the range of recent innovations in climate economics.

Climate sensitivity and the dismal theorem

In a widely cited assessment of the Stern Review, Weitzman (2007a) said that Stern was "right for the wrong reason." According to Weitzman, Stern was right to highlight the urgency of the climate problem but wrong to base that conclusion on a very low discount rate rather than on the fundamental problem of uncertainty. Weitzman's analysis of uncertainty has reshaped climate economics; it is the most important contribution to the field since the Stern Review.

The so-called dismal theorem (Weitzman 2009) is a densely mathematical demonstration that, under plausible assumptions and standard models, the marginal benefit of a reduction in greenhouse gas emissions is literally infinite. The two crucial assumptions leading to this result are 1), the structure of the earth's climate is so uncertain that our best estimates inevitably have a fat-tailed[1] probability distribution, and 2) the disutility of extreme outcomes is unbounded as they approach the limits of human survival.

Regarding the first assumption, the climate sensitivity parameter is a crucial determinant of the impacts of climate change: Higher values for this parameter imply higher temperatures and a greater likelihood of the catastrophic outcomes discussed in earlier chapters. Yet the climate sensitivity parameter remains uncertain (see Chapter 1). Large-scale experiments to determine its value are obviously impossible; knowledge of climate sensitivity gained through indirect inference is limited, and the uncertainty may be inherently irreducible (Roe and Baker 2007). Weitzman argues more generally that in a complex, changing system such as the climate, older information may become obsolete at the same time that new information arrives, imposing an upper limit on the amount of empirical knowledge that we can acquire. Therefore, we are forced to rely on a limited amount of data, implying that our best estimates follow a fat-tailed probability distribution with a fairly large probability of dangerously high climate sensitivity.

The second assumption involves climate damages. The proof of the dismal theorem depends only on the limit approached by climate damages in extreme cases. It assumes that at sufficiently high levels of climate sensitivity, climate change would be severe enough to destroy much or all of economic output, driving per capita consumption down to subsistence levels and below. The resulting welfare loss, in standard economic models, rises without limit as consumption falls toward the threshold for human survival.[2] These disastrous scenarios cannot be ruled out or even ruled sufficiently improbable due to the fat-tailed probability distribution for climate sensitivity.

When outcomes are uncertain, economic analysis typically calculates expected values, which are probability-weighted averages (or integrals) across all possible outcomes. The fat-tailed probability distribution means that the disastrous scenarios in the tail of the curve, which have extremely bad outcomes, are only moderately improbable. Therefore, their contribution to the weighted average is huge; they dominate the expected value of climate change mitigation. Infinite values, as in the dismal theorem, result when these extremes are so large that the expected value, calculated as the sum of an infinite series, or an integral, fails to converge.

Responses to the dismal theorem

The discussion prompted by the dismal theorem has transformed the economic understanding of climate uncertainty and has shifted attention away from expected or most likely impacts toward catastrophic risks. There have been numerous criticisms and disagreements with Weitzman's formulation of the problem; many of these comments can be interpreted as proposing alternative theoretical frameworks for analyzing catastrophic risk.

Nordhaus (2009) challenges both of the assumptions of the dismal theorem. In his view, the unbounded, fat-tailed distribution of possible outcomes conflicts with the possibility that scientific knowledge and principles might place an upper bound on climate sensitivity and damages, while the second assumption, unbounded negative utility as consumption approaches zero, unrealistically implies unlimited willingness to pay to avoid even very small risks to human survival. Nordhaus also explores conditions that lead the DICE model to predict a "catastrophic" outcome, which he defines as world consumption per capita falling 50 percent below the current level. He concludes that three factors must all be present to drive consumption below this threshold: high climate sensitivity, high damages (i.e., a damage function steeper than DICE assumes), and the absence of any mitigation policy.[3]

Pindyck (2011) accepts the dismal theorem's first assumption, the fat-tailed distribution of possible climate outcomes, but rejects the second assumption, marginal utility becoming infinite as consumption drops toward zero, on much the same grounds as Nordhaus. If a limit, even a very high one, is placed on marginal utility, Pindyck demonstrates that the fat-tailed distribution of climate outcomes is important but not necessarily decisive. Willingness to pay for abatement can be greater in a model with a thin-tailed distribution of outcomes, depending on the choice of other parameters.

Costello *et al.* (2010) pursue the opposite strategy, exploring the effects of changing the first assumption, i.e., imposing upper limits on climate sensitivity. Using a fat-tailed distribution for climate sensitivity and a very simplified model, they reproduce the dismal theorem result when climate sensitivity is unbounded, with willingness to pay to avoid climate change approaching 100 percent of GDP. When a high upper limit is placed on climate sensitivity – they experiment with limits from 20 to 50°C – then the paradoxical result disappears, and willingness to pay to avoid climate change drops below ten percent of GDP in most of their scenarios.[4]

Yohe and Tol (2007) acknowledge the logic of the dismal theorem and discuss its implications. As they point out, Tol also found that the marginal utility of emission reduction could become infinitely large in a FUND model scenario when lack of precipitation drove future incomes to subsistence levels in one region of the world (Tol 2003). There are several responses to this problem in Tol (2003), Yohe and Tol (2007), and other works by these authors.

One response from Yohe and Tol is that many potential climate catastrophes can be averted or moderated by a stringent policy of emission reduction, perhaps eliminating catastrophic risk and the accompanying infinite values. Another, seemingly inconsistent, response is that the same risks and infinite values might be present in both the base case and policy scenario but not in the difference between them. In that case, cost–benefit analysis could still be performed on the difference between the two scenarios, which is all that is needed for policy applications. Yohe and Tol conclude that the dismal theorem is of limited applicability to real-world problems.

Weitzman replies

In a recent paper, Weitzman responds to comments on the dismal theorem (Weitzman 2011). He begins with a challenge to standard cost–benefit analyses, reminiscent of Stern's approach: How could economic analysis of climate change be *unaffected* by deep uncertainty about extreme events? We are headed for atmospheric greenhouse gas concentrations more than twice as high as at any time in the last 800,000 years. The projected temperature that will result from this is extremely sensitive to the (unknown) shape of the probability distribution assumed for climate sensitivity, while the projected economic impact of climate change depends on arbitrary choices about the (unknown) shape of the damage function.

Weitzman maintains that the two pillars of the dismal theorem are sound: Our best estimate of the probability distribution of climate outcomes must be fat-tailed, because we have so little data about analogous past events, and the disutility of extreme outcomes must be unbounded, "because global stakeholders cannot short the planet as a hedge against catastrophic climate change" (Weitzman 2011, p. 15). As he concludes, "Non-robustness to subjective assumptions about catastrophic outcomes is an inconvenient truth to be lived with.... The moral of the dismal theorem is that, under extreme tail uncertainty, seemingly casual decisions about functional forms, parameter values, and tail fatness can dominate" the economic analysis of climate change (Weitzman 2011, p. 16).

Combined effects of multiple uncertainties

A number of recent studies have attempted to combine multiple dimensions of uncertainty, such as climate sensitivity and the shape of the damage function. The first study described here challenges the conventional wisdom that faster warming will be worse for the economy.

Nordhaus (2008) examines both climate and economic uncertainties, concluding that the economic factors are more important. He presents a small-scale Monte Carlo analysis with 100 iterations, in which he allows eight parameters in DICE to vary. He finds that temperature change over this century is positively correlated with consumption per capita at the end of the century. This occurs because he allows relatively large variation in economic growth (driven by assumptions about potential variation in productivity growth and population) but relatively small variation in climate impacts (driven by assumptions about climate sensitivity, the shape of the damage function, and the discount rate). High-growth scenarios have greater output and hence greater emissions, leading to warmer temperatures; in DICE, the resulting climate impacts reduce but do not reverse the benefits of economic growth, such as higher per capita consumption. For a rejoinder, insisting that income must decline with warming, see Ng and Zhao (2011).

Our own work has examined the effects of multiple uncertainties in DICE, including the climate sensitivity parameter and the shape of the damage function

(Ackerman *et al.* 2010; Ackerman and Stanton 2012). Under DICE-2007 default assumptions, the optimal policy involves very gradual abatement, taking 200 years to reach complete abatement of carbon emissions; despite moderate climate losses, per capita consumption grows throughout the simulation period. This endorsement of gradualism is robust under relatively large changes in either climate sensitivity or the shape of the damage function but not both together. Variation in both dimensions at once produces scenarios in DICE in which business-as-usual emissions would cause large economic losses and sharp drops in per capita consumption. The optimal policy becomes one of very rapid elimination of carbon emissions; taking into account just a few major uncertainties can increase the social cost of carbon by more than an order of magnitude. A similar analysis examines joint uncertainties in climate sensitivity and the shape of the damage function in the PAGE model, finding that fat-tailed probability distributions for both uncertainties can more than double the social cost of carbon (Pycroft *et al.* 2011).

Others have objected that uncertainty should be represented in the inner workings of a model, rather than repeatedly drawing parameters from a probability distribution and running a deterministic model for the chosen parameters. In a provocative mathematical and philosophical discussion of this point, Peters (2011) argues that Monte Carlo analysis of a deterministic model represents a misleading picture of the temporal dimension of uncertainty: it is, in effect, an average over parallel, deterministic universes, not a picture of sequential decision-making within a single dynamic process.

The simplest model of sequential decision-making under uncertainty assumes that key parameters are initially unknown, but will become known later. The focus is on the decisions made earlier, under uncertainty, or on the effects of learning at the later date. Such models have been variously described as stochastic optimization, discrete uncertainty models, or models of learning or hedging (Ackerman *et al.* 2012; Babonneau *et al.* 2011; Webster *et al.* 2008; Keller *et al.* 2004). The simplicity of this structure of uncertainty leads to tractable and transparent models – at the cost of ad hoc assumptions about the timing of learning.

At a deeper level, some models have attempted to address structural uncertainty about model relationships or probability distributions, sometimes referred to as ambiguity. A theory of ambiguity aversion has been developed (Klibanoff *et al.* 2005) and applied to climate policy (Millner *et al.* 2010); it achieves manageable solutions at the cost of assuming a known distribution of second-order preferences over first-order uncertainties. A more general treatment of structural uncertainty is provided by robust control models, exploring a zone of uncertainty around assumed model relationships and seeking solutions that are robust under alternate assumptions. For climate change, robust control methods seem to require arbitrary simplifications of the underlying dynamic model for the sake of tractability (Funke and Paetz 2010).

A more complete treatment of uncertainty over time can be achieved with dynamic programming methods, sequentially modeling short time steps and allowing incremental updating of Bayesian priors about key uncertainties.

Despite promising new developments, the complexity and computational requirements of dynamic programming, particularly when threshold effects are included, have limited many applications to simplified or stylized models (Crost and Traeger 2010; Lemoine and Traeger 2011; Lontzek and Narita 2011). An interesting study, using somewhat stylized representation of uncertainty (without threshold effects) and huge numbers of iterations in a DICE-like model, shows that failing to accurately account for risk can lead to substantial underestimation of the benefits of greenhouse gas abatement (Gerst *et al.* 2010). The study contrasts rapid and gradual abatement scenarios, finding that rapid abatement is preferable under most assumptions; gradual abatement is preferable only if the discount rate is very high *and* major uncertainties are ignored.

Risk aversion revisited

A final area of recent research on uncertainty leads to a deeper understanding of risk aversion and addresses problems related to the Ramsey equation (5.1) and the limitations of the constant relative risk aversion (CRRA) utility function (equation 5.2). One important result offers a resolution to the paradoxically conflicting meanings of η in the Ramsey equation – that is, the problem that greater risk aversion or inequality aversion today (larger η) seems to imply a higher discount rate and thus less concern for future outcomes. Other research explores alternative interpretations of risk aversion and, in some cases, alternative utility functions.

Newbold and Daigneault (2009) conduct a series of numerical simulation experiments to study the effects of uncertainty about climate sensitivity. In many but not all scenarios, they find a large, positive risk premium – defined as the difference between willingness to pay for emission reduction in a model with uncertain climate sensitivity, and willingness to pay in a deterministic version of the same model, using best guesses for uncertain parameters. Their estimates are sensitively dependent on assumptions about extreme conditions, such as climate losses at 10°C of warming or the level of subsistence consumption. Other studies have also attempted to calculate the risk premium that risk-averse individuals would be willing to pay for climate risk reduction; although there are many uncertainties surrounding the results, the risk premium is often substantial (Kousky *et al.* 2011; Cooke 2011).

Newbold and Daigneault's results demonstrate that under conditions of uncertainty, increases in η (a key parameter governing risk aversion and time preference in equations 5.1 and 5.2) can lead to greater willingness to pay for climate mitigation. If uncertainty is severe enough, the increase in risk aversion resulting from a higher value of η may outweigh the effect on time preference per se. Weitzman (2010b) suggests that this situation (higher η decreases the discount rate) is the norm, driven by the "fear factor" of risk aversion to potentially catastrophic shocks.

As noted in Chapter 5, the problems of interpretation of the Ramsey equation (5.1), limitations of CRRA utility, and multiple meanings of η also play central roles in the economics of financial markets, particularly in the analyses of the equity premium puzzle. The extensive research on the equity premium puzzle has produced a range of rival explanations (DeLong and Magin 2009), of which at least two have been echoed in climate economics. One group of theories proposes that the perceived risk of extreme losses is greater than is suggested by recent experience; a second group proposes a more complex, multidimensional interpretation of utility.

In the first group, emphasizing anticipation of extreme events, Weitzman's dismal theorem resembles, and is in part derived from, his earlier analysis of financial markets (Weitzman 2007b). Markets, not unlike the climate, have complex, changing structures in which old information becomes obsolete over time. This implies that investors can have only a limited amount of knowledge of the current structure of the market, so their best estimates of market returns follow a fat-tailed probability distribution with relatively high risks of extreme outcomes. Weitzman's work along these lines appears to be more influential in climate economics than in finance: the hypothesis that future risks of extreme events are outside the range of past experience is clearly consistent with climate science, but it is less obvious in finance, where there is a long history of abrupt market downturns and crashes.

Taking a different approach to extreme risk in finance, Barro, among others, argues that the twentieth-century history of major economic slumps is sufficient to explain extreme risk aversion and large equity premiums in financial markets around the world (Barro 2006). This is more controversial than it might seem at first glance: because virtually all the major downturns that drive Barro's result occurred in the first half of the twentieth century, this approach assumes that investors have very long memories. A recent climate-economics analysis using a modified version of DICE with a Barro-type calibration of risk aversion (implying $\eta = 6.7$) and a variant on the Ramsey equation concludes that standard models greatly underestimate the true willingness to pay for climate mitigation and that aggressive mitigation is more desirable with higher values of η (Gerst *et al.* 2011). This echoes the Newbold and Daigneault (2009) result discussed above.

A second group of theories calls for a more sophisticated approach to utility, separating the multiple roles played by η. The limited empirical research on this subject suggests that people do not apply a single standard to risk, inequality, and time preference – all of which are represented by η in the Ramsey equation. A survey of more than 3,000 respondents (an international, nonrandom "convenience sample" recruited over the Internet) asked questions designed to elicit preferences toward risk, inequality today, and inequality over time (Atkinson *et al.* 2009). The results show clear differences among all three, with median values of η falling between 3 and 5 for risk aversion, between 2 and 3 for inequality today, and above 8 for inequality over time. Correlations among individuals' responses in the three areas are weak. For additional experimental evidence on the distinction between preferences toward time and risk, see Coble and Lusk (2010). Older empirical estimates of η typically did not distinguish among these different roles. For example, an analysis of attitudes toward inequality revealed by the progressive income tax structures of OECD countries estimated an average of $\eta = 1.4$ (Evans 2005).

A more complex utility function is needed to allow explicit separation of attitudes toward risk and time, representing each with its own parameter. This approach has been developed and applied in the equity premium puzzle literature in finance; the best-known example is by Epstein and Zin (1989). It offers a theoretically elegant solution to the dilemmas of the multiple roles of η – at the cost of much-increased mathematical complexity and computational burden. The explicit treatment of risk makes each period's utility depend on expectations about the next period, leading to a recursive, or non-time-separable, utility function.

The use of such utility functions has been suggested in the empirical studies of risk and time preference. Atkinson *et al.* (2009) closes with a suggestion that Epstein-Zin preferences should be considered, while Coble and Lusk (2010) frame their analysis in terms of the Kreps–Porteus model, a precursor of Epstein and Zin. Perhaps the first application of this new class of utility functions in climate economics is Ha-Duong and Treich (2004), using a simplified climate model to demonstrate that the separation of risk aversion and time preference makes the optimal carbon tax much more sensitive to risk aversion.

Additional studies adopting the Epstein–Zin framework are now beginning to appear (Aase 2011; Ackerman *et al.* 2012; Crost and Traeger 2010; Jensen and Traeger 2011; Kaufman 2012). Although some DICE-based analyses find that the results are relatively insensitive to the value of the risk aversion parameter, this may be due to the difficulty of representing catastrophic risk within the DICE framework (Ackerman *et al.* 2012; Crost and Traeger 2010). A study assuming large catastrophic risks found willingness to pay was strongly influenced by risk aversion (Kaufman 2012).

These analyses do not exhaust the new approaches to risk that have been explored in recent climate economics. Yet another response to the equity premium puzzle has been mentioned at least once: Brekke and Johansson-Stenman (2008) discuss behavioral economics approaches to both finance and climate policy, concluding that the appropriate discount rate should be close to the risk-free rate (i.e., the rate of return on government bonds) – an idea that is discussed further in Chapter 7.

Looking more broadly at risk, Lowry (2010) argues that leading theories of well-being imply that the experience of risk itself is harmful. Ng (2010) demonstrates that if future utility is expected to grow, independently of consumption growth, then avoidance of catastrophic risks becomes more important. An empirical study finds that households do not have stable risk preferences across different risks; greater risk aversion is displayed for the larger risks involved in home insurance, as opposed to auto insurance (Barseghyan *et al.* 2011).

7 Public goods and public policy

Climate change poses unique economic problems that raise new, fundamental issues, both about uncertainty and about public goods and public policy. New economic analysis primarily concerned with uncertainty was covered in Chapter 6, while analyses primarily concerned with public goods and public policy issues are addressed in this chapter. The separation, however, is not a clean or unambiguous one, and the two chapters should be read together.

There are a number of reasons why climate policy choices might be made on a different basis from private investment decisions:

- Climate policy is intergenerational, involving actions now with major consequences far in the future. It is not clear that present value calculations and cost–benefit analysis have the same meaning when extended across a span of multiple generations. This gives rise to dilemmas in discounting and to alternative approaches to modeling intergenerational impacts.
- Public policy in general is different in scope from private market choices. For instance, society as a whole can afford to provide insurance that the private sector cannot against risks such as unemployment compensation and flood relief. The uncertain risks of catastrophe have inspired exploration of precautionary or insurance-like approaches to climate policy, reflected in alternative decision-making criteria.
- Public policy decisions are ideally made on a democratic basis, weighting all individuals' opinions equally; private market outcomes weight individual preferences in proportion to wealth. Public policy may incorporate equity concerns, choosing on ethical grounds to weight impacts and burdens on lower-income groups more heavily. Due to the global nature of the problem, contested questions of international equity are central to the search for an adequate climate solution.

There are four major sections in this chapter: new approaches to discounting, other analyses of intergenerational impacts, alternative decision-making criteria, and the complex issues surrounding global equity.

New approaches to discounting

Discounting permeates the economics of climate change. Even with deep uncertainty about climate sensitivity and economic costs, expressed via fat-tailed probability distributions, welfare estimates and optimal policy choices depend on time preference as well as tail risks (Dietz 2010). Much of the discussion of uncertainty in Chapter 6, particularly the new approaches to risk aversion, has a direct effect on discount rates and procedures. This section presents four additional topics related to discounting: incorporation of a preference for long-term sustainability, the effects of environmental scarcity, the extension of the Ramsey equation to include precautionary savings, and the appropriate interest rates to use under the descriptive approach to discounting.

When applied to intergenerational problems, simple approaches to discounting produce the unsettling result that with any significantly positive, constant discount rate, the far future does not matter. The logic of discounting, which is essential to cost–benefit analyses conducted over shorter time frames, clashes with the common conviction that climate change and long-run sustainability must be important.

One response is to assume that people place some value on long-term sustainability and current consumption. This is argued informally in a widely cited paper by Summers and Zeckhauser (2008) and formally in a mathematical model by Chichilnisky (2009), building on her earlier work in "axiomatizing sustainability." In both cases, the result is that the discount rate declines gradually to zero over time. Drawing on a similar motivation, a hybrid formulation, "sustainable discounted utilitarianism," sets the utility discount rate (i.e., the rate of pure time preference) to zero whenever future generations will be worse off than the present, but allows positive discount rates when the future will be better off (Dietz and Asheim 2012).

There are multiple arguments for declining discount rates. The behavioral economics evidence reviewed by Frederick *et al.* (2002) suggests that people reveal a preference for declining discount rates in their market behavior. An analysis of uncertainty about future interest rates by Weitzman (1998) demonstrates that the discount rate should gradually decline over time, from the expected value of future rates toward the lowest possible future rates. The valuation of long-term sustainability, as proposed by Summers and Zeckhauser, and by Chichilnisky, is a third independent argument for declining discount rates.

A second innovation involves the assumption of environmental scarcity. The growth model underlying the Ramsey equation assumes a single, undifferentiated output or equivalently perfect substitution among outputs. There is a long-standing debate in ecological economics about the degree of substitutability between marketed goods and environmental services; it is far from clear, in reality or in theory, that perfect substitution is the right assumption. If the two sectors are not close substitutes, and one is subject to absolute scarcity (i.e., no additional "natural environment" can be produced), the long-run price trends for the two sectors will diverge.

A two-sector model in which the output of ordinary goods can grow without limit but the supply of environmental services is constant or decreasing has striking implications for discounting (Hoel and Sterner 2007; Sterner and Persson 2008; Traeger 2011). Assuming that consumers obtain utility from both sectors and that there is limited substitution between them, economic growth leads to a steady increase in the relative price of environmental services. Even with a high discount rate, the change in relative prices can outpace the effect of discounting, so that the present value of future environmental services is rising rather than falling with time – implying that the optimal climate policy is a rapid reduction in carbon emissions. This model successfully formalizes an intuition often expressed by non-economists, namely that something seems wrong with applying the same discount rate to financial and environmental assets.

The third "new" approach to discounting is not, strictly speaking, an innovation; it is reasonably well known but routinely ignored. Examination of the theoretical derivation of the Ramsey equation shows that the usual form, as presented in Chapter 5, is only an approximation, valid when the parameters and the consumption growth rate are small (Ackerman *et al.* 2009; Dasgupta 2008). Even under that assumption, it is derived only for a single optimal growth path, assuming a known rate of growth of consumption. If the future rate of growth is uncertain, with an expected variance of σ^2, then under the common assumption of a constant relative risk aversion (CRRA) utility function (see equation 5.2), the Ramsey equation (5.1) becomes

$$\rho = \delta + \eta g - \frac{1}{2}\eta^2 \sigma^2 \tag{7.1}$$

The final term, which is always negative, can be interpreted as representing a precautionary savings motive. That motive becomes stronger as uncertainty (σ^2) increases; a lower discount rate implies greater concern for the future and hence a higher optimal savings rate. It also becomes stronger as risk aversion (η) increases, consistent with the everyday understanding of precaution. Indeed, this expanded form of the Ramsey equation shows one reason why it is possible that increases in η may lower the discount rate, as discussed in Chapter 6.[1] Simple applications of the Ramsey equation, however, rarely include the final, precautionary term. As a result, they overstate the appropriate discount rate under conditions of uncertainty about economic growth.

Descriptive discounting and the risk-free rate

A final point about discounting is also well-established in theory but frequently overlooked in practice. Under the descriptive approach to discounting, the appropriate discount rate depends on the risk profile of the asset being discounted. The risk profile of investment in climate protection could lead to the use of a very low discount rate.

Due to the declining marginal utility of additional consumption, the same monetary return on an investment yields more utility when incomes are low and less utility when incomes are high. In order to obtain equal utility from a range of investments, investors demand higher rates of return on assets that do best when incomes are high, such as equities. Risk-reducing assets – ones that do best when incomes are low, such as insurance – can pay lower rates of return; the rate of return on an insurance policy is typically negative. Government bonds are intermediate between these extremes, with almost no risk and the same low but positive rate of return whether incomes are high or low. (That is, the covariance of returns with personal income or per capita consumption is positive for equities, roughly zero for government bonds, and negative for insurance.)

To express the present value of the return on any asset in terms of utility, it should be discounted at its own rate of return: a high, positive rate for equities, positive but near zero for risk-free assets such as government bonds, and negative for insurance. Which of these does investment in climate protection most closely resemble?

Many analysts have used a rate of return on equity or on assets of average risk, assuming that investments in mitigation are competing with, and comparable to, ordinary investments in other sectors. Others, such as Howarth (2003), have argued that mitigation is at least risk neutral if not risk reducing and should be discounted at the rate of return on risk-free assets such as government bonds. The risk-free rate or lower is appropriate for discounting mitigation costs under the widely but not universally accepted conclusion that mitigation reduces overall economic risk.[2]

If anything, it appears that insufficient attention has been paid to the possibility that mitigation is risk reducing and therefore should be discounted at less than the risk-free rate. For additional analysis of circumstances under which the risk-free rate might be the appropriate discount rate, see Howarth (2009) and Brekke and Johansson-Stenman (2008). For an analysis of rates of return on multiple assets under uncertainty, concluding that the data support a rate of pure time preference close to zero, see Liu (2012).

Intergenerational impacts

Discounting – or more precisely, discounted utilitarianism – is not the only approach to the analysis of intergenerational impacts. A Rawlsian perspective argues instead for a duty to "avoid serious evil" for future generations (Hampicke 2011). A feminist economics perspective likewise rejects the mechanistic, disembodied rationality of utilitarianism, and calls for joint action focusing on avoiding the worst rather than achieving the optimal outcome (Nelson 2011).

In formal mathematical modeling, a leading alternative to discounting involves the use of overlapping generations (OLG) models. The standard framework of integrated assessment, shared by Stern, Nordhaus, and others, evaluates all present and future costs and benefits from the standpoint of the current generation – assuming either infinitely lived agents or a dictatorship of the present generation over its descendants. In contrast, OLG models allow separate treatment of the costs, benefits, and preferences of successive generations.

Proposed some time ago as a framework for modeling long-term sustainability (Howarth and Norgaard 1992), OLG models are an active area of research in recent climate economics. Such models can highlight the importance of abatement cost assumptions in determining the burden on successive generations and can estimate the point in time at which climate mitigation becomes a net benefit (Gerlagh 2007). One OLG model finds that the allocation of scarcity rents, such as the value of emissions permits, can determine the net present value of a climate policy; the same policy could have a negative bottom line (net costs to society) with grandfathered emission rights versus net benefits with per capita rights (Leach 2009). A formal OLG model with hyperbolic (declining) discount rates within each generation and extensive game-theoretic analysis reaches policy conclusions broadly compatible with the Stern Review (Karp and Tsur 2011).

One remarkable suggestion is that there is less of an intergenerational conflict than is commonly believed: in the presence of a large, unpriced externality, business-as-usual (i.e., no new mitigation efforts) is a distinctly suboptimal scenario. An optimal mitigation policy creates large welfare gains, allowing both current and future generations to be better off (Rezai *et al.* 2011).

Elaborating on this perspective, Karp and Rezai (2010) create an OLG model in which a carbon tax benefits the current older generation by increasing the scarcity and hence the value of that generation's capital assets, and benefits future generations by improving environmental quality. The current younger generation, which receives lower labor income due to the carbon tax, can be compensated by the current older generation, making everyone better off.

Another framework that addresses intergenerational issues is the relatively new technique of "real options" analysis applied to climate policy by Anda *et al.* (2009). In addition to the costs and benefits of a policy, real-options analysis calculates the value of maintaining the flexibility to achieve a desirable future goal, such as a low atmospheric concentration of greenhouse gases. Real-options analysis is developed by analogy to financial options, which guarantee to the buyer the right to purchase an asset at a future date. Under the assumption of great uncertainty, a mitigation policy that has substantial net costs – that is, its costs exceed its benefits, as conventionally defined – might have a real option value greater than its net costs: the policy could be valuable if it preserves the opportunity for decision makers a generation from now to change course and aim for lower-than-planned greenhouse gas concentration targets. Such a policy would be rejected by cost–benefit analysis but approved by real-options analysis.

Standards-based decision making

As an alternative to utility maximization, some economists have advocated a focus on avoiding the risks of possible climate catastrophes (e.g., Yohe and Tol

2007). This approach is not entirely new and has gone by various names, such as "safe minimum standards," "tolerable windows," and "precaution." It is often described as analogous to insurance against catastrophe, both in popular writing (e.g., Ackerman 2009) and formal research (e.g., Weitzman 2010a).

The insurance analogy is literally appropriate up to a point: as business enterprises that exist to manage risks, private insurers are increasingly addressing climate concerns and can play an essential role in promoting adaptation and improving disaster resilience (Mills 2009). There are limits, however, to private insurance. The increasing but unpredictable likelihood of extreme events may reduce the insurability of important risks related to natural disasters (Mills 2007). Public policy is essential to address the full range of climate risks.

Precautionary or insurance-like approaches to climate policy begin with a predetermined objective that is deemed necessary to avoid thresholds that could trigger catastrophic damages – or more precisely and modestly, to reduce risks of catastrophic damages to a very low level. The objective can be defined in terms of avoidance of specific discontinuities, such as the collapse of the Atlantic thermohaline circulation (Bahn *et al.* 2011) or the Western Antarctic Ice Sheet (Guillerminet and Tol 2008). It can also be defined in terms of an upper limit on allowable temperature increases (den Elzen *et al.* 2010) or an upper limit on atmospheric concentrations of greenhouse gases (Vaughan *et al.* 2009; Bosetti *et al.* 2009).

Standards-based analyses frequently find that an immediate, ambitious mitigation effort is needed either in general (den Elzen *et al.* 2010; Vaughan *et al.* 2009) or under stringent stabilization targets (Bosetti *et al.* 2009), or under an assumption of high climate sensitivity (Bahn *et al.* 2011).[3] With a predetermined standard in place, the economic problem becomes one of cost-effectiveness analysis, seeking to determine the least-cost strategy for meeting the standard. This is different from and more tractable than cost–benefit analysis. In a cost-effectiveness analysis, only the costs of mitigation need to be calculated, because the standard replaces the more problematic calculation of benefits (i.e., avoided damages).

In a broader sense, however, the cost-effectiveness analysis of meeting a standard can be seen as a special case of cost–benefit analysis in which the shadow price of the benefits (or the value of the avoided damages) has become infinite, or at least larger than the cost of maximum feasible abatement. A literally infinite value is not necessary; the same practical result will follow if damages become very large very quickly, implying that the marginal damage curve becomes nearly vertical. Under these circumstances, welfare optimization can lead to the same result as precautionary, standards-based policy making.

Weitzman's dismal theorem, concluding that greenhouse gas mitigation could have literally infinite value (see Chapter 6), is difficult to interpret, let alone incorporate into cost–benefit analysis. An infinite value implies the implausible conclusion that willingness to pay to avert climate change should approach 100 percent of GDP. The problem has been discussed in more general terms by Buchholz and Schymura (2012), who argue that any nonzero probability of unbounded losses creates the "tyranny of catastrophic risks." Weitzman himself suggests the alternative of assigning a large but finite value to the survival of humanity, akin to the "value of a statistical life" that is often used in cost–benefit analyses. This would eliminate the infinite value while still obtaining a large numerical result (Weitzman 2009). There is, however, little rigorous basis for such limits. In nontechnical terms, how could the extinction of the human race be said to represent only a finite loss of utility for the human subjects of the theory? Does this mean that there is some imaginable package of goods and services that is more valuable than the survival of the human race?

In a sense, estimates of infinite damages are irrelevant, as many authors have suggested. After all, the ability to pay for climate mitigation is finite, constrained by income. Indeed, for policy purposes, there is an even lower limit to relevant damage estimates. Once climate damages exceed the marginal cost of the maximum feasible scenario for emission reduction, it no longer matters how high the damages are: the policy recommendation will be the same, endorsing maximum feasible abatement. Our own analysis of uncertainty in climate damages finds worst-case estimates that are far above the marginal cost of a maximum feasible abatement scenario (Ackerman and Stanton 2012). While these estimates are clearly not infinite, they may be close enough to infinity for all practical purposes.

Of course, climate policy decisions, whether based on standards and precaution or on cost–benefit calculations, must be made in the context of deep uncertainty. A counterintuitive result (proved analytically for a simple model of eutrophication) is that in the presence of a threshold effect, there is a nonmonotonic relationship between the degree of uncertainty and the optimal level of precaution (Brozović and Schlenker 2011). Precaution is not needed when the threshold is known with certainty, and it has a limited probability of effectiveness when uncertainty is too great.

Climate policy discussion have given rise to classifications of differing levels of uncertainty, for example distinguishing uncertainty in events (such as daily weather), model parameters, model relationships, and subtler categories of confidence in our sources of knowledge (Spiegelhalter and Riesch 2011). There is a limited literature on decision making under extreme uncertainty, when the decision maker knows the set of all possible outcomes but not the probabilities of individual outcomes within that set (Ackerman 2008, Chapter 4). Under reasonable assumptions, such as risk aversion, the best decision under extreme uncertainty is based primarily or entirely on information about the worst-case outcome – just as suggested by the precautionary principle. For a recent discussion and proposal along these lines, see Farber (2011).

One rule for decisions under extreme uncertainty that has appeared in the recent climate literature is the minimax regret criterion. Assume that, facing an uncertain state of the world, you choose a course of action, and then the true state of the world becomes known. The "regret" associated with your choice is the difference between the utility under that choice and the greatest utility attainable from another choice for the same state of the world. The "maximum regret" for your choice is the greatest regret you would experience under any state of the world; it is the worst case for the choice you made. The minimax regret criterion picks the choice that has the smallest maximum regret; it is the choice for which the worst case looks least bad.

Using an integrated assessment model with a broad range of inputs and scenarios, Hof *et al.* (2010) find that the minimax regret criterion recommends more stringent mitigation than does a conventional cost–benefit analysis if either a low discount rate or the combination of high climate sensitivity and high damages is assumed. In the absence of these assumptions, the difference between the minimax regret criterion and cost–benefit analysis is much smaller. Minimax regret analysis has also been adapted for energy system planning under uncertainty (Li *et al.* 2011).

Using the FUND model, Anthoff and Tol (2010a) compare cost–benefit analysis and minimax regret (along with other decision criteria). Using a 1 percent rate of pure time preference and a rate of risk aversion (η) of 1, the carbon tax that maximizes expected welfare (the cost–benefit criterion) is $33 per ton of CO_2 in 2010. Varying interpretations of the minimax regret rule recommend carbon taxes of $27 to $46 per ton of CO_2 for the same year.

Global equity implications

Climate change is a completely global public good (or public bad). It is caused by worldwide emissions and can be controlled only by worldwide cooperation to reduce or eliminate those emissions. At the same time, the significant costs of climate protection must be borne by a very unequal world economy. Free-rider problems and debates over the appropriate formulas for burden-sharing will be endemic.

Economic theory has much more to say about efficiency than about equity, but economists have not been silent on the distributional issues surrounding climate policy. Here we review three areas of recent research and discussion: approaches to equity and redistribution in climate-economics models, equity-based proposals for international negotiations, and game-theoretic analyses of the prospects for international agreement.

Equity and redistribution in integrated assessment models

At any one point in time, costs and benefits are typically expressed, compared, and aggregated in monetary terms. For private market decisions, it is difficult to imagine the use of any other standard. Public policy, however, could be based on a different, equity-based standard. The fundamental principle of declining marginal utility implies that the same amount of money yields more utility to lower-income individuals.[4] Thus, equitable distribution of policy costs, if measured in utility, should place a smaller burden on low-income groups than would equitable distribution measured in money.

Attempting to implement this principle, several articles explore "equity weighting," a hybrid technique that modifies cost–benefit calculations to give greater weight to costs borne by lower-income regions. Hope (2008) argues that costs in each region should be multiplied by

$$\left(\frac{\text{world income per capita}}{\text{regional income per capita}} \right)^{\eta} \tag{7.2}$$

Because η, among its other roles, is the elasticity of marginal utility with respect to consumption, multiplication by this factor effectively converts climate costs from measurement in monetary terms to utility. Equal utility impacts rather than equal dollar impacts are given the same value wherever they occur. Using PAGE, Hope models greater equity weighting by increasing η and finds that it decreases the social cost of carbon: the increase in η increases the discount rate (using the simple form of the Ramsey equation, as seen in Chapter 5), which reduces the present value of future impacts.

A number of other studies of equity weighting use the FUND model. Anthoff, Hepburn and Tol (2009) experiment with several formulas for equity weighting, ranging from an approach that makes almost no difference to the social cost of carbon, to one that leads to very large increases under some scenarios. Anthoff, Tol and Yohe (2009) explore the interactions of pure time preference, uncertainty, and equity weighting, finding: "As there are a number of crucial but uncertain parameters, it is no surprise that one can obtain almost any estimate of the social cost of carbon." Equity weighting appears to generally increase the social cost of carbon in this analysis.

Anthoff and Tol (2010b) explore not only equity weights but also weights representing four different policies that might be followed by a national decision maker: sovereignty (ignoring all impacts abroad); altruism (taking into account all impacts abroad, regardless of source); good neighbor (taking account of the country's own impacts abroad); and compensation (payment is required for all of the country's international impacts). While equity weights roughly double the optimal carbon tax in this analysis, two of the national policies, good neighbor and compensation, cause even larger increases in the optimal carbon tax in high-income countries.

Another perspective suggests that a tilt toward equity should be a natural consequence of the assumption of diminishing marginal utility in climate-economics models. National, regional, or global utility is typically calculated as individual utility (at the mean per capita consumption level) multiplied by population. Under this approach, equalization of incomes between regions will always increase total utility.

This is reminiscent of early twentieth-century economic theory, which assumed that utility was measurable and comparable between individuals and that income must have a higher marginal utility for the poor. Leading economists of the day such as Marshall and Pigou knew that this created a presumption in favor of progressive redistribution. That school of thought was overturned by Robbins and others in the "ordinalist revolution" of the 1930s (Cooter and Rappoport 1984). The ordinalist view, which has dominated economic theory since that time, maintains that while each individual experiences diminishing marginal utility, it is impossible to compare one person's utility to that of another; utility is an ordinal rather than a cardinal magnitude.

Regardless of its theoretical merits, however, ordinalism offers little help in quantitative modeling of optimal decisions and social welfare. Perhaps solely for mathematical convenience, climate-economics modeling has rolled back the ordinalist revolution and reinstated cardinal utility and interpersonal comparisons. Why doesn't this create "equity weighting" by default?

There are two answers, one institutional and one technical. In institutional terms, significant transfers of resources from rich to poor nations are not common in reality; most models accordingly exclude this possibility without comment. In technical terms, regionally disaggregated models often use a procedure known as "Negishi welfare weighting" (Stanton 2011). Negishi introduced a method for the calculation of an equilibrium point in a general equilibrium model (Negishi 1972). It applies weights to each individual's utility, such that maximization of the weighted sum of utilities leads to the same outcome as a competitive market equilibrium. The Negishi weights are inversely proportional to marginal utility, so that Negishi-weighted marginal utility is equal for all. The Negishi solution thus counters the tendency toward income equalization that is built into the utility function; it maximizes a sum to which everyone's (weighted) utility contributes equally at the margin, implying that there are no welfare gains available from redistribution.

A new integrated assessment model, Climate and Regional Economics of Development (CRED), is designed to remove both the institutional and the technical obstacles to redistribution (Ackerman *et al.* 2011). CRED allows global income redistribution and evaluates its contribution to climate protection and to welfare maximization. When there are no constraints on redistribution, the optimal scenario involves massive transfers of resources from high-income countries in order to fund investment in mitigation and in economic development in low-income countries. This scenario has greater global welfare *and* better climate outcomes than any others in the model. Even when redistribution is constrained to much lower levels, it still makes an important, often decisive contribution to climate stabilization and raises overall welfare.

Global equity and international negotiations

A separate discourse about global equity has emerged in the process of international climate negotiations. International climate policy proposals focus on identifying each nation's responsibility for mitigating domestic emissions and on industrialized countries' unilateral responsibility to pay for emissions and adaptation measures in less-developed countries. While economics has much to say about the efficiency of emission reduction mechanisms and the likely distribution of their burden, it cannot solve the normative dilemmas posed in international negotiations: What determines a country's responsibility for global emissions reductions? Should rights to fill the limited atmospheric sink for greenhouse gases be allocated on a cumulative, historical basis or start with a clean slate today? Should these rights be considered on an equal per capita basis, and if so, how should population growth be treated? Do some countries have an obligation to pay for mitigation efforts outside of their own borders? Does this international obligation extend to adaptation measures that aim to limit exposure to climate damages?

This set of issues – often referred to as "burden sharing" – is at the heart of international climate negotiations. To cite one important dimension of the problem, the share of developed countries in global emissions is markedly larger over a longer time frame. An analysis by the World Resources Institute found that in 2000, the United States accounted for 21 percent of global greenhouse gas emissions and the EU-25 for another 14 percent. However, from 1990 through 2002, the U.S. share was 24 percent and the EU-25 share 17 percent. Over a much longer time span, from 1850 through 2002, U.S. emissions were 29 percent and the EU-25 countries' emissions 27 percent. Japan, having industrialized much more recently, was responsible for 4 to 5 percent of world emissions over any of these time frames (Baumert *et al.* 2005). As such, U.S. and EU (but not Japanese) obligations depend on the time period over which emissions are measured.

There is a growing literature on burden-sharing strategies that sets out general principles and specific plans for two sticky normative problems: how much each country should be permitted to emit and how much each country should pay for mitigation and adaptation efforts abroad.[5] Most proposals assume that each country is expected to pay for its own emissions abatement (an exception is noted below), although the sale of unused emissions rights to other countries is generally allowed. Proposals that have been raised in international negotiations or that exemplify alternative approaches to equity include:

- "Equal Per Capita Emissions Rights" would set a limit on global emissions and award emissions rights on an equal per capita basis. A country's allocation would be the sum of its residents' emissions rights. The global emissions target would be reduced over time, and national allocations would fall along with it (Agarwal and Narain 1991; Narain and Riddle 2007).
- "Individual Targets" is another variation on equal per capita rights. It uses the income distribution of each country to estimate how its greenhouse gas emissions are distributed among individuals. It then sets a consistent worldwide cap on individual emissions and derives the corresponding national emissions caps. No reductions are required for citizens of any nation whose emissions are equal to or lower than the target. The strategy aims to prevent high-emission individuals in low-emission countries from free riding by using the unclaimed rights of their poorer neighbors (Chakravarty *et al.* 2009).
- Another well-known proposal is "Contraction and Convergence," which creates a transition toward equal per capita rights. The global target for per capita emissions shrinks steadily toward a sustainable level. Countries with

per capita emissions above the global target have their emissions allocation reduced over time; countries below the global target receive gradual increases in their allocations. Using this strategy, global emissions would contract while per capita emissions among countries would converge (Global Commons Institute 2010).[6]

• "Greenhouse Development Rights" sets global mitigation targets and distributes the costs of meeting those targets on the basis of nations' capacities to pay for mitigation and adaptation and their responsibility for past and current emissions (e.g., cumulative emissions since 1990). These criteria are defined with respect to an income threshold. Only individuals with incomes above this threshold have a responsibility to help pay for global mitigation efforts, and a country's responsibility is the sum of its residents' responsibilities (Baer *et al.* 2007). Prominent Chinese economists have proposed a variant on this approach, "Revised Greenhouse Development Rights," which bases responsibility for the problem on cumulative emissions back to 1850 and places a greater obligation on industrialized countries to pay for emissions reductions (Fan *et al.* 2009).

Game theory and the prospects for agreement

The lengthy and frustrating process of international negotiation is far from guaranteed to be a success. A number of economists have analyzed the prospects for agreement in terms of game theory and strategic interaction. Barrett (2003) offers useful background in this area, combined with a historical treatment of negotiations. Wood (2011) provides an extensive review of the implications of game theory for climate policy. He concludes that mechanisms can be designed to promote cooperation, such as binding commitments to abatement conditional on actions taken by others. Milinski *et al.* (2008) introduce a collective-risk social dilemma in a controlled experiment designed to simulate the climate problem. People in a group are each given a sum of money from which they have to make individual contributions to a common investment. They can keep any leftover money if they collectively reach the investment target but not if they fail. Only half of the groups succeed; the investigators see a need for additional effort to convince people that they are at risk of grave individual loss.

Some investigations strike a more optimistic note. Rübbelke (2011) proposes that rich countries' funding of adaptation in developing countries, although not directly on the path to controlling emissions, may nonetheless improve the prospects of success in international negotiations by increasing the perception of fairness. Saul and Seidel (2011) analyze leadership in a game-theoretic model of cooperation, finding that increased leadership contributes to international cooperation. Testing this model against data on annual climate negotiations since 1995, they find that the extent to which the EU has exerted leadership is positively correlated with the progress achieved in the negotiations. DeCanio and Fremstad (2011) provide a comprehensive review of game-theoretic models for climate negotiation, emphasizing that the prisoner's dilemma is not necessarily the relevant framework, that multiple approaches to solutions (e.g., maximin versus Nash equilibrium) are possible, and that slight changes in preferences can dramatically change the prospects for agreement. In another study modeling the positions and interests of major countries in potential climate negotiations, DeCanio (2009) argues that the primary division is not between north and south but between those regions with large fossil fuel reserves, notably Russia and the Middle East, versus all others. DeCanio suggests that the decision by the United States about whether to ally with fossil fuel producers or with other developing countries will be crucial to the prospects for negotiation.

Part IV

Mitigation and adaptation

8 Economics and the climate policy debate

The global climate problem is not without solutions. A small amount of climate change is now locked in, but the serious impacts and potential catastrophes described in Chapters 3 and 4 are still avoidable if quick action is taken on emissions abatement. At the same time, sensible adaptive preparations could offer protection from impacts caused by past (and unavoidable near-term future) emissions. The nature of the climate problem (as explained in Chapters 5, 6, and 7), however, complicates economic analysis – and therefore policy decisions – related to climate change in ways that few, if any, other economic or environmental concerns have prepared us for: the magnitude of climate impacts is uncertain but potentially enormous; solutions require one generation to act to benefit a later generation; and the need for virtually worldwide cooperation appears to be inextricably linked to controversial issues of equity among countries and among income groups.

Newer economic research does a better job of accounting for these gnarly issues in its analysis and policy recommendations, but many existing models are well behind the state of the art, and improved methods for modeling uncertainty are still in active development throughout the field. Even more problematically, economic estimation of the value of climate damages is not based on anything like the complete contemporary understanding of damages presented earlier in this book. Instead, the best-known, most widely used climate-economics models rely on simple rule-of-thumb damage functions with little – and dated – empirical foundation. As a result, some economic models are still recommending very little short-run investment in climate mitigation.

The alternative "standards" or "cost-effectiveness" modeling approach (see Chapter 7) offers very different advice. When a standard is set for a maximum temperature increase or concentration level beyond which expected losses would be considered unacceptable, the resulting policy recommendations are consistent across studies released by different researchers: There is a need for rapid, sustained abatement. As explained in detail below, the goal of keeping global temperatures from rising more than 2°C requires that global greenhouse gas emissions peak almost immediately and fall rapidly thereafter. The higher and later that emissions peak, the faster and deeper the decline must be. In every recent mitigation scenario that offers at least a 50 percent chance of staying below a rise of 2°C (or meets a similar criterion related to atmospheric concentrations), emissions peak no later than 2020.

The 2°C guardrail

The goal of staying below 2°C of warming has become ubiquitous in climate policy discussion. It does not derive from economic analysis, and it is not necessarily the policy recommended by economic optimization models. Rather, it emerges from the standard-setting approach to climate policy; it represents a widely accepted estimate of a threshold for avoiding the worst damages from climate change. Citing AR3 (IPCC 2001) and Smith *et al.*'s (2009) update to its risk analysis, the Synthesis Report of the 2009 Copenhagen Climate Congress (Richardson *et al.* 2009) states:

> While there is not yet a global consensus on what levels of climate change might be defined to be "dangerous," considerable support has developed for containing the rise in global temperature to a maximum of 2°C above preindustrial levels. This is often referred to as "the 2°C guardrail." IPCC as well as more recent scientific research indicate that even with temperature rises less than 2°C impacts can be significant, although some societies could cope with some of these impacts through pro-active adaptation strategies. Beyond 2°C, the possibilities for the adaptation of society and ecosystems rapidly decline with an increasing risk of social disruption through health impacts, water shortages and food insecurity.

Some advocacy organizations call for still-deeper emissions cuts, either aiming to stay well below the 2°C guardrail under standard assumptions or anticipating stabilization targets that are consistent with 2°C warming at higher climate sensitivity values (on climate sensitivity, see Chapter 1). The Alliance of Small Island States – representing some of the populations most vulnerable to the first 2°C of temperature increase – supports a threshold "well below" 1.5°C above preindustrial levels, noting that its members are "profoundly disappointed by the lack of apparent ambition within the international climate change negotiations to protect [small island developing states] and other particularly vulnerable countries, their peoples, culture, land and ecosystems from the impacts of climate change" (Alliance of Small Island States 2009).

The German Advisory Council on Global Change (WGBU), which appears to have coined the term "2°C guardrail," asserts that this target has been acknowledged by 133 nations representing four-fifths of the world population and three-quarters of current greenhouse gas emissions; that many nations have adopted climate policies with the express purpose of limiting temperature increases to 2°C; and that climate scientists broadly support this goal (WGBU 2009).[1] The WGBU report goes on to invoke Article 3 of the United Nations Framework Convention on Climate Change (United Nations 1992):

The Parties should take precautionary measures to anticipate, prevent, or minimize the causes of climate change and mitigate its adverse effects. Where there are threats of serious or irreversible damage, lack of full scientific certainty should not be used as a reason for postponing such measures, taking into account that policies and measures to deal with climate change should be cost-effective so as to ensure global benefits at the lowest possible cost.

(WGBU 2009, p. 14)

WGBU suggests that signatories to the UNFCCC – now ratified by 165 nations – have agreed to approach decision making with regard to climate change from a precautionary, standards-based perspective and explores mitigation scenarios consistent with a 67 to 75 percent probability of keeping temperature increases below 2°C (WGBU 2009, pp. 22–34). These scenarios, together with other recent mitigation scenarios, are described in more detail in the next section.

Standards-based mitigation scenarios

According to a recent UK government study, the range of business-as-usual emissions scenarios described in Chapter 1 (from AR5 scenarios RCP 8.5 to RCP 4.5, corresponding roughly to the range from the IPCC's earlier A1FI to B1 scenarios) results in a 0 to 4 percent chance of keeping global mean temperature increases below 2°C and a 0 to 53 percent chance of staying below 3°C (Bernie 2010). In other words, even RCP 4.5 – corresponding to B1, the slowest-growing of the old IPCC scenarios – offers virtually no chance of staying below 2°C.

Two important measures of the pace of mitigation are the timing and the level of the peak in emissions. In the more optimistic RCP 4.5 scenario, emissions peak at 42 Gt CO_2 around 2035; in the more pessimistic RCP 8.5 scenario, emissions reach 106 Gt CO_2 by 2100 and are still rising.[2] (For comparison, global emissions were 34 Gt CO_2 or 44 Gt CO_2-e in 2005.[3]) Although RCP 4.5 would be a great improvement over RCP 8.5, even more needs to be done to meet standards such as a reasonable chance of staying below 2°C. Several studies have demonstrated how demanding that goal turns out to be.

The lowest AR5 Representative Concentration Pathway (RCP 3-PD) has about a 50 percent chance of keeping mean warming below 2°C, and rapid abatement is required to achieve that result. In this scenario, emissions peak at 38 Gt CO_2 around 2015, and there are small net negative emissions (that is, sequestration is greater than emissions) by 2090.[4] In the most ambitious mitigation scenarios, of which RCP 3-PD is an example, success in keeping temperatures low depends on the timing and the shape of the future emissions peak and on the trajectory after the peak. Table 8.1 presents a synopsis of 20 mitigation scenarios that either have at least a 50 percent chance of staying below 2°C or have low target concentrations, on the order of 350 to 450 ppm CO_2.

All 20 mitigation scenarios share several characteristics. Emissions peak in 2020, at the latest, and do not exceed 46 Gt CO_2 or 55 Gt CO_2-e. Emissions then

Table 8.1 Business-as-usual and mitigation scenarios: emissions and temperatures

	Peak emissions		Annual rate of decrease after emissions peak (%)	2100 concentration (CO_2/CO_2-e)	Chance of staying below:		
	Year	Level (Gt)			2°C	3°C	4°C
Business-as-usual range							
RCP 4.5	2035	42 CO_2	2.0	538/581	0.04	0.53	0.88
RCP 8.5	no peak	106 CO_2 (in 2100)	NA	936/1,231	0.00	0.00	0.06
Mitigation scenarios							
Ackerman et al. 2200	2010	39 CO_2	9.8	370/NA			
PIK Comparison	2015	31 CO_2	4.3	400/NA			
Hansen et al.:							
IPCC reserves	2005	46 CO_2	9.8	350/NA			
EIA reserves	2005	46 CO_2	4.5	400/NA			
Lowe et al.	2015		3.0		0.55		
RCP 3-PD	2015	38 CO_2	5.4	421/427	0.48	0.92	0.99
WGBU:							
Option 1	2011	32 CO_2	3.7		0.75		
Option 2a	2015	34 CO_2	5.3		0.67		
Option 2b	2020	37 CO_2	9.0		0.67		
Option 2c					0.67		
IEA:							
BLUE Map	2015	30 CO_2	2.2	445 in 2050/NA	0.50		
450 Policy Scenario	2020	47 CO_2-e	1.9	450/520			
Gohar and Lowe:							
A1B_2016: 4% zero	2016	55 CO_2-e	3.0	NA/461	0.57	0.92	0.99
A1B_2016: 5% zero	2016	55 CO_2-e	4.0	NA/447	0.63	0.95	0.99
A1B_2016: 9% zero	2016	55 CO_2-e	9.0	NA/426	0.74	0.96	1.00
A1FI_2016: 3%	2016	50 CO_2-e	3.0	NA/488	0.48	0.92	0.99
A1FI_2016: 5%	2016	50 CO_2-e	5.0	NA/471	0.56	0.95	0.99
B2_2016: 3%	2016	44 CO_2-e	3.0	NA/515	0.55	0.95	1.00
B2_2016: 5%	2016	44 CO_2-e	5.0	NA/460	0.62	0.97	1.00
McKinsey 400ppm	2015	46 CO_2-e	3.1–6.5	NA/480 in 2065	0.70–0.85		

Sources: RCP emissions and concentration data: International Institute for Applied Systems Analysis (2009); Bernie (2010); Ackerman et al. (2009); PIK: Edenhofer et al. (2010); Kitous et al. (2010); Magne et al. (2010); Leimbach et al. (2010); Barker and Scrieciu (2010); van Vuuren et al. (2010); other scenarios: Hansen et al. (2008); Lowe et al. (2009); WGBU (2009); International Energy Agency (2010; 2008); Gohar and Lowe (2009); McKinsey & Company (2009).

fall rapidly, at rates of 2 to 10 percent each year. The higher and later that emissions peak, the more rapid the subsequent decline.[5] The scenarios have another similarity not represented in the circumscribed data in Table 8.1: the higher and later that emissions peak, the more necessary it becomes to drive annual emissions down to zero or even to net negative levels toward the end of this century. Rogelj *et al.* (2011) find that scenarios with a greater than 66 percent chance of staying below 2°C require emissions to peak by 2020. In their review of emission limits consistent with the RCP scenarios, Arora *et al.* (2011) conclude that limiting warming to 2°C in this century is unlikely.

Most of the listed scenarios either do not report data for years later than 2050 or show temperatures that continue to climb after 2100 (for some models, the probabilities shown are the chance of staying below 2°C through 2100). Lowe *et al.* (2009) suggest that there would be very little reduction in temperature in the century after peak warming was reached. Other studies suggest that peak temperatures will not decline for several hundred years (see Chapter 1).[6] Joshi *et al.* (2011) calculate that the 2°C threshold may be exceeded as early as 2040, and that even in lower emission scenarios, regional 2°C degree averages are likely to be exceeded by 2040.

At present, there is no international accord aimed at a global emissions peak in the next five or ten years followed by steep annual reductions. Few – if any – countries have made internal commitments consistent with these global reductions. For comparison, the voluntary terms of the Copenhagen Accord – formalized in the Cancún Agreements – would allow global emissions to exceed 50 Gt CO_2-e in 2020, an increase of 1 percent per year over 2005 levels (United Nations Environment Programme 2010; Bernie 2010; Höhne *et al.* 2012).[7] Recent (failed) proposals for U.S. climate legislation called for annual emission reduction of about 1 percent each year through 2020, 2 percent through 2030, and 6 percent thereafter (Stanton and Ackerman 2010).

There is an extensive economics literature on the choice of policy instruments, addressing such questions as the merits of carbon taxes versus cap-and-trade systems, revenue recycling options, and border tax adjustments and other policies to address the carbon "leakage" that would occur if carbon-intensive production moves to countries with weak or non-existent emission limits (among many others, Fischer and Fox 2011; Bushnell and Mansur 2011; Pezzey and Jotzo 2012). We have not attempted to review that literature; the issues we are addressing here, such as the need for rapid emission reduction, could be expressed through any of several policy instruments. From this perspective, a very high carbon tax may be more fundamentally similar to a very stringent cap-and-trade system (since both would provide incentives for rapid reduction) than to a very low carbon tax. The targeted level of emissions and pace of reduction, not the choice of policy instrument, is the crucial dimension on which climate policies should be measured.

Climate action agenda

No one action can solve the climate problem. Steep and immediate emissions reductions will require policy measures on many fronts, including international agreements, market incentives, government regulations, and investment in technical innovation. Chapters 9, 10 and 11 explore the key elements necessary to portray climate policy options in economic analysis: the technology and economics of both mitigation and adaptation.

Chapter 9, "Technologies for mitigation," looks at strategies for reducing annual emissions and even achieving negative net emissions by removing greenhouse gases from the atmosphere. The technologies reviewed run the gamut from well-understood energy efficiency, fuel switching, and tree planting to nascent climate engineering proposals such as painting roofs and roadways white, and fertilizing the oceans so that they grow more carbon-sequestering algae. This chapter also profiles the technology choices made in the more sector- and fuel-specific of the low-temperature mitigation policies above – the International Energy Agency's BLUE Map, McKinsey's 400 ppm CO_2-e concentration trajectory, and the range of technology proposals in the Potsdam Institute for Climate Change Research (PIK) comparison project.

Chapter 10, "Economics of mitigation," reviews new developments in portraying mitigation in climate economics. Technology prices that remain static or decrease steadily with time are a poor representation of the real-world effects of learning and innovation; newer models are exploring ways to endogenize technological change. Widely divergent assumptions about oil prices, found in recent climate policy assessments, can be one of the strongest determinants of abatement costs. Controversy continues about the accuracy of negative abatement cost projections and assumptions regarding the energy-efficiency rebound effect. The latest literature on both topics is discussed in the context of climate-economics modeling.

Even if rapid mitigation succeeds, temperatures are still expected to rise by another 0.1 to 0.6°C and sea levels by another 0.1 to 0.3 m by 2100 (see Chapter 1). These unavoidable future changes, added to the warming and other changes that have already occurred, will pose ongoing challenges of adaptation for vulnerable regions around the world. Chapter 11, "Adaptation," touches briefly on adaptation technologies – which are largely dissimilar across regions – and then reviews the literature regarding this relatively new area of economic modeling: the costs of climate adaptation and its interactions with mitigation efforts and economic development.

9　Technologies for mitigation

Models targeted at limiting global mean temperature increases share a common policy prescription: immediate, rapid reductions in greenhouse gas emissions. There is much less agreement, however, regarding the best method of achieving these reductions. Each mitigation scenario makes a unique set of choices regarding not only where reductions should be made and who should pay for them (as described in Chapter 7), but also in the optimal mix of technologies to bring about these changes. Reduction in fossil fuel combustion is at the heart of every mitigation scenario, but in order to maintain low temperatures and minimize climate damages, more far-reaching, innovative abatement measures will also be required.

Either in place of the deepest near-term cuts in fossil fuel use (in less ambitious plans) or along with these cuts (in more ambitious plans), alternative mitigation strategies such as afforestation and carbon capture and sequestration are a key ingredient. A subset of mitigation methods is often classified as "geoengineering" or "climate engineering" – purposeful attempts to intervene in the climate system, with the goal of reducing radiative forcing and forestalling temperature increases (Shepherd *et al.* 2009). These proposed methods have received some attention in the economics literature and in policy circles, but to date they lack commercial applications or even large-scale demonstrations.[1]

Still, future technological innovation will no doubt include methods either not yet imagined or ill-regarded today. Here we discuss three categories of mitigation options, some currently feasible and some the topics of current research and future aspirations:

- reducing emissions, including both CO_2 and non-CO_2 greenhouse gases, as well as point-source carbon capture and sequestration;
- removing greenhouse gases from the atmosphere, including afforestation and reforestation, enhanced sequestration, air capture, and ocean fertilization;
- directly reducing radiative forcing (black carbon reduction and solar radiation management).

We do not attempt comprehensive coverage of the widely discussed options for reduction of fossil fuel emissions, but instead concentrate on newer and less familiar options that are of potential importance for future mitigation policies. The chapter concludes with a brief overview of the mix of technologies employed in some of the more detailed low-temperature mitigation scenarios shown in Chapter 8.

Reducing emissions

Slowing the emission of CO_2 and non-CO_2 greenhouse gases is an essential first step in every mitigation strategy. In many of the low-temperature mitigation scenarios, annual emissions are nearly eliminated by the late twenty-first century.

Carbon dioxide

CO_2 emission reduction strategies focus on energy-efficiency improvements and fuel switching for electricity generation, transportation, buildings, and industry. The IEA's BLUE Map scenario (International Energy Agency 2008) calls for sustained global energy-efficiency gains of 1.7 percent per year, with end-use efficiency accounting for 36 percent of 2050 emissions reductions (compared to business-as-usual projections). Many energy-efficiency measures are thought to have low or negative costs, although efficiency gains may be accompanied by smaller "rebound" efficiency losses, and controversy continues about interpretation of negative-cost measures. Both negative-cost abatement and rebound effects are discussed in Chapter 10.

Mitigation scenarios call for the gradual decarbonization of the power-generation sector, with the remaining fossil fuel and biomass generators using carbon capture and sequestration technology (discussed below). A variety of low and no-carbon generation options, including renewable fuels such as hydro-power, solar, wind, and geothermal power, together with nuclear energy and some switching to less carbon-intensive fossil fuels (from coal to natural gas, for example), will be needed to reach these goals, especially as demand for electricity increases around the world (International Energy Agency 2008). According to McKinsey & Company (2009), low-carbon power generation has the potential to supply 70 percent of global electricity by 2030.

Transportation emissions can be reduced by behavioral changes, public investment in mass transit, and fuel-efficiency improvements. The ambitious goal of fuel switching poses more of a technological challenge. Today the vast majority of vehicles are powered by petroleum; mass production of alternative-fuel vehicles is impeded by their need for a very different fueling infrastructure – e.g., electric outlets and battery-charging stations in the place of gas stations. Electric-powered vehicles, including plug-in hybrids and those using hydrogen fuel cells, also will necessitate the generation of additional electricity. IEA's BLUE Map scenario requires a significant share of electric-, hydrogen-, and biofuel-powered light-duty vehicles, while its emissions reductions from other forms of transit – trucks, buses, rail, air, and water – focus primarily on efficiency gains (Köhler *et al.* 2010; International Energy Agency 2008). A study of

California's targets for steep emission reductions by 2050 concluded that the targets can only be met if transportation and other sectors are powered by decarbonized electricity (Williams *et al.* 2011).

While commercial and residential buildings contribute a relatively small share of total CO_2 emissions, switching to less carbon-intensive fuels for space and water heating is still crucial to mitigation strategies that limit temperature increases to 2°C. Heat pumps, solar water heating, biofuels, and lower-intensity fossil fuels such as natural gas are all potential tactics. The IEA emphasizes the importance of transitioning from "traditional" biomass technologies, still used widely around the world, to cleaner "modern" biomass technologies, in particular, dimethyl ether biogas, which is nontoxic and can be produced from a variety of feedstocks (International Energy Agency 2008). Industrial processes contributed 22 percent of 2005 global emissions, and that share is expected to grow over the next decades. In the McKinsey & Company (2009) 400 ppm CO_2-e stabilization scenario, reductions to industrial emissions account for 16 percent of total mitigation.

Non-CO_2 greenhouse gases

Several non-CO_2 gases make important contributions to radiative forcing (see Chapter 1). Where anthropogenic increases to CO_2 have added 1.66 W/m² to the global energy balance, other long-lived gases jointly add slightly less than 1 W/m² (methane, 0.48 W/m²; nitrous oxide, 0.16 W/m²; and all halocarbons combined, 0.34 W/m²), and ozone adds another net 0.30 W/m² (–0.05 W/m² for stratospheric ozone and 0.35 W/m² for tropospheric). Eliminating all emissions of these gases would be equivalent to a 77 percent decrease in CO_2 emissions. While the bulk of CO_2 emissions come from energy production, most non-CO_2 greenhouse gases do not. Most methane and nitrous oxide emissions result from land-use changes, agriculture, and waste management, and most halocarbons result from industrial processes (Weyant *et al.* 2006).

Agriculture and land-use changes contribute about 30 percent of all emissions (measured in CO_2 equivalents), the second largest share of anthropogenic greenhouse gases after CO_2 (IPCC 2007d, *Working Group III* Technical Summary; Weyant *et al.* 2006). Methods proposed for reducing agricultural methane and nitrous oxide emissions include changes to the rate or type of fertilizer applied, tilling practices, and feed for livestock (Beach *et al.* 2008). There are, however, many constraints to implementation, both technical and economic. Carbon sequestration in soil is complex: the rate of sequestration declines as soil and ecosystem carbon storage capacity reaches a maximum; its contribution to global mitigation is difficult to measure due to questions of additionality,[2] and some related feedback processes are still not well understood. It may also be the case that carbon sequestration practices in one location tend to push cheaper high-carbon-emitting agricultural practices to other areas rather than eliminating them (Smith *et al.* 2007).

Carbon capture and sequestration

Anthropogenic CO_2 can be captured before its release into the atmosphere and then sequestered by direct injection into underground storage – a process referred to as carbon capture and sequestration (CCS).[3] Several CCS pilot projects are currently in operation, but technical and political hurdles still impede widespread implementation (Haszeldine 2009; Herzog 2011). Both the capture and storage phases of CCS face remaining challenges. Carbon capture must be comprehensive (all or nearly all carbon emissions captured from a source) but not too energy intensive. Several potentially viable carbon capture technologies exist, but challenges lie in scaling these methods up while keeping costs and energy use low, and limiting further environmental burdens from process by-products and pollutants (Liu and Gallagher 2009; Kanniche *et al.* 2010; House *et al.* 2011).

Post-combustion capture – using, for example, amine scrubbing – requires large facilities for the treatment of enormous volumes of gas (Rochelle 2009). Alternatively, fossil fuels can be combusted in near-pure-oxygen environments in a process referred to as "oxy-combustion" or "oxyfuels." This method requires lower temperatures for combustion, allowing CO_2 to be captured in its liquid form, and obviates the need for chemical solvents such as amine. To date, only a few small pilot projects are using oxyfuels. In a third method, pre-combustion gasification of fossil fuels forms carbon monoxide, which is converted to CO_2 and captured, and hydrogen, which is used as a clean fuel (the sole by-product of hydrogen combustion is water). High costs of retrofitting plants for pre-combustion gasification have derailed some pilot projects (Hart and Gnanendran 2009; Olajire 2010; Kanniche *et al.* 2010). No method is a clear winner, though there may be a trend toward using pre-combustion for newly built plants and post-combustion for retrofits (Haszeldine 2009). Most of the recently built or planned fossil fuel-burning plants in the EU have not been designed to be ready for installation of CCS (Graus *et al.* 2011).

Carbon storage presents additional challenges. After CO_2 has been captured, it must be transported to a suitable location and stored. CO_2 could be transported by fossil-fuel-powered vehicles, but the volumes are significant, and the attendant transportation emissions could be large. The alternative is construction of a new network of CO_2 pipelines, moving the gas from power plants to appropriate disposal sites, such as oil and gas fields under either dry land or ocean. The investment necessary to create such an infrastructure would be substantial (Haszeldine 2009).

Another concern is the potential for CO_2 injected into subsurface geological formations to leak back in the atmosphere. Leakage would not only risk increased atmospheric concentrations of CO_2, but if released in bursts of concentrated CO_2, it would also threaten human health (Fogarty and McCally 2010). Leakage from subsea CO_2 injection could result in considerable ocean acidification and oxygen depletion (Shaffer 2010). On a global scale, substantial space is available for this kind of storage, but careful site selection is essential (Orr 2009; Szulczewski *et al.* 2012).

These obstacles notwithstanding, CCS is expected to be a major source of emissions reduction in many of the mitigation scenarios discussed in Chapter 8, with one-third or more of all electricity generated with fossil fuel and biomass technologies using CCS by 2050 (Edenhofer *et al.* 2010). IEA's BLUE Map (International Energy Agency 2010b) assumes that in 2050, carbon capture applies to 55 percent of power-generation emissions, 21 percent of industry emissions, and 24 percent of transportation emissions, noting that there is also "an urgent need to accelerate the demonstration of CCS in the power sector and to develop comprehensive regulatory approaches to enable its large-scale commercial deployment" (p. 11). An analysis of deployment strategies projected commercial rollout of CCS between 2015 and 2020 and global rollout between 2020 to 2025 (Gibbins and Chalmers 2008).[4]

Removing greenhouse gases from the atmosphere

The higher and later that emissions peak, the lower and more quickly they will have to fall to keep warming below 2°C. Many low-temperature mitigation scenarios include measures to increase the rate of CO_2 sequestration on land and in oceans. In some scenarios, sequestration is so large in scale that net emissions become negative later in this century.

Afforestation and reforestation

Expanding forested areas and avoiding new deforestation are essential components of many rapid mitigation scenarios. Estimates of the technical potential for near-term reforestation range from 186 to 1,023 g C/m^2 per year, depending on the type of forest (Alexandrov *et al.* 2002, p. 302). AR4 considered both economic feasibility and technical potential in presenting a range of 1 to 14 Gt CO_2 sequestration from afforestation each year (IPCC 2007d, *Working Group III*, Technical Summary). To put these numbers in context, terrestrial systems absorbed 3.3 Gt CO_2 in 2005, while the net annual addition to atmospheric concentrations from all sources and sinks was 15.0 Gt CO_2 (IPCC 2007e, *Working Group I*, Technical Summary).

A recent IPCC technical paper reports the results of two new studies of afforestation's potential for mitigation. One finds 12.5 Gt CO_2 of feasible potential emission reductions by 2030, virtually all in less-developed countries, at average prices lower than $2 per ton. The second uses a bottom-up methodology to identify 2.0 Gt CO_2 of mitigation potential in 2020 at $15 per ton (United Nations Framework Convention on Climate Change 2008). Stern's *Blueprint for a Safer Planet* (2009) calls for spending $15 billion per year to combat deforestation in tropical countries, sequestering 3.0 Gt CO_2 per year at $5 per ton, and Hansen *et al.*'s (2008) 350 ppm CO_2 trajectory requires sequestration of 6.5 Gt CO_2 per year by 2030 from a combination of afforestation and biochar (charcoal stored in soil, discussed below). As discussed in Chapter 3, newer research demonstrates that afforestation and reforestation efforts should take place in tropical countries to have the best effect on global temperatures. Adding to forested areas in temperate zones has a neutral net effect on radiative forcing, while in boreal forests the net effect is an increase in warming.

Enhanced sequestration

There may also be some scope for purposefully enhancing the biological and geological processes that remove carbon dioxide from the atmosphere, with the object of increasing net carbon storage. Plants rely on photosynthesis, the process of converting CO_2 into glucose, as their source of energy. Sugar from photosynthesis builds plant matter, or biomass, which may be burned or may undergo aerobic decomposition by bacteria and fungi, releasing CO_2 back into the atmosphere. To the extent that plant matter is placed in longer-term storage, as wood in trees or in organic material that enters into soils without decomposition, CO_2 is effectively removed from atmospheric stores. Enhanced sequestration initiatives increase the share of biomass carbon that is stored in trees and soil, often through land-use decisions. For example, the United Nations Reducing Emissions from Deforestation and Forest Degradation (REDD) program is attempting to create a financial incentive for carbon sequestration in forests and a system for their long-term sustainable management (UN-REDD Programme n.d.).

Carbon sequestration in agricultural soils can be enhanced by the carefully calibrated application of nitrogen fertilizers and tillage of biomass (Lu *et al.* 2009). The full life-cycle impacts of these practices, however, warrant careful consideration: the greenhouse gases released during the production and distribution of fertilizer have been estimated to surpass the carbon sequestered in agricultural soils using enhancement methods (Schlesinger 2010).

One of the most discussed methods for enhanced sequestration is biochar. Charcoal, a form of black carbon, can be mixed into soils, increasing their carbon storage. A higher share of charcoal in the composition of soil also slows the rate at which soil emits CO_2, a feedback mechanism that may be misspecified in general circulation models (Lehmann *et al.* 2008). Stable long-term storage of black carbon in soil depends on the action of microorganisms and on limiting human disturbance such as tilling, fire, and land-use changes (Czimczik and Masiello 2007).

Worldwide, of the 222 Gt CO_2 converted by photosynthesis each year, an estimated 10 percent is potentially available for biochar, including crop and forestry residue and animal waste. Conversion of this 22 Gt CO_2 to charcoal could offset the combustion of fossil fuels generating 6.6 Gt of emissions and could sequester an additional 11.0 Gt as biochar. Combined, these effects would exceed net addition to atmospheric concentrations from all sources and sinks (annually, 15.0 Gt CO_2, or 26.4 Gt in fossil fuel and cement emissions, less 11.4 Gt of net oceanic and terrestrial contributions[5]). The systemic effects of such a large-scale effort at biochar are not well understood; climate feedback mechanisms and biological effects on soil biota require substantial additional study (Amonette *et al.* 2007). In comparisons of different uses of biomass, biochar outperformed biofuels except where these fuels displaced coal-fired electricity generation (Fowles 2007; Gaunt and Lehmann 2008). A full life-cycle assessment of biochar concluded that transportation distances are an important obstacle to the economic viability of any large-scale biochar scheme (Roberts *et al.* 2010).

Air capture

Air capture is a variant of carbon capture and sequestration in which CO_2 is harvested directly from ambient air (Keith 2009). While it would, in some ways, be far simpler to capture the more concentrated CO_2 that is an effluent from power plants and many industrial processes, air capture may hold some advantages. It could be used to remove emissions from mobile and other small-scale sources, and if conducted on a large enough scale it could – like afforestation – affect a net removal of CO_2 already present in the atmosphere. Some studies have gone so far as to suggest that a viable air capture strategy reduces the need for short-run precautionary mitigation (Keith *et al.* 2005). While air capture is generally thought to be prohibitively expensive, some studies have disagreed, suggesting that the unit cost of air capture would be similar to that of other mitigation methods (Pielke Jr. 2009).

Ocean fertilization

Certain areas of ocean may be "iron limited," implying that iron fertilization could lead to blooms of diatoms (a type of algae), effectively sequestering carbon when plant material from these blooms sinks to the deep ocean. Iron enrichment experiments on a scale of 25 to 225 km^2 have been conducted in the equatorial Pacific, subarctic Pacific, and Southern oceans. Unfortunately, despite strong responses in diatom blooming, these experiments show very little carbon removed to the deep ocean (Strong *et al.* 2009).[6] Initial results from the 300 km^2 LOHAFEX study conducted in 2009 suggest that carbon in algae becomes remineralized, returning to surface waters (National Institute of Oceanography 2009). Two natural experiments in iron fertilization (one from upwelling along islands in the Southern Ocean, the other due to a volcanic eruption in the Aleutian Islands) also showed algae blooms but little or no carbon sequestration (Tilmes *et al.* 2008; Pollard *et al.* 2009). In 2008, the London Convention on Marine Pollution and the UN Convention on Biological Diversity placed an effective moratorium on further ocean iron fertilization experiments, with the exception of small-scale legitimate scientific research projects. As of 2010, these experiments must be assessed and approved by the London Convention (International Maritime Organization 2010).

Reducing radiative forcing

Several additional mitigation technologies aim to enhance albedo, directly decreasing radiative forcing. Keeping the earth cool by increasing albedo would not necessarily preserve current precipitation patterns nor would it keep ocean CO_2 concentration from rising.

Black carbon reduction

Black carbon (soot) absorbs solar radiation in the atmosphere and decreases surface albedo (impeding reflection and allowing further radiation to be absorbed), especially when deposited on ice and snow (for further discussion, see Chapter 1). Black carbon is second only to CO_2 among anthropogenic influences on radiative forcing, so cleaning up this pollutant has enormous potential for climate change mitigation. Post-combustion capture (filtration) and storage are far more straightforward for black carbon than for CO_2. Burning biomass, heavy fuel oils, and coal are the primary sources of black carbon. Fuel switching and filtration could greatly limit these emissions, reducing a major source of warming (Ramanathan and Carmichael 2008; Wallack and Ramanathan 2009).

Black carbon's contribution to radiative forcing is determined by the source of the emissions. Black carbon from fossil fuels is twice as powerful a warming agent as black carbon from biomass. Moreover, emissions of black carbon are often combined with sulfates and organic aerosols, resulting in negative forcings: that is, they reflect solar radiation and reduce warming. Calculations of the impact of black carbon reduction initiatives, therefore, need to include the net effects of decreased positive forcings from CO_2 and black carbon and decreased negative forcings from other aerosols. Mitigation strategies for black carbon may be more effective if they start by reducing emissions from fuels with high black-carbon-to-sulfate ratios (Ramana *et al.* 2010).[7]

Solar radiation management

Solar radiation management describes a diverse set of proposals for reducing warming by reflecting sunlight away from the earth's atmosphere. Methods range from giant sunshades in space to land-use modifications aimed at increasing surface albedo. Painting roofs and roads white (or using light-colored materials to construct them) has the potential to transform the albedo effect of developed areas from heat sink to heat reflector. Levinson and Akbari (2009) report that painting 80 percent of U.S. commercial rooftops white would result in an annual cooling energy savings of 10.4 TWh, increased heating energy use of 133 million therms (equivalent to about 4 TWh), net energy cost savings of $735 million, and CO_2 reductions of 6.2 million metric tons. Another study estimates that a 10 percent global increase in urban albedo would increase outgoing radiation by 0.5 W/m^2 while slightly reducing mean surface temperatures (Menon *et al.* 2010). Increasing the solar reflectance of urban roofs and pavement would also lessen heat island effects and improve outdoor air quality (Akbari *et al.* 2009; Jacobson and Ten Hoeve 2012).

Other solar radiation management proposals include the problematical idea of increasing the concentration of aerosols such as sulfates in the atmosphere

(Lenton and Vaughan 2009; Goes *et al.* 2011). Releasing sulfate aerosols into the stratosphere could mimic the global cooling effects of volcanic eruptions, although it would have no effect on ancillary negative impacts of high atmospheric CO_2 concentration, such as ocean acidification. Offsetting a 760 ppm concentration of CO_2 (twice today's levels of CO_2) would require the release of 1.5–3.0 Mt of sulfur every year, depending on the size of the particles and their stability over time. Larger aerosol particles (like those from volcanic eruptions) are less effective at reflecting radiation than are smaller ones (Rasch *et al.* 2008).

For this strategy to be effective, stratospheric sulfate injections would have to continue for thousands of years due to millennial persistence of CO_2 in the atmosphere. If stratospheric aerosol levels are not maintained, there is potential for rapid warming of up to 5°C within several decades, which would be more damaging than would gradual warming of the same amount (Brovkin *et al.* 2008). Stratospheric sulfate injections may also disrupt the Asian and African summer monsoons, jeopardizing food supplies for much of the world's population (Robock *et al.* 2008). Other potential feedback effects from stratospheric sulfates include a reduction in global precipitation and increased rates of polar ozone depletion (Bala *et al.* 2008; Tilmes *et al.* 2008). Even if global average temperatures were stabilized via sulfate aerosols, the effects on polar temperatures would be less certain (McCusker *et al.* 2012).

Mitigation scenarios in climate-economics models

All the mitigation scenarios discussed in Chapter 8 draw from the same palette of technologies, but each one paints a different picture of emission reductions and accelerated sequestration; none includes direct reductions to radiative forcing.

IEA's BLUE Map scenario relies on a combination of fuel switching, carbon sequestration, and efficiency measures. By 2050, emissions are 48 Gt CO_2 lower than business-as-usual projections. Thirty-six percent of this reduction comes from end-use fuel and electricity efficiency improvements, 21 percent from renewable electricity generation sources, 19 percent from CCS power generation and industrial production, 11 percent from end-use fuel switching, 7 percent from power-generation efficiency and fuel switching, and 6 percent from nuclear. Abatement costs range from $200 to $500 per ton of CO_2 in 2050, depending on the degree of optimism regarding technological innovation. In IEA's more stringent "450 Scenario," global oil production peaks around 2020, and the deepest emissions cuts (relative to baseline growth) take place in the United States, the European Union, Japan, China, and India. By 2035, the nuclear share of power generation doubles, renewables account for 45 percent of global generation, half of all coal-fired plants are fitted with carbon capture and sequestration, and 70 percent of all car sales are of hybrid or electric models (International Energy Agency 2008; International Energy Agency 2010a).[8]

In McKinsey's 450 ppm CO_2-e scenario, 70 percent of all abatement potential comes from developing countries, including 22 percent from China alone.

Projected 2030 emissions fall from 70 Gt CO_2-e in the baseline to 38 Gt CO_2-e. This mitigation strategy includes 22 percent from transport, buildings, and waste; 21 percent from afforestation, reforestation, and changes to agricultural management; 17 percent from industrial emissions (including energy-efficiency measures); 11 percent from renewable electricity generation; 7 percent from CCS; 6 percent from other power sector measures; and 5 percent from nuclear. Abatement costs range from \$90 to \$150 per ton of CO_2 in 2030. In the McKinsey 400 ppm CO_2-e scenario, behavior changes and additional, higher-cost technical measures reduce emissions by another 9 Gt CO_2-e (McKinsey & Company 2009).

An inter-model comparison project examined scenarios from five models that stabilize carbon dioxide concentrations at 400 ppm by 2100. The rapid mitigation required to meet this target was achieved in different ways by each model. Shares of mitigation, across the models, range from 29 to 50 percent for fossil fuels and biomass without CCS, 29 to 36 percent for fossil fuels and biomass with CCS, 4 to 53 percent for renewables, and 11 to 21 percent for nuclear. Abatement costs in these scenarios range from \$150 to \$500 per ton of CO_2 in 2050 (Edenhofer *et al.* 2010; Kitous *et al.* 2010; Magne *et al.* 2010; Leimbach *et al.* 2010; Barker and Scrieciu 2010; van Vuuren *et al.* 2010).

10 Economics of mitigation

Estimates of the cost of mitigation differ by orders of magnitude – with all-important implications for the public debate about climate policy. The Stern Review (Stern 2006) projects that most climate damages could be avoided and the climate stabilized at an annual cost of about 1 percent of world output. On the other hand, Lomborg (2010) argues that the cost of staying under 2°C of warming could be 12.9 percent of world output in 2100. In recent U.S. debates, the extreme positions regarding action or inaction to confront climate change have been based on extreme estimates of costs: business lobbies opposed to climate policy have relied on consultant studies showing ruinous costs from even small initiatives, while environmental groups have developed their own studies showing little or no net cost from ambitious "win-win" solutions (Ackerman *et al.* 2009; Ackerman *et al.* 2010).

In the short run, the costs of climate policy depend on empirical information about current technologies and prices. Much has been written about this, and our discussion here is far from comprehensive. Even in short-run cost calculations, there are major differences in several areas, including the evaluation of both renewable energy and nuclear power. Is renewable energy currently or soon to be a competitive alternative to fossil fuels, or is additional research and development needed to reach that point? A recent review of numerous mitigation scenarios found that, while all scenarios relied on the expansion of renewable energy, there was no simple relationship between the stringency of climate targets and the projected extent of renewable energy use (Krey and Clarke 2011). Policies that address the unique characteristics of renewable technologies may be needed in order to achieve their potential for emission reduction (Arent *et al.* 2011), including investment in upgrading the electricity grid (Joskow 2012).

The economic comparison of renewable and conventional energy technologies depends on assumptions about externalities, sometimes referred to as the "co-benefits" of emission reduction (Borenstein 2012). Externality costs are substantial, amounting to more than twice the value added by coal-fired power plants in one major study, even without including a price for carbon emissions (Muller *et al.* 2011). The unpriced benefits of solar power in New York State have been estimated at $0.15–$0.40 per kwh (Perez *et al.* 2011). On the other hand, most studies to date of the relatively new technology of shale gas extraction ("fracking") have been sponsored by the industry, and have minimized or omitted externality costs (Kinnaman 2011).

The role of nuclear power is another area of conflicting assumptions, with some analysts arguing that there is no other feasible route to a low-carbon global energy system by mid-century. Many of the low-carbon scenarios discussed in Chapters 8 and 9 rely on significant amounts of nuclear power. Others have concluded that the much-advertised "nuclear renaissance" was already failing before the Fukushima accident in 2011, a victim of ever-rising costs and competition from cheaper alternatives (Thomas 2012; Mez 2012; Davis 2012).

These controversial topics, however, are the easy, short-run questions. As the time frame of the analysis lengthens toward a century or more, as it must to encompass the climate crisis, the anticipated future evolution of technology becomes more and more important. What will the energy technologies of the twenty-second century look like, and what will they cost? This seems like a subject for science fiction rather than economic analysis. Yet even fiction has failed to foreshadow the future of technology in decades past. A half-century ago, most science fiction still imagined that computers would keep getting bigger and bigger as they became more powerful. Economists face a similar challenge today: Gazing deep into our climate models, how accurately can we imagine the future of, for instance, photovoltaic cells?

The Stern Review sidestepped many of the difficult issues about costs, relying instead on the fact that two separate methodologies – a consensus of published model estimates and a new study of energy technology costs – both implied costs of roughly 1 percent of world output to meet the Stern Review's emission reduction targets. Yet for ongoing analysis exploring other scenarios, a deeper look at mitigation costs is needed – both in the areas where recent research has been active and in other areas that deserve more attention.

This chapter explores four difficult issues in the economics of mitigation. First, endogeneity in technological change and learning effects is an area of active research: does technological progress just happen, or can we influence its pace and direction? Second, one of the greatest uncertainties in the global economy, the future price of oil, has an inescapable influence on climate policy costs. Given the importance of the topic, far too little has been said about oil prices and climate costs. Third, bottom-up empirical studies repeatedly identify opportunities to reduce emissions at zero or negative net costs, a possibility that seems to be ruled out by economic theory. This is an area where data development has run ahead of economic analysis. Finally, rebound losses that shrink energy-efficiency gains are sometimes touted as being greater than the savings themselves. Recent research finds these losses to be no greater than 50 percent of savings in the worst cases, and usually much less. For many sectors, rebound effects are trivial.

Endogenous technical change and learning effects

Modeling the sources of technical change is always challenging (Clarke *et al.* 2008). Many models have adopted a simple ad hoc solution to the "science-fiction" problem of predicting the technologies of the far future: assume a constant annual rate of technical change. In energy models, this is often called the rate of autonomous energy-efficiency improvement (AEEI), where change is "autonomous" in the sense of occurring independently of policy or experience. The DICE model, for example, assumes that the cost of achieving any given level of emission reduction is a fraction of GDP. That fraction decreases at a fixed rate over time (Nordhaus 2008). This assumption makes it cheaper to wait to reduce emissions, contributing to the gradual "climate policy ramp" recommendation that emerges from Nordhaus' analyses with DICE.

An alternative assumption is more realistic but also more difficult to model. To quote one of the Stern Review team's responses to critics, "[T]echnical progress does not appear exogenously with the 'passage of time' ... but endogenously with investment in R&D, demonstration and deployment" (Dietz *et al.* 2007, p. 236). The Stern Review surveyed cost estimates from many existing models, and also developed its own estimates of the likely evolution of costs of a range of energy technologies over the next several decades. Both the average of model estimates and the Stern Review's own technology cost estimates assumed that climate policy would lead to moderate cost reductions over time (Stern 2008; Dietz *et al.* 2007).

Learning curves, or "learning by doing" effects, have been studied since the 1930s. While most commonly applied to cost estimates of energy supply technologies, learning curves are equally applicable to energy demand technologies (Weiss *et al.* 2010). The unit costs of many new technologies gradually reduce over a period of time as the cumulative volume of production increases. Unfortunately, it is difficult to tell how rapid the reductions will be and how long they will continue. For an attempt at predicting learning curves for energy technologies, see Alberth (2008). The best available learning curves clearly outperform a simple time trend, but the data remain noisy. See also Gillingham *et al.* (2008) on the problematic empirical evidence underlying the current modeling of endogenous technical change.

Kemfert and Truong (2007) review past studies of learning effects in energy technologies and test their importance in the WIAGEM (World Integrated Assessment General Equilibrium Model). They distinguish between endogenous technical change (unit costs go down as cumulative production goes up) and induced technical change (targeted climate policies such as research and development reduce new technology costs). With endogenous technical change included in the baseline, the addition of induced technical change reduces the costs of meeting stringent CO_2 targets by about 20 percent by 2100. In a study using the E3MG model, Barker *et al.* (2008) find that inducing technological change with a high carbon price is insufficient for reaching a 50 percent decrease in CO_2 emissions by 2050. To achieve this reduction, they model targeted investments in low-greenhouse-gas technologies using part of the revenues collected from auction or tax revenues.

In another detailed study, Kypreos (2007) uses MERGE to model many individual energy technology costs, including separate treatment of endogenous and induced technical change. Every doubling of cumulative production is assumed to reduce unit costs by 20 percent. In addition, every doubling of the accumulated stock of knowledge lowers the cost of new technologies by 15 percent. The stock of knowledge is increased by research and development spending but depreciates over time. These assumptions lower the cost of meeting a 450 ppm CO_2 target by almost 50 percent by 2100, compared to a baseline without learning. A similar finding is reached with a different model in Gerlagh (2008). Studies of specific technologies show similar results; for example, Ek and Söderholm (2010) look at learning curves and public investments in European wind power, finding a decline in both costs and government expenses.

Others have analyzed the effects of induced technological change on the optimal time path of mitigation. In several studies, the possibility of reducing costs through learning leads to an early surge in investment, accelerating mitigation. Greaker and Pade (2009) find high carbon taxes in the near future may be justified in order to spur investment in research and development if there are positive knowledge spillovers. Hart (2008) concludes that, with induced technological change and positive knowledge spillovers, the optimal carbon tax may need to be higher than the Pigouvian tax in order to stimulate investment in emissions reduction.

Policy choice becomes more complex in an environment with learning effects. On the one hand, policies to promote innovation are not, alone, enough to achieve common mitigation targets (Bosetti *et al.* 2011). On the other hand, carbon prices alone are also inadequate; a much-discussed recent analysis identifies plausible conditions under which the optimal policy combines carbon prices with subsidies for innovation (Acemoglu *et al.* 2012). Rout *et al.* (2010) conclude that early subsidization of "climate friendly" technologies may help make them cost-competitive more quickly and is more effective than subsidization at later stages. Fischer and Newell (2007) find that such positive knowledge spillovers have a discernible effect on the relative cost of alternative climate policy instruments.

Climate R&D investments may also have an opportunity cost: they may "crowd out" other R&D investments, dampening overall gains from induced technological change. Popp and Newell (2009) find only limited and sector-specific evidence for crowding out from investments in energy R&D. Gillingham *et al.* (2008) explore tensions between spillover and crowding-out effects across a broad selection of climate-economics models.

A more complex pattern is described by Alberth and Hope (2007). Using the PAGE model, they find that with learning, the optimal pace of mitigation is slightly slower in the near future, because investment is initially focused on learning about new technologies, but then substantially faster in later years as the new technologies are applied. They discuss the political difficulties of mobilizing the resources required in this scenario for exploration of unproven new technologies and the risks of failure of those technologies. A more gradual learning process may be the more prudent course.

Some studies have identified contradictory influences on timing of mitigation. Ingham *et al.* (2007) argue that the possibility of learning leads to delays in anticipation of obtaining better information, while the risks of irreversibility of damages result in earlier mitigation. Improved adaptation possibilities may ease the irreversibility constraint and thus delay mitigation. The study finds the combined effects of such factors to be ambiguous but small. Lange and Treich (2008) explore the effect of learning on the optimal mitigation path, finding that it is ambiguous and depends on the details of model specification.

The effect of learning may also depend on the manner in which economic policy is modeled. Using a modified version of DICE, Webster *et al.* (2008) find that the possibility of future learning has little effect in a conventional cost–benefit framework but is potentially more important in a standards-based cost-effectiveness framework, where a fixed target must be met. Lee *et al.* (2010) examine the impact of high regulatory standards, or "technology forcing," on automobile makers in the United States and find that regulation played an important role in leading to innovations and determining the subsequent direction of technological change.

Other analyses of learning can have unexpected results. Vona and Patriarca (2011), focusing on the rate of diffusion of new "green" products, find that per capita income is the limiting factor in developing countries, while income inequality is often the limiting factor in high-income countries. Optimistic pictures of learning are challenged by Oppenheimer *et al.* (2008), who note that incorrect learning may lead away from the right answers. They argue that such "negative learning" has happened at times in climate science when models are mis-specified. Negative learning can occur even when Bayesian analysis is correctly applied, as Oppenheimer *et al.* illustrate in a modified version of DICE.

Oil prices and climate policy costs

One of the greatest gaps in the recent literature is the lack of attention to the role of oil prices, and fossil fuel prices in general, in determining the cost of emission reduction. As the McKinsey abatement cost studies (discussed in the next section) make clear, a typical emission reduction measure consists of a capital expenditure that reduces fossil fuel consumption over its lifetime. The capital costs are almost independent of fossil fuel prices; the market value of the fuel savings is, of course, determined by fuel prices. Thus, the net cost of most emission reduction technologies should be negatively correlated with fuel prices.

Fossil fuel price assumptions play an important though little-noticed part in recent political debates over climate policy. The extreme views of climate policy cost, cited above, are based in part on clashing fossil fuel price projections. Those who view climate policy as prohibitively expensive assume that fossil fuel prices will be low. In contrast, detailed studies from environmental groups finding net benefits from emission reduction often rest on oil price projections of $100 per barrel or more – a level which seemed quite high a few years ago (Ackerman *et al.* 2009; Ackerman *et al.* 2010). While there are other differences between these two camps, their fossil fuel price assumptions alone would ensure substantially different evaluations of climate policy costs.

A handful of studies have examined the connections between climate policy and oil prices. Rozenberg *et al.* (2010) show that climate policies are a valuable hedge against uncertainties in oil markets. In their words, "climate policies are less costly when oil is scarce because, in addition to their benefits in terms of avoided climate impacts, they bring important co-benefits in terms of resilience to oil scarcity" (p. 666). Climate policies have been shown to provide important hedges against oil price rises in California (Fine *et al.* 2012) and in the European Union (Maisonnave *et al.* 2012). An explicit focus on hedging oil price uncertainties may lead to technology choices that are not simply the average of deterministic scenarios, such as short-lifespan investments that keep future options open (Usher and Strachan 2012).

Higher oil prices lead to some reduction in fossil fuel consumption and carbon emissions, but demand, especially in transportation, is relatively inelastic – implying that both price and non-price policies will be needed to reduce emissions (Knittel 2012). Similarly, Vielle and Viguier (2007) argue that higher oil prices are no substitute for sensible climate policies. Oil price increases are both less efficient and less equitable than is a climate policy designed to reduce emissions. And because alternative energy producers will be among the beneficiaries of carbon reduction policies, it is not surprising to find that higher oil prices increase the stock prices of alternative energy companies (Henriques and Sadorsky 2008).

In simpler analyses and cost estimates, fossil fuel prices will inevitably be treated as exogenous. This understandable simplification leads, however, to the problem faced by the dueling political advocates: fossil fuel price assumptions go a long way toward determining the results. An adequate, comprehensive analysis of climate economics should make fossil fuel consumption and prices endogenous. Mitigation strategies reduce the long-run demand for conventional fuels and should have long-run effects on prices.

Modeling fossil fuel prices is a daunting challenge. It involves enormous uncertainties about the extent of reserves, the availability and environmental impacts of "dirty" supplies such as oil shale and tar sands, oligopoly behavior in a complex geopolitical context, and the potential for substitution of alternative fuels. Speculation cannot be ruled out, and appears to have been important in recent market volatility (Kaufmann 2011). Nonetheless, an endogenous treatment of fossil fuel prices is an essential part of the puzzle, required for a complete economic analysis of the costs and benefits of climate policy. This is an area where more research is clearly needed.

Negative-cost abatement: does it exist?

Disaggregated, bottom-up studies of the potential for energy savings and emission reduction routinely find substantial opportunities with negative net costs – that is, cases where energy savings quickly outweigh the initial costs. Such negative-cost abatement opportunities present a challenge to economic theory, reflected in the old saying about $20 bills on the sidewalk. If energy savings are available at a net economic benefit, why hasn't someone already found it profitable to invest in them? A common response from economists is that there must be unobserved costs which explain the failure of consumers and businesses to make the seemingly free investments (Allcott and Greenstone 2012).

The debate about negative-cost savings is an old one, and there is relatively little new academic research in this area. The important innovation is in the realm of data, in the comprehensive empirical studies from McKinsey & Company, an international consulting firm, which develop marginal abatement cost curves for the world and for major countries and regions (e.g., McKinsey & Company 2009 for the world; Creyts *et al.* 2007 for the United States). The McKinsey studies find large savings available at negative cost, implying very low estimates of average abatement costs. They are widely cited and are now treated as an established data source in many contexts.

The older research literature in this area offers several possible explanations for the "efficiency paradox," or the "efficiency gap" (between the cost-minimizing level of investment in energy efficiency and the actual level). Market failures and barriers may discourage investment in low-cost efficiency measures; examples include misplaced incentives, unpriced costs and benefits, incomplete information, capital market barriers, and incomplete markets for efficiency (Brown 2001). Consumer reluctance to invest in efficiency measures could reflect extremely high discount rates for such purchases, possibly due to uncertainty and incomplete information. Households may avoid investments in efficiency unless payback times are very rapid. Business investment in energy efficiency may be shaped by organizational and institutional factors that, in practice, cause systematic deviations from profit-maximizing behavior (DeCanio 1998).

In another theory that implies the existence of $20 bills on the sidewalk, the Porter hypothesis (Porter and van der Linde 1995) asserts that carefully designed regulation can create a competitive advantage and increase profits for regulated firms – controversially implying that the firms were not maximizing profits prior to the regulation. Bréchet and Jouvet (2009) review the Porter hypothesis literature and provide a microeconomic rationale for no-regret abatement options. Regulation may lead a firm to invest in learning about additional production techniques, and while initially costly, the learning process can lead to the discovery of profitable long-run production possibilities.

Little has been written about the McKinsey marginal abatement cost curves in academic research. Murphy and Jaccard (2011) critique the McKinsey curves, developing alternative estimates with higher costs; their model assumes very high discount rates, some intangible costs of efficiency measures, and some general equilibrium effects. In the CRED climate-economics model (discussed in Chapter 7), the McKinsey curves are used as the basis for the model's estimate of abatement costs, with one major modification (Ackerman and Bueno 2011). McKinsey's negative-cost abatement measures are arbitrarily assumed to have a small but positive cost, while the McKinsey data on positive-cost abatement measures are used to estimate CRED's abatement cost curves. A comparison of the CRED calculations to abatement cost curves from MIT's EPPA model shows that the two models make broadly similar estimates.

In a study estimating global abatement costs, Cline (2010) compares CRED's McKinsey-based estimates, the comparable cost estimates from a new version of RICE (a regionally disaggregated version of DICE), and a synthesis of estimates from several models in the Energy Modeling Forum (EMF). The three estimates are strikingly different, with RICE in the middle; the CRED cost estimates are lower, often one-third of those of RICE, while the original EMF estimates are far above RICE by up to an order of magnitude (Cline also suggests a modification that lowers the EMF estimates). The lack of consensus shows that, even apart from the issue of negative-cost abatements, there are serious disagreements and issues to be resolved about the costs of climate protection.

Rebound effects: do they reverse efficiency gains?

An important ongoing controversy in energy and climate economics is the existence of a "rebound effect," where energy-efficiency gains are reduced by other related market effects. Savings from energy efficiency (an effective increase in disposable income) may be spent on other goods, which in turn require energy to produce. In addition, supply-side energy-efficiency measures may lower the unit cost of energy, driving up the quantity demanded. Steinhurst and Sabodash (2011) identify three possible forms of the rebound effect:

- negative rebound, where energy savings are higher than expected;
- typical rebound, where energy savings are less than expected;
- backfire, or the "Jevons paradox," where energy savings are negative (that is, overall energy use increases as a consequence of an energy-efficiency measure).

While much has been written about the dangers of energy-efficiency backfire, most actual rebound effects result in losses but are not large enough to erase savings, in part because energy is only a small share of total purchases and because savings from energy efficiency are correspondingly small (Steinhurst and Sabodash 2011). Warnings about backfire date back to William Stanley Jevons' book *The Coal Question* (1865) and surface periodically as contrarian arguments against otherwise-desirable efficiency measures. Recent examples of this genre include Sorrell (2009), Herring and Sorrell (2009), and Jenkins *et al.* (2011).

Hard evidence for rebound effects approaching or exceeding 100 percent, however, is rare. Jenkins *et al.* (2011) largely suggest that it is important to consider the possibility that rebound might reach 100 percent. Empirical research, on the other hand, finds distinctly smaller rebound effects. A review of this literature shows rebound losses of 10–30 percent for residential space heating, 0–50 percent for residential space cooling, <10–40 percent for residential water heating, 5–12 percent for residential lighting, 0 percent for residential appliances,

10–30 percent for automobiles, 0–2 percent for commercial lighting, and 0–20 percent for commercial process uses (Ehrhardt-Martinez and Laitner 2010).[1] One study of the rebound effect in U.S. transportation estimates it at 11–19 percent (Su 2012); another study estimates it at about 11 percent today, and declining as average incomes rise (Greene 2012, Table A1).

In a historical analysis of lighting, Tsao *et al.* (2010) demonstrate that the development of new technologies has generated considerable growth in the consumption of energy but that these large rebounds have not resulted in backfire. Historically, savings from energy-efficiency measures have been positive when GDP and population growth are taken into account. Goldstein *et al.* (2011) show that, despite a broad mandate for energy efficiency starting in the 1970s, California's energy consumption per capita has remained steady while the rest of the United States' energy consumption per capita has grown by more than half.

Using the E3MG climate-economics model, Barker *et al.* (2009) model the potential rebound effects resulting from climate policy. They distinguish among direct, indirect, and economy-wide rebound effects, and they estimate that direct rebound effects, resulting from the use of more energy-efficiency devices, would reduce savings globally by about 10 percent. With indirect effects (lower unit energy costs increase the quantity of energy demanded) and economy-wide effects (lower energy prices deflate the overall price level) included, overall reductions to savings are estimated as 31 percent in 2020 and 52 percent in 2030. Ehrhardt-Martinez and Laitner (2010) estimate the direct rebound effect to be a 10 to 30 percent loss of energy-efficiency savings and the total effect to be a 40 percent loss.

Druckman *et al.* (2011) estimate the potential rebound effect of UK households' greenhouse gas abatement actions at 34 percent, but find that if savings are targeted toward spending on goods and services with low greenhouse gas intensities, the losses can be reduced to 12 percent. Using evidence from a computable general equilibrium of the Chinese economy, Liang *et al.* (2009) identify smaller rebound effects for policies that combine a carbon tax with subsidies to primary energy producers as compared to producer subsidies alone.

In short, empirical research on the rebound effect shows that it is real but modest in size. Estimates of 10 to 30 percent seem common, with some larger and some smaller. Actual evidence of backfire, or rebound effects of 100 percent or more, appears to be nonexistent. Perhaps most promising is the possibility that well-designed policies could reduce the extent of rebound, thus maximizing gains from energy efficiency. Even when careful calculation of losses due to rebound are included, energy efficiency remains a very low-cost option for reducing emissions.

11 Adaptation

Past greenhouse gas emissions have already altered the earth's climate, "locking in" some amount of additional change to temperatures, sea levels, and precipitation patterns that can no longer be avoided (see Chapter 1). Even the ambitious mitigation scenarios described in Chapter 8 that limit global mean warming to 2°C would not prevent all significant future damages (see Chapters 3 and 4). The large and diverse set of measures aimed at reducing vulnerability to these damages and enhancing resilience with regard to changing climatic conditions is collectively referred to as adaptation. AR4 reviewed the limited state of the adaptation literature as of 2007, explaining:

> Adaptation occurs in physical, ecological, and human systems. It involves changes in social and environmental processes, perceptions of climate risk, practices and functions to reduce potential damages or to realize new opportunities.... In practice, adaptations tend to be on-going processes, reflecting many factors or stresses, rather than discrete measures to address climate change specifically.
>
> (IPCC 2007a, *Working Group II*, Chapter 17.4)

While adaptation investments have great potential to lessen near-term climate damages, the economics of estimating adaptation costs is complicated by inter-relations among adaptation, mitigation, and economic development. For many developing countries, the "additionality" of adaptation aid – over and above current development funding – is a central issue (Fankhauser and Burton 2011; Smith *et al.* 2011). For others, especially small island states, the question of whether the international community will provide compensation for irreversible losses is a key issue (Grenada 2011; Barnett and Dessai 2002). Still others, in particular those with extensive fossil fuel resources, call for a definition of "adaptation" that is broad enough to include economic losses due to emission mitigation efforts by other countries (Kingdom of Saudi Arabia 2011; Barnett and Dessai 2002).

Higher projections for likely future temperatures together with limited success in international climate negotiations suggest the need to plan for adaptation to temperature rises as high as 4°C in this century (Smith *et al.* 2011). Fair treatment of developing countries is of the utmost importance to a successful outcome from current climate policy negotiations. Adaptation investments, including funding from rich countries for adaptation in poor countries, will be an essential component of a comprehensive international climate policy. Nonetheless, near-term adaptation investment choices have little impact on the modeling of optimal mitigation scenarios, and climate-economics models that incorporate explicit adaptation decisions have concluded that rapid emissions abatement should take precedence in the next few decades. In this chapter, we briefly sketch out the wide range of adaptation technologies and then focus on the very serious challenges that exist to the inclusion of adaptation investment in climate-economics models.

Adaptation technology

The technology of adaptation varies from setting to setting and includes a broad swath of building, infrastructure, and energy technologies, as well as numerous public health and even poverty reduction measures. The inclusive definition of "adaptation" – reducing vulnerability and enhancing resilience – makes for a very big tent, with room for most investments in economic development to also be classified as adaptation. A lexicon of types of adaptation may serve as an illustration (IPCC 2007a, *Working Group II*, Chapter 17; Smith 1997; Margulis *et al.* 2008; de Bruin *et al.* 2009).

- *Reactive adaptation* occurs after and in response to climate change; *anticipatory adaptation* precedes and prepares for climate change. Reliance on reactive measures may avoid unnecessary precautionary investments but would fail to avert irreversible damage, and could lead to short-term, high-cost solutions. Anticipatory adaptation also includes investments in innovation to develop new adaptive measures.
- *Planned adaptation* is the result of public policy decisions; *autonomous adaptation* is the result of actions by households, businesses, and communities. Both planned and autonomous adaptation can be either reactive or anticipatory.
- *Induced adaptation* refers to unplanned adjustments to new climatic conditions, including transition costs and transition time. In economic models, *implicit adaptation* is built into the climate damage function, so the damage function actually models residual damages after the assumed optimal adaptation. *Explicit adaptation* is modeled separately from climate damages.
- *Nonoptimal adaptation* is inefficient or poorly suited to actual circumstances; *maladaptation*, which may be a response to climate change or to climate policies, increases vulnerability or reduces resilience to new climatic conditions.
- *Hard adaptation measures* offer an "engineering" response using built infrastructure; *soft adaptation measures* include early warning systems, community preparedness programs, zoning, and water price adjustments. The terms

hard adaptation measure and *soft adaptation measure* are also used to distinguish between built infrastructure (such as dikes and seawalls) and measures that enhance natural systems (such as rehabilitating sand dunes, salt marshes, and barrier islands).

Most of these types of adaptation have potential relevance to many of the areas of climate impacts discussed in Chapters 3 and 4. In AR4, disparate examples of damages that could be ameliorated by adaptation include sea-level rise, saltwater intrusion into aquifers, storm surges, permafrost melt, change in ice cover, loss of snow, glacier melt, extreme temperatures, droughts, and floods (IPCC 2007a, *Working Group II*, Chapter 17). The economic sectors most likely to be impacted are agriculture, forestry, fishing, and tourism. Infrastructure will be affected in a wide range of climates and settings, especially indoor climate control, roads and railways, and coastal property. In addition, to the extent that energy demands will increase with climate change, new investments in energy infrastructure may be viewed as adaptation.

Unlike mitigation technologies, which are often applicable across nations and latitudes, adaptation technologies are extremely localized. The types of expected damages are different in each locality, as are the solutions considered most technically sound and culturally appropriate.

Adaptation and mitigation

Any estimation of the costs of adaptation is necessarily contingent on a scenario of future mitigation. Temperature and other climatic changes will depend on the amount and pace of emissions abatement together with climate sensitivity (see Chapter 1), and potential damages will depend on these climate outcomes. In optimization models that compare costs and benefits of climate policy, damages are equal to abatement costs at the margin. Thus, in any optimal scenario, marginal abatement cost equals the value of marginal averted damages (i.e., the social cost of carbon). Adaptation investments, in turn, affect the social cost of carbon (or marginal damages) and, therefore, the optimal level of mitigation. The endogeneity of adaptation and mitigation is extremely challenging to model (Warren 2011). The optimal mix of adaptation, mitigation, and investment in innovation will vary by time and scenario (Agrawala *et al.* 2010; Anda *et al.* 2009).

Model results are very sensitive to choice of damage function (as discussed in Chapter 2) and the local or regional distribution of damages (Agrawala *et al.* 2010). Unit adaptation costs also vary by region, economic sector, and time period. For accurate modeling, each of these factors should be considered in determining the exposure of assets and costs of "climate proofing" (Agrawala and Fankhauser 2008). The omission of a region's or sector's damages or adaptation costs has the potential to distort optimal mitigation recommendations, but a comprehensive catalog of all potential damages and adaptive measures is not feasible (Stern 2006). Modeling the stock (investment) and flow (operations and maintenance) dimensions of adaptation is an additional complication (Callaway 2004).

The greatest challenge for integrated assessment modeling, both with and without explicit adaptation, is the uncertainty inherent in the climate and economic systems (see Chapter 6). The magnitude, type, and timing of impacts are highly uncertain, as are the costs of new technology (see Chapter 9) and the effectiveness of anticipatory adaptation measures (Wilby and Dessai 2010). The interdependence of adaptation, mitigation, and technical innovation compounds uncertainties in each of these areas (Anda *et al.* 2009; Smith 1997). Uncertainty regarding future climate outcomes can have the effect of limiting adaptation measures to short-run adjustments or increasing the risks of nonoptimal adaptation or maladaptation (Callaway 2004).

Adaptation and economic development

Another challenge for incorporating adaptation into climate-economics models is the substantial overlap between measures that enhance resilience to climate changes and measures that will enhance the quality of life regardless of climate change. Many adaptation measures lead double lives as sensible improvements for economic development (Anda *et al.* 2009; Fankhauser and Schmidt-Traub 2011). Two specific concerns are of particular importance to climate-economics modeling.

First, baseline GDP and population assumptions are important to delineating adaptation investments (specifying what is and what is not adaptation), even in no-adaptation scenarios. If real GDP per capita is expected to grow over time, especially in developing countries, then today's levels of public infrastructure, quality of housing, and energy-generation and delivery systems are likely a poor proxy for future levels. With higher incomes, the capital stock vulnerable to climate damage will be larger, but it is also likely that new investments built by a richer population will be more robust to climate change. Development substantially increases the potential damages from climate change, and the recent literature regarding adaptation finance highlights issues of "climate proofing" development (Fankhauser and Schmidt-Traub 2011; Smith, Dickinson *et al.* 2011).

A related issue is the uncertain impact of climate change on GDP growth. Overall, the economics literature suggests an inverse relationship between temperature and income: countries with higher average temperatures have lower GDP per capita (Dell *et al.* 2009), and temperature increases over the past 50 years have been associated with reduced economic growth in poorer countries but have had little effect on economic growth in richer countries (Dell *et al.* 2008). Other studies have reported that higher temperatures are a risk factor with an adverse effect on global economic growth (Bansal and Ochoa 2010). In most climate-economics models, however, higher temperatures occur in low or slow mitigation scenarios with high GDP growth; lower temperatures occur only when a share of GDP is diverted from standard investment into abatement. The existence of an inverse relationship between temperature and GDP growth suggests, again, that damages functions used in integrated assessment models (IAMs) are very likely mis-specified (as discussed in Chapter 2), particularly at lower levels of temperature change.

Second, even after baseline GDP per capita growth is accounted for, some proposed climate change adaptation measures will still overlap with more general improvements for economic development. Improving sanitation and water delivery, and providing universal protection from diseases such as malaria, would save millions of lives every year, regardless of future climate change. Flood protection, high-tech irrigation systems, and energy-efficiency measures will lower costs even if only the lowest climate change damages come to pass. Without these measures, lower-income populations, especially in developing countries, would be still more vulnerable to climate change. In modeling adaptation investments, IAMs need to account for social benefits that increase welfare above and beyond negating potential climate damages.

New developments in economic modeling of adaptation

Several research groups are actively engaged in bringing adaptation investment choices into climate-economics models. De Bruin *et al.* (2009) modify the DICE and RICE climate-economics models to incorporate explicit adaptation decisions; they examine interactions between adaptation and mitigation as well as the distribution of adaptation costs across regions. They construct regional adaptation cost curves where the costs and benefits (damages reductions) of adaptation are restricted to occur only in the same period. The most efficient policy for reducing climate damages is found to be a mix of adaptation and mitigation investments. (See also de Bruin *et al.* 2007.)

Agrawala *et al.* (2010) extend de Bruin *et al.*'s AD-DICE and AD-RICE models and also present modifications to the WITCH model. For all three models, the representation of adaptation has been improved to include both flows of adaptation costs and benefits over time and the stock of climate-adaptation-related capital. The authors' AD-WITCH model allows for anticipatory investments in adaptation capacity, as well as reactive actions designed to reduce same-period climate damages. The study finds that adaptation measures can be a cost-effective policy choice, with benefit-to-cost ratios of 1.8 in AD-DICE and 2.0 in AD-WITCH. In AD-RICE and AD-WITCH, South Asia and sub-Saharan Africa had the highest adaptation costs, while the United States, Japan, and China had the lowest.

Bosello (2010) adds planned adaptation to the FEEM-RICE model. This study finds that a combination of adaptation, mitigation, and technology innovation investments is necessary to keep climate damages small, and suggests that the best intertemporal allocation of investment funds would involve rapid anticipatory mitigation measures, together with adaptation investments, to counteract residual damages in later decades. Other studies reach a similar conclusion: adaptation investments should not be permitted to crowd out near-term mitigation investments

(Carraro *et al.* 2010; The World Bank and United Nations 2010). Rapid emissions reductions are the top priority for immediate climate policy spending

Estimates of global adaptation costs

Several recent studies have attempted to estimate the costs of near-term adaptation measures. Agrawala *et al.* (2008) reviewed an array of sectoral, national, and global multi-sectoral estimates and found substantial variations. The World Bank projected $9 billion to $41 billion in annual costs to developing countries; the Stern Report $4 billion to $37 billion, an Oxfam paper at least $50 billion, and a United Nations Development Programme study $86 billion to $109 billion (by 2015). Agrawala also reviewed estimates from the United Nations Framework Convention on Climate Change (UNFCCC), which put annual global adaptation costs at $44 billion to $166 billion per year, including $28 billion to $67 billion for developing countries. Of the global total, $8 billion to $130 billion would be required for infrastructure investments, $14 billion for agriculture, $11 billion each for water systems and coastal zones, and $5 billion for human health.[1] Similarly, Narain *et al.* (2011) estimate a price tag of $70 to $100 billion per year from the adaptation of developing countries to 2°C warming.

Based on this review, Agrawala *et al.* (2008) find that the multi-sectoral estimates face "serious limitations," most notably due to their sensitivity to assumptions about two parameters for which there is little reliable information: the proportion of assets and financial flows exposed to climate risk, and the incremental cost of "climate proofing" those assets. They also raise concerns about the lack of direct attribution to specific adaptation activities, the lack of consideration of the benefits of adaptation investments, and issues of double counting and scaling up to global levels. Thus, they conclude, "the 'consensus' on global adaptation costs, even in order of magnitude terms, may be premature" and not useful for decision making (p. 14).

Parry *et al.* (2009) find that the UNFCCC underestimated adaptation costs in included sectors by a factor of two to three, and omitted other important adaptation costs, including health costs in high-income countries and ecosystems protection. By 2030, they estimate that annual costs to developing countries will be $134 billion to $230 billion. A recent World Bank study (2010) estimated $80 billion to $90 billion in 2030 adaptation costs for developing countries, including $29 billion each in coastal zones and infrastructure.

A recent analysis of adaptation and development costs by Smith *et al.* (2011) finds that a large share of estimated adaptation costs coincides with development expenditures, and that a considerable share of current development expenditures goes to climate-sensitive projects. The analysis concludes that coordination of adaptation and development investments could make both funding streams more effective.

Conclusion

In the years since AR4 and the Stern Report, climate science has made great leaps in understanding the likely pace and extent of climate impacts. The uncertainties inherent in predicting climate change are now better understood and better represented in forecasts. In order to be relevant and useful in policy making, climate economics must catch up with climate science. Our review of the latest literature brings to light the most critical improvements needed to assure that climate-economics models are based on the best possible scientific knowledge. In our judgment, the following elements are essential to a state-of-the-art, policy-relevant climate-economics analysis.

Climate-economics models should use an up-to-date representation of the climate system, including non-declining temperatures on a timescale of several centuries.

The latest general circulation models (GCMs) draw on the current state of the art in climate science to produce a more detailed – and more complicated – representation of the planet's physical systems. The climate is not a simple, predictable system. The important effect of atmospheric concentrations of CO_2 on future temperatures is shaped by multiple, complex interactions, some of them of uncertain strength. The number of interacting factors affecting the future climate is immense; predictions are complicated by many feedback effects. Today's GCMs incorporate more interactions among systems and take account of irreducible uncertainty in future outcomes. The result is a more accurate and detailed range of likely temperatures, precipitation patterns, and rates of sea-level rise.

The IAMs of climate economics cannot match the overwhelming level of detail embodied in GCMs. Instead, IAMs use simplified representations of the climate system that are designed to approximate GCM results, given the same emission inputs and baseline climate. Of course, calibrating IAMs to the GCMs of five or ten years ago is not sufficient to policy-relevant climate-economics analysis. To achieve the state of the art in climate-economics modeling, IAMs should emulate the state of the art in climate science by approximating the latest suite of GCM results.

One new scientific finding that is critically important to policy results is the relationship between peak greenhouse gas concentrations and temperatures. After reaching their high point, temperatures are unlikely to decline for the next several hundred years. This means that "overshoot" scenarios are no longer viable options for policy analysis. While it is possible to exceed target concentrations and then gradually reduce atmospheric levels to a lower stabilization trajectory, this course of action will not have the previously anticipated effect of quickly reducing global temperatures. Climate-economics analyses should model non-declining temperatures to avoid producing infeasible policy recommendations.

Outcomes from climate change are uncertain, and climate-economics modeling results should reflect this uncertainty.

Climate science projects a range of outcomes from bad to much worse; climate economics should do the same. Future economic growth rates and the carbon intensity of future technologies are not known; nor, therefore, are future emissions. The relationships among greenhouse gases, radiative forcing, and temperature change are thought to be irreducibly uncertain – creating a much broader, possibly unbounded range of risks, and thereby posing a fundamental challenge to climate economics. The pace of sea-level rise will depend, in part, on the timing of irreversible and potentially abrupt threshold events, such as large ice sheets breaking apart or shifts in ocean circulation, with important implications for damage estimates. Forecasts of precipitation levels and storm frequency and intensity depend on the assumptions made about emissions, climate sensitivity, and ocean circulation, as well as inherently unpredictable weather patterns.

New approaches to risk aversion that raise the possibility of improved modeling frameworks are a promising area in recent climate-economics research. The intriguing parallels to new developments in finance suggest that this could be part of a broader rethinking of the economics of markets, risk, and uncertainty. Short of such paradigm-changing innovations, however, there is much that can be done to improve the treatment of uncertainty in existing models.

Either by drawing from an assumed distribution of parameter values – producing a range of results instead of a single best guess – or by using the more complicated approach of modeling multiple future states of climate outcomes within the IAM structure, climate-economics models should incorporate uncertainty. At a minimum, results should be presented for values corresponding to the low end (e.g., first to tenth percentiles), the median, and the high end (e.g., 90th to 99th percentiles) of an up-to-date climate sensitivity probability distribution. Alternatively, models can use a climate-sensitivity distribution to estimate the probability of exceeding set temperature-increase thresholds, such as 2°C, 3°C, and 4°C.

Climate-economics models should incorporate up-to-date scientific findings on the expected physical and ecological impacts of climate change.

Many economic models arrive at a policy recommendation by evaluating trade-offs among abatement investments, other investments, and current consumption in order to find the spending mix that maximizes global utility. In these welfare-optimization models, utility is extremely sensitive to assumptions made about the relationship between emissions and climate damages: if damages are assumed to be only trivially increasing as emissions rise, these models recommend little or no spending on mitigation.

At present, the functions representing damages in many of the best-known welfare-optimization models appear to have no basis whatsoever in the current scientific literature on climate impacts. This fundamental disconnect between physical impact analysis and economic impact analysis undermines the models' relevance to climate policy.

To accurately model monetary damages as a function of temperature, IAMs should incorporate recent scientific findings on sector-specific damages, regional variation in vulnerability and in baseline climate, human communities' reliance on ecological systems, and uncertainty in impact assessments, especially in the long run. Both low- and high-temperature damages must be subjected to serious, detailed economic evaluation. In particular, the common but entirely unsubstantiated practice of assuming that damages grow with the square of temperature should be discarded.

Methods for modeling adaptation investment choices within IAMs are still under development. Endogeneity between adaptation and mitigation and the overlap between adaptation and economic development present significant analytical challenges. In the absence of a clear, widely adopted method for incorporating adaptation as a separate investment choice, some IAM damage functions represent climate impacts after an arbitrary, assumed level of adaptation. Policy recommendations will be strongly dependent on this assumed adaptation level, and it is therefore imperative that model results be presented with an explicit explanation of the degree of adaptation that they assume.

If damages cannot be accurately represented in welfare-optimization models, economists should instead use a standards-based approach.

Accurate modeling of the relationship among emissions, temperatures, and damages is a daunting task. The data requirements for such an endeavor are overwhelming, and no simple function can represent sector- and region-specific damages. The uncertainties, large enough to make modeling difficult at low temperatures, are imponderable at high temperatures. If damages cannot be modeled in a way that reflects current scientific knowledge, welfare-optimizing models cannot offer good policy advice. Fortunately, there is another approach that obviates the need to model damages in IAMs: the widely used standards-based, or precautionary, approach.

A standards-based approach to climate-economics analysis replaces welfare maximization with cost minimization, identifying the least-cost method of achieving a particular climate outcome – for example, keeping temperature increases below a threshold such as 2°C. Although they are derived from different theoretical frameworks, the welfare-optimization and cost-effectiveness approaches are functionally equivalent when the damage function used for utility maximization reflects a near-vertical relationship between temperatures and damages. This implies that, beyond some threshold, even a small increase in temperature results in an unacceptably large increase in damages.

The assumption of an extremely steep damage function at some point not far beyond the 2°C threshold seems well-founded in science, and is ubiquitous in climate policy discussions. It also fits a broadly accepted normative standpoint: temperature increases above this level would create too great a possibility of catastrophic damages for the most vulnerable in our own generation and for future generations, and should therefore be avoided even if the necessary precautionary actions are costly. Standards-based models take the near-vertical temperature-damage relationship as a given and focus on trade-offs regarding where and when to use particular abatement technologies in order to minimize the global costs of meeting the standard.

All climate-economics analyses should be accompanied by an explanation of what discount rate was chosen and why.

Climate change results from a form of pollution that has global and long-lasting effects, and appropriate responses will also be global and long lasting in nature. Climate change is a public problem that requires public policy solutions. The distinction between public and private decision making is important in the choice of a discount rate, both in utility modeling in welfare-optimizing models and in the evaluation of abatement costs in standards-based models. When decisions involve multiple generations, as well as populations within the current generation that cannot plausibly be said to share common preferences or objectives with regard to climate policy, the discount rate is an ethical construct rather than an empirical observation.

Welfare-optimizing models seek to maximize utility functions, which include parameters quantifying the importance of equity, both within and across generations. The public nature of the climate problem and its long timeframe – decisions made today will have potentially enormous impacts on the well-being of future generations – point to the appropriateness of a low and perhaps declining discount rate and/or other approaches to intergenerational equity. In standards-based (cost-effectiveness) models, the focus on nearer-term abatement investments makes discounting choices less crucial and makes a market-based discount rate more appropriate. Even for cost-effectiveness models, however, many major investments last for decades; it may be important to analyze decisions extending beyond the current generation. Thus the same long-run considerations can arise in discounting abatement costs.

Regardless of model type and approach to discounting, climate-economics results should be presented together with an explicit statement of what discount rate was used and why. Where the case for using a particular discount rate is weak or ambiguous, presenting modeling results across a range of discount rates may improve policy relevance.

Policy relevance in climate economics depends on the ability to present impacts not just for the world as a whole but also by region or income group.

It is simply not plausible that the welfare of the world's economically, culturally, and geographically diverse population can be well represented by the single "representative agent" of abstract economic theory. Despite the global-public-goods aspect of the problem, there is wide regional variation in economic and physical vulnerability, baseline climate, and expected climate damages, as well as in energy infrastructure, abatement options, and technical costs. Under any climate policy, some members of the current generation will benefit from averted damages, improved access to more reliable energy sources, or jobs in green industry. Others will suffer net losses due to higher taxes, energy costs, or carbon charges, or from residual damages that occur despite mitigation and adaptation investments.

The diversity of climate effects around the world calls for at least the inclusion of multiple interests within a single objective function or for multiple objective functions across geographic regions. At a minimum, any climate-economics model should consider the concerns of poor and rich countries separately and should have the means to present results by region or other relevant grouping.

In a similar vein, climate-economics models that act as if the distribution of income is immutable (using Negishi weighting) should be explicit regarding limitations they have placed on interregional transfers or investments. Assumptions regarding the global distribution of income – and opportunities (or lack thereof) for changing it – are of paramount importance to international climate policy negotiations.

Abatement costs should be modeled as both determining and determined by abatement investments.

With an appropriate temperature-damage relationship, or a standards-based approach, the question of *what* to do about climate change has a clear answer: stop increases to global emissions as soon as possible, with rapid and sustained annual decreases thereafter. The question of *how* to reduce annual net emissions cost-effectively, however, still requires substantial exploration. This is an area where climate economics can make an important contribution to the decisions made in international climate policy negotiations and in domestic policy decisions around the world.

For all types of climate-economics analysis, abatement cost assumptions are key determinants of policy recommendations. Ideally, IAMs should model technological change endogenously, taking into account learning and price reductions that grow with investments in a particular technology. Abatement costs should not be modeled as purely a function of time or as a deadweight cost to society; research and development investment in emissions mitigation has clear benefits in improving future technological innovation, lowering energy costs, and providing jobs and income.

Modeling abatement choices and costs is complicated not only by endogeneity with respect to investment decisions but also by several ongoing controversies in the field of climate economics. Our review of this literature suggests, on the one hand, that negative-cost abatement options (the fabled "low-hanging fruit"), while perhaps exaggerated at times, really do exist and should be taken seriously in economic analysis. On the other hand, while the rebound effect (reducing the potential of energy-efficiency measures) also exists, backfire (a rebound large enough to erase energy-efficiency gains) is the economics equivalent of an urban legend.

Finally, abatement cost estimates include another critical assumption that should be made explicit when presenting modeling results: fossil fuel price assumptions are a significant determinant of the comparative affordability of different abatement measures. A complete analysis of climate economics would make these prices endogenous, but this would require a level of complexity beyond the scope of most modeling efforts (and would, in any case, introduce new uncertainties). As with other assumptions in climate-economics models, assumptions about future fossil fuel prices should be presented explicitly, along with an explanation of the choices made. Where these choices may seem especially arbitrary, the policy relevance of model recommendations would be improved by presenting results across a range of possible future fossil fuel prices.

In the end, analyzing climate change is not an academic exercise. The climate crisis is an existential threat to human society; it poses unprecedented challenges and demands extraordinary levels of cooperation, skill, and resource mobilization to craft and enact policies that will create a sustainable future. Getting climate economics right is not about publishing the cleverest article of the year but rather about helping solve the dilemma of the century. The tasks ahead are daunting, and failure, unfortunately, is quite possible. Better approaches to climate economics will allow economists to be part of the solution rather than part of the problem.

Notes

1 Climate science for economists

1 Globally averaged marine surface monthly mean CO_2 concentration was 394 ppm in May 2012 (NOAA Earth System Research Laboratory 2012).

2 RCP Database (International Institute for Applied Systems Analysis 2009). The two scenarios are named for their radiative forcing pathways, which lead to 8.5 and 4.5 W/m^2 in 2100.

3 See also Clarke *et al.* (2007).

4 The EMF exercise compared ten integrated assessment models; see Energy Modeling Forum (2009).

5 International Energy Agency (2008).

6 The UK government's AVOID program has also released an update of climate science literature since AR4 with similar findings. See Warren *et al.* (2009).

7 The economic downturn led to a reduction in global emissions beginning in 2009. It is not clear how long the downturn, or the reduction in emissions, will last, but preliminary data from the IEA in 2011 suggest that CO_2 emissions were greater in 2010 than in 2008.

8 According to Solomon, Plattner *et al.* (2009) and Gillett *et al.* (2011), temperatures are expected to increase along with CO_2 concentrations but will remain roughly constant (within ±0.5°C) for about 2,000 years after CO_2 concentrations peak. Near-constant temperatures result from a balance between 1) the decrease in radiative forcing due to shrinking CO_2 concentrations; and 2) gradually rising ocean temperatures, which will slow down the transfer of heat from the atmosphere to the oceans.

9 For a more detailed review of recent research on overshoot, see Warren *et al.* (2009).

10 See Solomon *et al.* (2009). Results assume a climate sensitivity of 3.2°C.

11 See NOAA Earth System Research Laboratory (2010) for a discussion of the radiative forcings of greenhouse gases and an index of these gases' impacts on the global energy balance over time.

12 For reviews of the state of research on aerosols and climate change, see Rosenfeld *et al.* (2008) and Stevens and Feingold (2009).

13 Radiative forcing in 2005 relative to 1750.

14 Shindell and Faluvegi (2009) discuss advances in measuring the long-term impact of emissions and aerosols on radiative forcings, including interaction effects. For a critique of Ramanathan and Carmichael (2008), see Zarzycki and Bond (2010). Note that both CO_2 and black carbon can contribute more than half of anthropogenic radiative forcing, because there are also negative contributions, e.g., from other aerosols.

15 For a detailed synthesis of recent literature on black carbon and tropospheric ozone, see United Nations Environment Programme and World Meteorological Organization (2011).

16 Intergovernmental Panel on Climate Change (2007e), *Working Group I*, Technical Summary.

17 For a technical critique of this analysis of feedbacks, see Zaliapin and Ghil (2010) and the original authors' response (Roe and Baker 2011).
18 The IPCC ranks the likelihood of climate sensitivity falling within this range as "likely," indicating a 17th to 83rd percentile confidence interval, and states that it is "very unlikely" (less than ten percent probability) that climate sensitivity would be below 1.5°C (see IPCC 2007e, *Working Group I*, Box 10.2).
19 See Warren *et al.* (2009), section A.8, for a discussion of several additional recent studies on climate sensitivity.
20 The Interagency Working Group's report (2010) on *Social Cost of Carbon* uses a truncated version of the Roe and Baker distribution, asserting that this distribution provides the IPCC climate sensitivities with the most up-to-date information about the tails of the distribution. The Working Group calibrates and truncates the Roe and Baker distribution using three constraints derived from AR4: (1) setting the median equal to 3°C, (2) two-thirds probability of falling between 2.0°C and 4.5°C, and (3) zero probability of being less than 0°C or greater than 10°C.
21 NOAA Earth System Research Laboratory (2012); IPCC (2007e), *Working Group I*, Technical Summary, p. 25.
22 Equilibrium temperature may not be reached for centuries or millennia after peak concentration, but most of the temperature change occurs within a few decades; the time lag to reach equilibrium temperature is longer with higher climate sensitivity (Hansen *et al.* 2005; IPCC 2007e, *Working Group I*, Chapter 10).
23 According to AR4, models suggest "the possibility of a decrease in the number of relatively weak hurricanes, and increased numbers of intense hurricanes. However, the total number of tropical cyclones globally is projected to decrease" (IPCC 2007e, *Working Group I*, Technical Summary, p. 74).
24 Grossman and Morgan (2011) offer a discussion of the scientific uncertainty involved in modeling tropical cyclones.
25 End-of-century (2081–2100) precipitation under A1B relative to 1981–2000.
26 Lu (2009) notes that there is significant uncertainty regarding future Sahel drying, because it is influenced by 1) sea-surface temperature changes over all the world's oceans; and 2) the radiative effects of greenhouse gas forcing on increased land warming, which can lead to monsoon-like conditions.
27 Sea-level rise is relative to 1990 levels. IPCC sea-level rise ranges reported as 5 to 95 percent of the spread of model results. For background on the SRES scenarios, see Nakicenovic *et al.* (2000).
28 Kemp *et al.* (2011) find instead that sea levels have risen at a rate of 2.1 mm per year since the late nineteenth century, compared to 0.6 mm per year in the proceeding four centuries.
29 Based on annual estimated sea-level rise from 2003 to 2008.
30 Baselines for these projections are slightly different. Projections are relative to 1990 sea level for AR4 according to Vermeer and Rahmstorf (2009) and Jevrejeva *et al.* (2010); relative to 2001–5 for Horton *et al.* (2008); and relative to 2000 for Grinsted *et al.* (2009).
31 In this context, "recent" refers to sea-level rise from 1961 to 2004.
32 For a more detailed review of recent research on sea-level rise, see Warren *et al.* (2009).

2 Damage functions and climate impacts

1 This account is based on FUND version 3.5 and its technical documentation (www.fund-model.org/FundDocTechnicalVersion3.5.pdf), dated May 2010, the latest available documentation as of mid-2012. A modified form of FUND 3.5 was used in the U.S. Interagency Working Group analysis discussed in the text.

2 Richard Tol has objected to the citation and description of Ackerman and Munitz (2012), which occurs here and in Chapter 4. The article, however, is part of the peer-reviewed literature. The journal in which it appears, *Ecological Economics*, considered and turned down Tol's request for a retraction or correction of the article. See the response to Ackerman and Munitz by David Anthoff and Richard Tol (doi:10.1016/j. ecolecon.2012.06.012), the reply by Ackerman and Munitz (doi:10.1016/j. ecolecon.2012.06.023), and the editor's letter on these comments (doi:10.1016/j. ecolecon.2012.06.007), all in *Ecological Economics*, 2012.

3 This account is based on DICE-2007, the latest complete version available as of mid-2012 (http://nordhaus.econ.yale.edu/DICE2007.htm). At that time, DICE-2009 was available only in an incomplete and undocumented "beta" version that did not yet include the major announced innovation of a separate sea-level-rise module.

4 U.S. cities with annual average temperatures close to 68°F include Houston, Texas; Jacksonville, Florida; and New Orleans, Louisiana (www.cityrating.com/averagetemperature.asp).

5 U.S. cities with annual average temperatures close to 65°F include Dallas, Texas; Montgomery, Alabama; and San Diego, California (www.cityrating.com/averagetemperature.asp).

6 Hanemann compared his estimates to the DICE-1999 values; Hanemann's figures are almost exactly 4 times the DICE-1999 estimates, which is equivalent to 2.4 times the DICE-2007 values.

7 Nordhaus presents some numerical estimates of damages at 6°C, suggesting they are between 8 percent and 11 percent of output (Nordhaus 2007). These estimates are not well documented and do not appear to be used in the calibration of DICE.

8 Equation (2.3) is our re-estimate of the Weitzman damage function, estimated by minimizing the sum of squared differences from the DICE damage estimate at 2.5°C and Weitzman's estimates at 6°C and 12°C. It differs only trivially from Weitzman's version. See Ackerman and Stanton (2012) for more discussion.

3 Climate change impacts on natural systems

1 The Economics of Ecosystems and Biodiversity [TEEB] (2008), www.teebweb.org.

2 TEEB (2008), p. 35; Bakkes *et al.* (2008). Welfare cost of €50 billion (in 2007 currency) converted to dollars at 1.36 dollars per euro.

3 Globally averaged marine surface monthly mean CO_2 concentration for May 2012, NOAA Earth System Research Laboratory (2012).

4 Relative to 1990 carbon emissions.

5 Diadromous fish spend part of their life cycle in marine waters and part in fresh water; salmon are a well-known example.

4 Climate change impacts on human systems

1 Agricultural value added as a share of GDP for 2008 (World Bank Open Data, http://data.worldbank.org/).

2 http://nordhaus.econ.yale.edu/Accom_Notes_100507.pdf, pp. 23–4.

3 A third photosynthetic pathway exists in some plants subject to extreme water stress, such as cacti and succulents; it is not important in agriculture.

4 This article has been criticized by Tubiello *et al.* (2007); the original authors respond in Ainsworth *et al.* (2008).

5 Degree days are often used to measure seasonal totals of heat or cold, relative to a baseline temperature. Relative to a 30°C baseline, a day with an average temperature of 32°C would represent two degree days. The new threshold models typically add up such calculations for every day in the growing season to create their temperature variables.

6 For reviews of earlier studies in this area, see Cline (2007) and Schlenker *et al.* (2005).

7 Cline's (2007) results are the average of six A2 scenarios, with a mean climate sensitivity of 3.3°C.

8 In this study, profits are defined as the difference between market revenues and costs of production, as reported in the U.S. Census of Agriculture at five-year intervals.

9 The 100th meridian is a north-south line that forms the eastern edge of the Texas Panhandle and roughly bisects the Dakotas. It is traditionally taken as an approximation of the precipitation threshold for rain-fed agriculture: most of the area east of the 100th meridian has at least 20 inches of rain per year and does not rely on irrigation, while most of the area west of the line, excluding the Northwest coast, has less than 20 inches of rain and must rely on irrigation.

10 That is, the study measures growing-season total degree days in two different ways. First, it calculates degree days relative to the 8°C threshold, up to a cap of 32°C. The study adds up such calculations for every day in the growing season to measure beneficial heating. Harmful, excessive heating was calculated by adding up similar calculations relative to a 34°C baseline for every day when temperatures exceeded that baseline.

11 Personal communication, Michael Hanemann, July 2011.

12 See Cline (2007), Table 5.8 and p. 72.

13 World Resources Institute (2000).

14 Gamble *et al.* (2008) and Costello, Abbas *et al.* (2009) come to a very similar set of conclusions for the United States.

15 AR4 (IPCC 2007a, *Working Group II*, Chapter 8) summarizes these findings through 2007. More recent research includes Jackson *et al.* (2010); Knowlton *et al.* (2009); and Ostro *et al.* (2009).

16 The original study is Bosello *et al.* (2006). For a critique, see Ackerman and Stanton (2008). For the original authors' response, see Bosello *et al.* (2008).

17 Kinney (2008) and Bell *et al.* (2008) both review the literature on ancillary benefits from greenhouse gas mitigation through 2007.

5 Climate economics before and after the Stern Review

1 Knight's terminology, although well-known in economics (see Runde 1998 for a contemporary discussion), is not universally accepted or applied. The field of risk assessment sometimes uses the terms "known uncertainty" and "unknown uncertainty," which roughly correspond to Knight's "risk" and "uncertainty" (Daneshkhah 2004). Informal usage, including portions of the text of this report, often treats "risk" and "uncertainty" as synonyms. For instance, the common expression "catastrophic risk" does not always imply knowledge of probabilities.

2 Personal communication regarding PAGE09, Chris Hope, November 2010.

3 For additional views from the early stages of the discussion, see Portney and Weyant (1999), a widely cited collection of essays.

6 Uncertainty

1 In a "fat-tailed" probability distribution, the probability of extreme outcomes approaches zero more slowly than does an exponential function; examples include the Student's t-distribution, Pareto, and other power law distributions. A "thin-tailed" distribution approaches zero more rapidly than does an exponential function; the normal distribution is thin-tailed.

2 This feature is often attributed to the "constant relative risk aversion" (CRRA) utility function, but the same problem would arise with any function that assigns an infinite disutility to the extinction of the human race. CRRA utility is proportional to a negative

power of per capita consumption or to the logarithm of per capita consumption, either of which tends toward negative infinity as per capita consumption goes to zero.

3 DICE does not model adaptation, so adaptation policy options are not discussed. Climate damages that cause catastrophic drops in consumption, however, are likely to be too severe to handle with adaptation.

4 Note that these high values for climate sensitivity are upper limits on the probability distribution, not averages.

7 Public goods and public policy

1 Differentiation of equation (7.1) shows that the discount rate is a decreasing function of η whenever $g < \eta \sigma^2$.

2 The common assumption is that the scenarios where mitigation has its greatest value, i.e., cases where temperatures and climate impacts are growing most rapidly, are ones where the economy is weakest, due to climate damages. In that case, the returns on mitigation are negatively correlated with overall market returns, justifying the use of a discount rate below the risk-free rate. The surprising finding by Nordhaus (2008) of a positive correlation between economic growth and temperature, cited in Chapter 6, would contradict this conclusion, suggesting that returns on mitigation are positively correlated with overall market returns. The Nordhaus finding, however, appears to be an outlier, reflecting the fact that his analysis encompasses a wide range of assumed economic uncertainty but only a narrow range of climate uncertainty.

3 For a review of the recent literature of climate economics models, including those models classified under "cost minimization," see Stanton *et al.* (2009). For an expanded discussion of cost-effectiveness modeling in climate economics, see Stanton and Ackerman (2009).

4 The question of interpersonal comparison of utility is addressed below.

5 See also Stanton and Ackerman (2009).

6 For an additional proposal closely resembling contraction and convergence, see Gao (2007).

8 Economics and the climate policy debate

1 See also Allison *et al.* (2009) and Ackerman *et al.* (2010; 2009).

2 RCP Database, version 2.0 (International Institute for Applied Systems Analysis 2009).

3 Climate Analysis Indicator Tool (World Resources Institute 2012), http://cait.wri.org.

4 RCP 3-PD has a 48 percent chance of staying below 2°C and a 92 percent chance of staying below 3°C (Bernie 2010). See International Institute for Applied Systems Analysis (2009) for RCP emissions data.

5 The 2200 scenario of Ackerman *et al.* (2009), which has both an early peak and a rapid decline thereafter, was designed to stabilize at 350 ppm CO_2 by 2200 without requiring negative net emissions.

6 For a detailed assessment of emissions pathways likely to avoid dangerous climate change, see Anderson and Bows (2011). Their analysis considers the role of non-CO_2 gases and disaggregates emissions into those of Annex I and non-Annex I countries.

7 Kartha and Erickson (2011) review four pledge analyses, including UNEP (2010) and two that contain pledges made since the Cancún Agreements, and find that developing countries have, collectively, pledged more emissions reductions than did Annex I nations – but the global totals fall well short of any 2°C pathway.

9 Technologies for mitigation

1 For additional discussion of uncertainty regarding geoengineering methods, see Blackstock and Long (2010), Blackstock *et al.* (2009), and Vaughan and Lenton (2011).

2 Additionality in greenhouse gas mitigation refers to the net impact of any measure, beyond policies and practices that are already in place. A new mitigation initiative could lack additionality if it crowds out existing actions, or merely formalizes actions that are already taking place, without increasing total abatement. For a discussion of additionality in relation to the Kyoto Protocol's Clean Development Mechanism, see Schneider (2009).
3 For a detailed discussion of CCS technologies, see the September 25, 2009, special issue of *Science* magazine, titled "Carbon Capture and Sequestration."
4 See also Florin and Fennell (2010).
5 IPCC (2007e), *Working Group I*, Chapter 7.3.
6 See also Harvey (2008).
7 See also United Nations Environment Programme and World Meteorological Organization (2011).
8 Note that these projections were made and published before Japan's 2011 nuclear disaster. Newer projections may well downgrade the importance of nuclear power's contribution to total future energy production.

10 Economics of mitigation

1 See also Sorrell (2007).

11 Adaptation

1 See Agrawala *et al.* (2008), Table 2.6 for a summary. The studies reviewed are The World Bank (2006); Stern (2006); Oxfam International (2007); United Nations Development Programme (2007); and United Nations Framework Convention on Climate Change (2007).

References

Aase, K.K. (2011). *The Long Term Equilibrium Interest Rate and Risk Premiums Under Uncertainty*. NHH Department of Finance & Management Science Discussion Paper No. 2011/4. Norwegian School of Economics and Business Administration (NHH). Available at http://papers.ssrn.com/sol3/papers.cfm?abstract_id=1774704.

Acemoglu, D., Aghion, P., Bursztyn, L. and Hemous, D. (2012). "The environment and directed technical change." *American Economic Review* 102(1), 131–66. DOI: 10.1257/aer.102.1.131.

Ackerman, F. (2008). *Poisoned for Pennies: The Economics of Toxics and Precaution*. Washington, DC: Island Press.

Ackerman, F. (2009). *Can We Afford the Future? The Economics of a Warming World*. London: Zed Books.

Ackerman, F. and Bueno, R. (2011). *Use of McKinsey Abatement Cost Curves for Climate Economics modeling*. SEI Working Paper WP-US-1102. Somerville, MA: Stockholm Environment Institute-U.S. Center. Available at http://sei-us.org/publications/id/362.

Ackerman, F. and Finlayson, I. (2006). "The economics of inaction on climate change: A sensitivity analysis." *Climate Policy* 6(5), 509–26.

Ackerman, F. and Munitz, C. (2012). "Climate damages in the FUND model: A disaggregated analysis." *Ecological Economics* 77, 219–24. DOI: 10.1016/j.ecolecon.2012.03.005.

Ackerman, F. and Stanton, E.A. (2008). "A comment on 'Economy-wide estimates of the implications of climate change: Human health'." *Ecological Economics* 66(1), 8–13. DOI: 10.1016/j.ecolecon.2007.10.006.

Ackerman, F. and Stanton, E.A. (2011). *The Last Drop: Climate Change and the Southwest Water Crisis*. Somerville, MA: Stockholm Environment Institute-U.S. Center. Available at http://sei-us.org/publications/id/371.

Ackerman, F. and Stanton, E.A. (2012). "Climate risks and carbon prices: Revising the social cost of carbon." *Economics: The Open-Access, Open Assessment E-Journal* 6(2012–10). DOI: 10.5018/economics-ejournal.ja.2012–10.

Ackerman, F., DeCanio, S., Howarth, R. and Sheeran, K. (2009). "Limitations of integrated assessment models of climate change." *Climatic Change* 95(3–4), 1–19.

Ackerman, F., Stanton, E.A. and Bueno, R. (2010). "Fat tails, exponents, extreme uncertainty: Simulating catastrophe in DICE." *Ecological Economics* 69(8), 1657–65. DOI: 10.1016/j.ecolecon.2010.03.013.

Ackerman, F., Stanton, E.A. and Bueno, R. (2011). "CRED: A new model of climate and development." *Ecological Economics* (forthcoming). DOI: 16/j.ecolecon.2011.04.006.

Ackerman, F., Stanton, E.A. and Bueno, R. (2012). *Epstein-Zin Utility in DICE: Is Risk Aversion Irrelevant to Climate Policy?* E3 Network. Available at www.e3network.org/papers/EZ_utility_in_DICE.pdf.

Ackerman, F., Stanton, E.A., DeCanio, S.J. *et al.* (2009). *The Economics of 350: The Benefits and Costs of Climate Stabilization.* Portland, OR: Economics for Equity and the Environment Network. Available at http://sei-us.org/publications/id/31.

Ackerman, F., Stanton, E.A., DeCanio, S.J. *et al.* (2010). "The economics of 350." *Solutions* 1(5).

Ackerman, F., Stanton, E.A., Hope, C. and Alberth, S. (2009). "Did the Stern Review underestimate U.S. and global climate damages?" *Energy Policy* 37(7), 2717–21. DOI: 10.1016/j.enpol.2009.03.011.

Adams, H.D., Guardiola-Claramonte, M., Barron-Gafford, G.A. *et al.* (2009). "Temperature sensitivity of drought-induced tree mortality portends increased regional die-off under global change-type drought." *Proceedings of the National Academy of Sciences of the United States of America* 106(17), 7063–6. DOI: 10.1073/pnas.0901438106.

Agarwal, A. and Narain, S. (1991). *Global Warming in an Unequal World: A Case of Environmental Colonialism.* New Delhi: Centre for Science and the Environment.

Agrawala, S., Bosello, F., Carraro, C., de Bruin, K., De Cian, E., Dellink, R. and Lanzi, E. (2010). *Plan or React? Analysis of Adaptation Costs and Benefits Using Integrated Assessment Models.* OECD Environment Working Papers No. 23. Paris: OECD Publishing. Available at www.oecd-ilibrary.org/environment/plan-or-react_5km975m3d5hb-en.

Agrawala, S., Crick, F., Jetté-Nantel, S. and Tepes, A. (2008). "Empirical estimates of adaptation costs and benefits: A critical assessment." In S. Agrawala and S. Fankhauser, eds. *Economic Aspects of Adaptation to Climate Change: Costs, Benefits and Policy Instruments.* Paris: OECD Publishing, pp. 29–84. Available at www.oecd-ilibrary.org/environment/economic-aspects-of-adaptation-to-climate-change/empirical-estimates-of-adaptation-costs-and-benefits-a-critical-assessment_9789264046214-4-en.

Agrawala, S. and Fankhauser, S., eds. (2008). *Economic Aspects of Adaptation to Climate Change: Costs, Benefits and Policy Instruments.* Paris: OECD Publishing. Available at www.oecd-ilibrary.org/environment/economic-aspects-of-adaptation-to-climate-change_9789264046214-en.

Ainsworth, E.A., Leakey, A.D.B., Ort, D.R. and Long, S.P. (2008). "FACE-ing the facts: Inconsistencies and interdependence among field, chamber and modeling studies of elevated CO_2 impacts on crop yield and food supply." *New Phytologist* 179(1), 5–9. DOI: 10.1111/j.1469–8137.2008.02500.x.

Ainsworth, E.A. and McGrath, J.M. (2010). "Direct effects of rising atmospheric carbon dioxide and ozone on crop yields." *Climate Change and Food Security.* Advances in Global Change Research 37(Part II), 109–30. DOI: 10.1007/978–90–481–2953–9_7.

Akbari, H., Levinson, R., Rosenfeld, A.H. and Elliot, M. (2009). "Global cooling: Policies to cool the world and offset global warming from CO_2 using reflective roofs and pavements." Presented at the Second International Conference on Countermeasures to Urban Heat Islands, September 21–23, 2009, Berkeley, CA. Available at http://escholarship.org/uc/item/9hb8n851.

Alberth, S. (2008). "Forecasting technology costs via the experience curve – Myth or magic?" *Technological Forecasting and Social Change* 75(7), 952–83. DOI: 10.1016/j.techfore.2007.09.003.

Alberth, S. and Hope, C. (2007). "Climate modelling with endogenous technical change: Stochastic learning and optimal greenhouse gas abatement in the PAGE2002 model." *Energy Policy* 35(3), 1795–1807. DOI: 10.1016/j.enpol.2006.05.015.

Alexandrov, G.A., Oikawa, T. and Yamagata, Y. (2002). "The scheme for globalization of a process-based model explaining gradations in terrestrial NPP and its application." *Ecological Modelling* 148(3), 293–306. DOI: 10.1016/S0304–3800(01)00456–2.

Allcott, H. and Greenstone, M. (2012). "Is there an energy efficiency gap?" *Journal of Economic Perspectives* 26(1), 3–28. DOI: 10.1257/jep. 26.1.3.

Alliance of Small Island States (2009). *Declaration on Climate Change 2009.* Available at www.sidsnet.org/aosis/documents/AOSIS%20Summit%20Declaration%20Sept%20 21%20FINAL.pdf.

Allison, I., Alley, R.B., Fricker, H.A., Thomas, R.H. and Warner, R.C. (2009). "Ice sheet mass balance and sea level." *Antarctic Science* 21(05), 413. DOI: 10.1017/ S0954102009990137.

Allison, I., Bindoff, N., Bindschadler, R. *et al.* (2009). *The Copenhagen Diagnosis, 2009: Updating the World on the Latest Climate Science.* Sydney, Australia: The University of New South Wales Climate Change Research Centre (CCRC). Available at www. copenhagendiagnosis.org.

Amonette, J., Lehmann, J. and Joseph, S. (2007). "Terrestrial carbon sequestration with biochar: A preliminary assessment of its global potential." Presented at the American Geophysical Union, December 10–14, 2007, San Francisco, CA. Available at http:// adsabs.harvard.edu/abs/2007AGUFM.U42A..06A.

Anda, J., Golub, A. and Strukova, E. (2009). "Economics of climate change under uncertainty: Benefits of flexibility." *Energy Policy* 37(4), 1345–55. DOI: 10.1016/j. enpol.2008.11.034.

Anderson, G.B. and Bell, M.L. (2010). "Heat waves in the United States: Mortality risk during heat waves and effect modification by heat wave characteristics in 43 U.S. communities." *Environmental Health Perspectives* 119(2), 210–18. DOI: 10.1289/ehp. 1002313.

Anderson, K. and Bows, A. (2011). "Beyond 'dangerous' climate change: Emission scenarios for a new world." *Philosophical Transactions of the Royal Society A: Mathematical, Physical and Engineering Sciences* 369(1934), 20–44. DOI: 10.1098/ rsta.2010.0290.

Anenberg, S.C., Schwartz, J., Shindell, D. *et al.* (2012). "Global air quality and health co-benefits of mitigating near-term climate change through methane and black carbon emission controls." *Environmental Health Perspectives* 120(6), 831–9. DOI: 10.1289/ ehp. 1104301.

Anthoff, D. and Tol, R.S.J. (2010a). *Climate Policy under Fat-Tailed Risk: An Application of FUND.* ESRI Working Paper No. 348. Dublin, Ireland: Economic and Social Research Institute. Available at www.esri.ie/UserFiles/publications/WP348/WP348. pdf.

Anthoff, D. and Tol, R.S.J. (2010b). "On international equity weights and national decision making on climate change." *Journal of Environmental Economics and Management* 60(1), 14–20. DOI: 10.1016/j.jeem.2010.04.002.

Anthoff, D., Hepburn, C. and Tol, R.S.J. (2009). "Equity weighting and the marginal damage costs of climate change." *Ecological Economics* 68(3), 836–49. DOI: 10.1016/j.ecolecon.2008.06.017.

Anthoff, D., Tol, R.S.J. and Yohe, G.W. (2009). "Discounting for climate change." *Economics: The Open-Access, Open-Assessment E-Journal* 3(2009–24), Special Issue: Discounting the Long–Run Future and Sustainable Development. DOI: 10.5018/ economics-ejournal.ja.2009–24.

Archer, D., Buffett, B. and Brovkin, V. (2009). "Ocean methane hydrates as a slow tipping point in the global carbon cycle." *Proceedings of the National Academy of Sciences* 106(49), 20596–20601. DOI: 10.1073/pnas.0800885105.

Arent, D.J., Wise, A. and Gelman, R. (2011). "The status and prospects of renewable energy for combating global warming." *Energy Economics* 33(4), 584–93. DOI: 10.1016/j.eneco.2010.11.003.

Armour, K.C., Eisenman, I., Blanchard-Wrigglesworth, E., McCusker, K.E. and Bitz, C.M. (2011). "The reversibility of sea ice loss in a state-of-the-art climate model." *Geophysical Research Letters* 38(16), L16705. DOI: 10.1029/2011GL048739.

Arora, V.K. and Montenegro, A. (2011). "Small temperature benefits provided by realistic afforestation efforts." *Nature Geoscience* 4(8), 514–18. DOI: 10.1038/ngeo1182.

Arora, V.K., Scinocca, J.F., Boer, G.J., *et al.* (2011). "Carbon emission limits required to satisfy future representative concentration pathways of greenhouse gases." *Geophysical Research Letters* 38(5), L05805. DOI: 10.1029/2010GL046270.

Arrow, K., Parikh, J., Pillet, G., *et al.* (1996). "Chapter 2: Decision-making frameworks for addressing climate change." In J.P. Bruce, H. Lee and E.F. Haites, eds. *Climate Change 1995: Economic and Social Dimensions of Climate Change – Contribution of Working Group III to the Second Assessment Report of the IPCC.* New York: IPCC and Cambridge University Press.

Arrow, K.J. (2007). "Global climate change: A challenge to policy." *The Economists' Voice* 4(3), Article 2. DOI: 10.2202/1553–3832.1270.

Atkinson, G., Dietz, S., Helgeson, J., Hepburn, C. and Sælen, H. (2009). "Siblings, not triplets: Social preferences for risk, inequality and time in discounting climate change." *Economics E-Journal* 3(2009–26). DOI: 10.5018/economics-ejournal.ja.2009–26.

Auffhammer, M., Ramanathan, V. and Vincent, J.R. (2011). "Climate change, the monsoon, and rice yield in India." *Climatic Change* 111(2), 411–24. DOI: 10.1007/s10584–011–0208–4.

Babonneau, F., Haurie, A., Loulou, R. and Vielle, M. (2011). "Combining stochastic optimization and Monte Carlo simulation to deal with uncertainties in climate policy assessment." *Environmental Modeling & Assessment* 17(1–2), 51–76. DOI: 10.1007/s10666–011–9275–1.

Baer, P., Athanasiou, T. and Kartha, S. (2007). "The right to development in a climate constrained world: The Greenhouse Development Rights Framework." Available at www.boell.de/ecology/climate/climate-energy-966.html.

Bahn, O., Edwards, N.R., Knutti, R. and Stocker, T.F. (2011). "Energy policies avoiding a tipping point in the climate system." *Energy Policy* 39(1), 334–48. DOI: 10.1016/j.enpol.2010.10.002.

Bahr, D.B., Dyurgerov, M. and Meier, M.F. (2009). "Sea-level rise from glaciers and ice caps: A lower bound." *Geophysical Research Letters* 36(3). DOI: 10.1029/2008GL036309.

Bala, G., Caldeira, K., Wickett, M., Phillips, T.J., Lobell, D.B., Delire, C. and Mirin, A. (2007). "Combined climate and carbon-cycle effects of large-scale deforestation." *Proceedings of the National Academy of Sciences* 104(16), 6550–55. DOI: 10.1073/pnas.0608998104.

Bala, G., Duffy, P.B. and Taylor, K.E. (2008). "Impact of geoengineering schemes on the global hydrological cycle." *Proceedings of the National Academy of Sciences of the United States of America* 105(22), 7664–9. DOI: 10.1073/pnas.0711648105.

Balachandran, S. and Rajeevan, M. (2007). "Sensitivity of surface radiation budget to clouds over the Asian monsoon region." *Journal of Earth System Science* 116(2), 159–69. DOI: 10.1007/s12040–007–0016–4.

Balshi, M.S., Mcguire, A.D., Duffy, P., Flannigan, M., Kicklighter, D.W. and Melillo, J. (2009). "Vulnerability of carbon storage in North American boreal forests to wildfires during the 21st century." *Global Change Biology* 15(6), 1491–1510. DOI: 10.1111/j.1365–2486.2009.01877.x.

Bamber, J.L., Riva, R.E.M., Vermeersen, B.L.A. and LeBrocq, A.M. (2009). "Reassessment of the potential sea-level rise from a collapse of the west Antarctic ice sheet." *Science* 324(5929), 901–3. DOI: 10.1126/science.1169335.

Bansal, R. and Ochoa, M. (2010). *Temperature, Aggregate Risk, and Expected Returns.* Durham, NC: Duke University. Available at www.business.smu.edu.sg/disciplines/finance/Research%20Seminars/papers/RaviBansal_27May10.pdf.

Ban-Weiss, G.A., Cao, L., Bala, G. and Caldeira, K. (2011). "Dependence of climate forcing and response on the altitude of black carbon aerosols." *Climate Dynamics* 38(5–6), 897–911. DOI: 10.1007/s00382–011–1052-y.

Barker, T. and Scrieciu, S. (2010). "Modeling low climate stabilization with E3MG: Towards a 'New Economics' approach to simulating energy-environment-economy system dynamics." *Energy Journal* 31(Special Issue 1), 137–64.

Barker, T., Dagoumas, A. and Rubin, J. (2009). "The macroeconomic rebound effect and the world economy." *Energy Efficiency* 2(4), 411–27. DOI: 10.1007/s12053–009–9053-y.

Barker, T., Scrieciu, S.S. and Foxon, T. (2008). "Achieving the G8 50 target: Modelling induced and accelerated technological change using the macro-econometric model E3MG." *Climate Policy* 8, S30–S45. DOI: 10.3763/cpol.2007.0490.

Barnett, J. and Dessai, S. (2002). "Articles 4.8 and 4.9 of the UNFCCC: Adverse effects and the impacts of response measures." *Climate Policy* 2(2–3), 231–9. DOI: 16/S1469–3062(02)00023–2.

Barrett, S. (2003). *Environment and Statecraft: The Strategy of Environmental Treaty-Making.* Oxford: Oxford University Press.

Barro, R.J. (2006). "Rare disasters and asset markets in the twentieth century." *Quarterly Journal of Economics* 121(3), 823–66. DOI: 10.1162/qjec.121.3.823.

Barseghyan, L., Prince, J. and Teitelbaum, J.C. (2011). "Are Risk preferences stable across contexts? Evidence from insurance data." *American Economic Review* 101(2), 591–631. DOI: 10.1257/aer.101.2.591.

Barsugli, J.J. (2009). "Comment on 'Global warming and United States landfalling hurricanes' by Chunzai Wang and Sang-Ki Lee." *Geophysical Research Letters* 36(1). DOI: 10.1029/2008GL034621.

Battles, J., Robards, T., Das, A. and Stewart, W. (2009). "Projecting climate change impacts on forest growth and yield for California's Sierran mixed conifer forests." California Climate Change Center paper CEC-500-2009-047-D. Available at www.energy.ca.gov/2009publications/CEC-500–2009–047/CEC-500–2009–047-F.PDF.

Baum, S.D. (2009). "Description, prescription and the choice of discount rates." *Ecological Economics* 69(1), 197–205. DOI: 10.1016/j.ecolecon.2009.08.024.

Baumert, K.A., Herzog, T. and Pershing, J. (2005). *Navigating the Numbers: Greenhouse Gas Data and International Climate Policy.* Washington, DC: World Resources Institute. Available at www.wri.org/publication/navigating-the-numbers.

Beach, R.H., DeAngelo, B.J., Rose, S., Li, C., Salas, W. and DelGrosso, S.J. (2008). "Mitigation potential and costs for global agricultural greenhouse gas emissions." *Agricultural Economics* 38(2), 109–15. DOI: 10.1111/j.1574–0862.2008.00286.x.

Bell, M.L., Davis, D.L., Cifuentes, L.A., Krupnick, A.J., Morgenstern, R.D. and Thurston, G.D. (2008). "Ancillary human health benefits of improved air quality resulting from climate change mitigation." *Environmental Health* 7(1), 41. DOI: 10.1186/1476–069X-7–41.

Benford, G. (1999). *Deep Time: How Humanity Communicates Across Millennia.* New York: Bard Books.

Bentz, B. (2008). *Western U.S. Bark Beetles and Climate Change.* Available at www.fs.fed.us/ccrc/topics/bark-beetles.shtml.

Bernie, D. (2010). *Temperature Implications from the IPCC 5th Assessment Representative Concentration Pathways (RCP).* Work Stream 2, Report 11 of the AVOID Programme (AV/WS2/D1/R11). London: Met Office Hadley Centre. Available at www.metoffice.gov.uk/avoid/files/resources-researchers/AVOID_WS_D1_11_20100422.pdf.

Bernstein, A.S. and Myers, S.S. (2011). "Climate change and children's health." *Current Opinion in Pediatrics* 23(2), 221–6. DOI: 10.1097/MOP.0b013e3283444c89.

Biasutti, M. and Sobel, A.H. (2009). "Delayed Sahel rainfall and global seasonal cycle in a warmer climate." *Geophysical Research Letters* 36(23). DOI: 10.1029/2009 GL041303.

Blackstock, J.J. and Long, J.C.S. (2010). "The Politics of Geoengineering." *Science* 327(5965), 527. DOI: 10.1126/science.1183877.

Blackstock, J.J., Battisti, D.S., Caldeira, K. *et al.* (2009). *Climate Engineering Responses to Climate Emergencies.* Santa Barbara, CA: Novim. Available at http://arxiv.org/abs/0907.5140.

Blum, M.D. and Roberts, H.H. (2009). "Drowning of the Mississippi Delta due to insufficient sediment supply and global sea-level rise." *Nature Geoscience* 2(7), 488–91. DOI: 10.1038/ngeo553.

Boé, J., Hall, A. and Qu, X. (2009). "September sea-ice cover in the Arctic Ocean projected to vanish by 2100." *Nature Geoscience* 2(5), 341–3. DOI: 10.1038/ngeo467.

Boisvenue, C. and Running, S.W. (2006). "Impacts of climate change on natural forest productivity – Evidence since the middle of the 20th century." *Global Change Biology* 12(862–82). DOI: 10.1111/j.1365–2486.2006.01134.x.

Bonan, G.B. (2008). "Forests and climate change: Forcings, feedbacks, and the climate benefits of forests." *Science* 320(5882), 1444–9. DOI: 10.1126/science.1155121.

Borenstein, S. (2012). "The private and public economics of renewable electricity generation." *Journal of Economic Perspectives* 26(1), 67–92. DOI: 10.1257/jep. 26.1.67.

Bosello, F. (2010). *Adaptation, Mitigation and "Green" R&D to Combat Global Climate Change: Insights From an Empirical Integrated Assessment Exercise.* Sustainable Development Series, 22.2010. Venice, Italy: Fondazione Eni Enrico Mattei. Available at www.feem.it/userfiles/attach/20103151713534NDL2010–022.pdf.

Bosello, F., Roson, R. and Tol, R.S.J. (2006). "Economy-wide estimates of the implications of climate change: Human health." *Ecological Economics* 58(3), 579–91.

Bosello, F., Roson, R. and Tol, R.S.J. (2008). "Economy-wide estimates of the implications of climate change – a rejoinder." *Ecological Economics* 66(1), 14–15. DOI: 10.1016/j.ecolecon.2007.03.013.

Bosetti, V., Carraro, C., Duval, R. and Tavoni, M. (2011). "What should we expect from innovation? A model-based assessment of the environmental and mitigation cost implications of climate-related R&D." *Energy Economics* 33(6), 1313–20. DOI: 10.1016/j.eneco.2011.02.010.

Bosetti, V., Carraro, C., Sgobbi, A. and Tavoni, M. (2009). "Delayed action and uncertain stabilisation targets: How much will the delay cost?" *Climatic Change* 96(3), 299–312. DOI: 10.1007/s10584–009–9630–2.

Botzen, W.J.W. and van den Bergh, J.C.J.M. (2012). "How sensitive is Nordhaus to Weitzman? Climate policy in DICE with an alternative damage function." *Economics Letters* 117(1), 372–4. DOI: 10.1016/j.econlet.2012.05.032.

Braat, L. and ten Brink, P., eds. (2008). *The Cost of Policy Inaction: The Case of Not Meeting the 2010 Biodiversity Target.* Wageningen and Brussels: Study for the European Commission, DG Environment (ENV.G.1/ETU/2007/0044). Available at http://ec.europa.eu/environment/nature/biodiversity/economics/pdf/copi.zip.

Bréchet, T. and Jouvet, P.-A. (2009). "Why environmental management may yield no-regret pollution abatement options." *Ecological Economics* 68(6), 1770–77. DOI: 10.1016/j.ecolecon.2008.11.007.

Brekke, K.A. and Johansson-Stenman, O. (2008). "The behavioural economics of climate change." *Oxford Review of Economic Policy* 24(2), 280–97. DOI: 10.1093/oxrep/grn012.

Brovkin, V., Petoukhov, V., Claussen, M., Bauer, E., Archer, D. and Jaeger, C. (2008). "Geoengineering climate by stratospheric sulfur injections: Earth system vulnerability to technological failure." *Climatic Change* 92(3–4), 243–59. DOI: 10.1007/s10584–008–9490–1.

Brovkin, V., Raddatz, T., Reick, C.H., Claussen, M. and Gayler, V. (2009). "Global bio-geophysical interactions between forest and climate." *Geophysical Research Letters* 36(L07405). DOI: 10.1029/2009GL037543.

Brown, M.A. (2001). "Market failures and barriers as a basis for clean energy policies." *Energy Policy* 29(14), 1197–1207. DOI: 10.1016/S0301–4215(01)00067–2.

Brozović, N. and Schlenker, W. (2011). "Optimal management of an ecosystem with an unknown threshold." *Ecological Economics* 70(4), 627–40. DOI: 10.1016/j.ecolecon.2010.10.001.

Buchholz, W. and Schymura, M. (2012). "Expected utility theory and the tyranny of catastrophic risks." *Ecological Economics* 77, 234–9. DOI: 10.1016/j.ecolecon.2012.03.007.

Buddemeier, R.W., Lane, D.R. and Martinich, J.A. (2011). "Modeling regional coral reef responses to global warming and changes in ocean chemistry: Caribbean case study." *Climatic Change* 109(3–4), 375–97. DOI: 10.1007/s10584–011–0022-z.

Bushnell, J.B. and Mansur, E.T. (2011). "Vertical targeting and leakage in carbon policy." *American Economic Review* 101(3), 263–7. DOI: 10.1257/aer.101.3.263.

Byatt, I., Castles, I., Goklany, I.M. *et al.* (2006). "The Stern review: A dual critique – Part II: Economic aspects." *World Economics* 7(4), 199–229.

Callaway, J.M. (2004). "Adaptation benefits and costs: Are they important in the global policy picture and how can we estimate them?" *Global Environmental Change Part A* 14(3), 273–82. DOI: 16/j.gloenvcha.2004.04.002.

Carlson, K.M., Curran, L.M., Ratnasari, D. *et al.* (2012). "Committed carbon emissions, deforestation, and community land conversion from oil palm plantation expansion in West Kalimantan, Indonesia." *Proceedings of the National Academy of Sciences* 109(19), 7559–64. DOI: 10.1073/pnas.1200452109.

Carpenter, K.E., Abrar, M., Aeby, G. *et al.* (2008). "One-third of reef-building corals face elevated extinction risk from climate change and local impacts." *Science* 321(5888), 560–63. DOI: 10.1126/science.1159196.

Carraro, C., Bosello, F. and De Cian, E. (2010). *Climate Policy and the Optimal Balance between Mitigation, Adaptation and Unavoided Damage.* Department of Economics, Working Paper No. 09/WP/2010. Venice: Ca' Foscari University of Venice. Available at http://ideas.repec.org/p/ven/wpaper/2010_09.html.

Carter, R.M., de Freitas, C.R., Goklany, I.M., Holland, D. and Lindzen, R.S. (2006). "The Stern review: A dual critique – Part I: The science." *World Economics* 7(4), 165–98.

Cazenave, A., Dominh, K., Guinehut, S. *et al.* (2009). "Sea level budget over 2003–2008: A reevaluation from GRACE space gravimetry, satellite altimetry and Argo." *Global and Planetary Change* 65(1–2), 83–8. DOI: 10.1016/j.gloplacha.2008.10.004.

Chakravarty, S., Chikkatur, A., de Coninck, H., Pacala, S., Socolow, R. and Tavoni, M. (2009). "Sharing global CO_2 emission reductions among one billion high emitters." *Proceedings of the National Academy of Sciences* 106(29), 11884–8. DOI: 10.1073/pnas.0905232106.

Charlson, R.J., Ackerman, A.S., Bender, F.A.-M., Anderson, T.L. and Liu, Z. (2007). "On the climate forcing consequences of the albedo continuum between cloudy and clear air." *Tellus B* 59(4), 715–27. DOI: 10.1111/j.1600–0889.2007.00297.x.

Chaves, L.F. and Koenraadt, C.J.M. (2010). "Climate change and highland malaria: Fresh air for a hot debate." *The Quarterly Review of Biology* 85(1), 27–55. DOI: 10.1086/650284.

Chen, C.-C., McCarl, B. and Chang, C.-C. (2011). "Climate change, sea level rise and rice: Global market implications." *Climatic Change* 110(3–4), 543–60. DOI: 10.1007/s10584–011–0074–0.

Chen, I.-C., Hill, J.K., Ohlemuller, R., Roy, D.B. and Thomas, C.D. (2011). "Rapid range shifts of species associated with high levels of climate warming." *Science* 333(6045), 1024–6. DOI: 10.1126/science.1206432.

Chen, J.L., Wilson, C.R., Blankenship, D. and Tapley, B.D. (2009). "Accelerated Antarctic ice loss from satellite gravity measurements." *Nature Geoscience* 2(12), 859–62. DOI: 10.1038/ngeo694.

Cheung, W.W.L., Lam, V.W.Y., Sarmiento, J.L., Kearney, K., Watson, R. and Pauly, D. (2009). "Projecting global marine biodiversity impacts under climate change scenarios." *Fish and Fisheries* 10(3), 235–51. DOI: 10.1111/j.1467–2979.2008.00315.x.

Cheung, W.W.L., Lam, V.W.Y., Sarmiento, J.L., Kearney, K., Watson, R., Zeller, D. and Pauly, D. (2010). "Large-scale redistribution of maximum fisheries catch potential in the global ocean under climate change." *Global Change Biology* 16(1), 24–35. DOI: 10.1111/j.1365–2486.2009.01995.x.

Chichilnisky, G. (2009). "Avoiding extinction: Equal treatment of the present and the future." *Economics: The Open-Access, Open-Assessment E-Journal* 3(2009–32), Special Issue: Discounting the Long–Run Future and Sustainable Development. DOI: 10.5018/economics-ejournal.ja.2009–32.

Chu, J.T., Xia, J., Xu, C.-Y. and Singh, V.P. (2009). "Statistical downscaling of daily mean temperature, pan evaporation and precipitation for climate change scenarios in Haihe River, China." *Theoretical and Applied Climatology* 99(1–2), 149–61. DOI: 10.1007/s00704–009–0129–6.

Clarke, L., Edmonds, J., Jacoby, H. *et al.* (2007). *Scenarios of Greenhouse Gas Emissions and Atmospheric Concentrations.* Final Report, Synthesis and Assessment Product 2.1, U.S. Climate Change Science Program and Subcommittee on Global Change Research. Washington, DC: U.S. Department of Energy, Office of Biological & Environmental Research. Available at www.climatescience.gov/Library/sap/sap2–1/finalreport/.

Clarke, L., Weyant, J. and Edmonds, J. (2008). "On the sources of technological change: What do the models assume?" *Energy Economics* 30(2), 409–24. DOI: 10.1016/j.eneco.2006.05.023.

Clement, A.C., Burgman, R. and Norris, J.R. (2009). "Observational and model evidence for positive low-level cloud feedback." *Science* 325(5939), 460–64. DOI: 10.1126/science.1171255.

Cline, W.R. (1992). *The Economics of Global Warming*. Washington, DC: Institute of International Affairs.

Cline, W.R. (2007). *Global Warming and Agriculture: Impact Estimates by Country*. Washington, DC: Center for Global Development & Peterson Institute for International Economics. Available at www.cgdev.org/content/publications/detail/14090.

Cline, W.R. (2010). *Carbon Abatement Costs and Climate Change Finance*. Draft, November 11, 2010. Washington, DC: Peterson Institute for International Economics.

Coble, K.H. and Lusk, J.L. (2010). "At the nexus of risk and time preferences: An experimental investigation." *Journal of Risk and Uncertainty* 41(1), 67–79. DOI: 10.1007/s11166–010–9096–7.

Cogley, J.G. (2010). "A more complete version of the World Glacier Inventory." *Annals of Glaciology* 50(53), 32–8. DOI: 10.3189/172756410790595859.

Colbert, A.J. and Soden, B.J. (2012). "Climatological variations in North Atlantic tropical cyclone tracks." *Journal of Climate* 25(2), 657–73. DOI: 10.1175/JCLI-D-11–00034.1.

Connor, J.D., Schwabe, K., King, D. and Knapp, K. (2012). "Irrigated agriculture and climate change: The influence of water supply variability and salinity on adaptation." *Ecological Economics* 77, 149–57. DOI: 10.1016/j.ecolecon.2012.02.021.

Cooke, R.M. (2011). *A Shapley Value Approach to Pricing Climate Risks*. Economics E-journal Discussion Paper 2011–17. Available at www.economics-ejournal.org/economics/discussionpapers/2011–17.

Cooley, S.R. and Doney, S.C. (2009). "Anticipating ocean acidification's economic consequences for commercial fisheries." *Environmental Research Letters* 4(2), 024007. DOI: 10.1088/1748–9326/4/2/024007.

Cooter, R. and Rappoport, P. (1984). "Were the ordinalists wrong about welfare economics?" *Journal of Economic Literature* XXII, 507–30.

Costello, A., Abbas, M., Allen, A. *et al.* (2009). "Managing the health effects of climate change." *The Lancet* 373(9676), 1693–1733. DOI: 10.1016/S0140–6736(09)60935–1.

Costello, C.J., Deschênes, O. and Kolstad, C.D. (2009). *Economic Impacts of Climate Change on California Agriculture*. CEC-500–2009–043-F. Santa Barbara, CA: California Climate Change Center. Available at www.energy.ca.gov/2009publications/CEC-500–2009–043/CEC-500–2009–043/CEC-500–2009–043-F.PDF.

Costello, C.J., Neubert, M.G., Polasky, S.A. and Solow, A.R. (2010). "Bounded uncertainty and climate change economics." *Proceedings of the National Academy of Sciences of the United States of America* 107(18), 8108–10. DOI: 10.1073/pnas.0911488107.

Creyts, J., Derkach, A., Nyquist, S., Ostrowski, K. and Stephenson, J. (2007). *Reducing U.S. Greenhouse Gas Emissions: How Much at What Cost?* U.S. Greenhouse Gas Abatement Mapping Initiative, Executive Report. McKinsey & Company and The Conference Board. Available at www.mckinsey.com/clientservice/ccsi/pdf/US_ghg_final_report.pdf.

Crimmins, S.M., Dobrowski, S.Z., Greenberg, J.A., Abatzoglou, J.T. and Mynsberge, A.R. (2011). "Changes in climatic water balance drive downhill shifts in plant species' optimum elevations." *Science* 331(6015), 324–7. DOI: 10.1126/science.1199040.

Crost, B. and Traeger, C. (2010). "Risk and aversion in the integrated assessment of climate change." CUDARE Working Paper 1104 UC Berkeley. Available at http://escholarship.org/uc/item/1562s275.

Czimczik, C.I. and Masiello, C.A. (2007). "Controls on black carbon storage in soils." *Global Biogeochemical Cycles* 21(GB3005). DOI: 10.1029/2006GB002798.

Dadvand, P., Basagaña, X., Sartini, C. *et al.* (2011). "Climate extremes and the length of gestation." *Environmental Health Perspectives* 119(10), 1449–53. DOI: 10.1289/ehp. 1003241.

Daneshkhah, A.R. (2004). *Uncertainty in Probability Risk Assessment: A Review*. Sheffield, UK: University of Sheffield.

Dasgupta, P. (2007). "Comments on the Stern Review's Economics of Climate Change (revised December 12, 2006)." *National Institute Economic Review* 199(1), 4–7.

Dasgupta, P. (2008). "Discounting climate change." *Journal of Risk and Uncertainty* 37(2–3), 141–69. DOI: 10.1007/s11166–008–9049–6.

Dasgupta, S., Laplante, B., Murray, S. and Wheeler, D. (2009). *Sea-Level Rise and Storm Surges: A Comparative Analysis of Impacts in Developing Countries*. Policy Research Working Paper 4901. The World Bank Development Research Group, Environment and Energy Team. Available at http://econ.worldbank.org/research.

Dasgupta, S., Laplante, B., Murray, S. and Wheeler, D. (2010). "Exposure of developing countries to sea-level rise and storm surges." *Climatic Change* 106(4), 567–79. DOI: 10.1007/s10584–010–9959–6.

Davidson, E.A. and Janssens, I.A. (2006). "Temperature sensitivity of soil carbon decomposition and feedbacks to climate change." *Nature* 440(7081), 165–73. DOI: 10.1038/nature04514.

Davis, L.W. (2012). "Prospects for nuclear power." *Journal of Economic Perspectives* 26(1), 49–66. DOI: 10.1257/jep. 26.1.49.

de Bruin, K., Dellink, R. and Agrawala, S. (2009). *Economic Aspects of Adaptation to Climate Change: Integrated Assessment Modelling of Adaptation Costs and Benefits*. No. 6. OECD Publishing. Available at www.oecd-ilibrary.org/environment/economic-aspects-of-adaptation-to-climate-change_225282538105.

de Bruin, K.C., Dellink, R.B. and Tol, R.S.J. (2007). *AD-DICE: An Implementation of Adaptation in the DICE Model*. Working Paper FNU-126. Hamburg: Research Unit Sustainability and Global Change, Hamburg University. Available at www.fnu.zmaw. de/fileadmin/fnu-files/publication/working-papers/addicewp.pdf.

De'ath, G., Lough, J.M. and Fabricius, K.E. (2009). "Declining coral calcification on the Great Barrier Reef." *Science* 323(5910), 116–19. DOI: 10.1126/science.1165283.

DeCanio, S.J. (1998). "The efficiency paradox: Bureaucratic and organizational barriers to profitable energy-saving investments." *Energy Policy* 26(5), 441–54. DOI: 10.1016/S0301–4215(97)00152–3.

DeCanio, S.J. (2009). "The political economy of global carbon emissions reductions." *Ecological Economics* 68(3), 915–24.

DeCanio, S.J. and Fremstad, A. (2011). "Game theory and climate diplomacy." *Ecological Economics* (forthcoming). DOI: 10.1016/j.ecolecon.2011.04.016.

Dell, M., Jones, B.F. and Olken, B.A. (2008). *Climate Change and Economic Growth: Evidence from the Last Half Century*. NBER Working Paper No. 14132. Cambridge, MA: National Bureau of Economic Research. Available at www.nber.org/papers/w14132.

Dell, M., Jones, B.F. and Olken, B.A. (2009). *Temperature and Income: Reconciling New Cross-Sectional and Panel Estimates*. NBER Working Paper No. 14680. Cambridge, MA: National Bureau of Economic Research. Available at www.nber.org/papers/w14680.

DeLong, J.B. and Magin, K. (2009). "The U.S. Equity Return Premium: Past, Present, and Future." *Journal of Economic Perspectives* 23(1), 193–208. DOI: 10.1257/jep. 23.1.193.

den Elzen, M.G.J., van Vuuren, D.P. and van Vliet, J. (2010). "Postponing emission reductions from 2020 to 2030 increases climate risks and long-term costs: A letter." *Climatic Change* 99(1–2), 313–20. DOI: 10.1007/s10584–010–9798–5.

Deschênes, O. and Greenstone, M. (2007). "The economic impacts of climate change: Evidence from agricultural output and random fluctuations in weather." *The American Economic Review* 97(1), 354–85. DOI: 10.1257/aer.97.1.354.

Deser, C., Tomas, R., Alexander, M. and Lawrence, D. (2010). "The seasonal atmospheric response to projected Arctic sea ice loss in the late twenty-first century." *Journal of Climate* 23(2), 333–51. DOI: 10.1175/2009JCLI3053.1.

Deutsch, C.A., Tewksbury, J.J., Huey, R.B., Sheldon, K.S., Ghalambor, C.K., Haak, D.C. and Martin, P.R. (2008). "Impacts of climate warming on terrestrial ectotherms across latitude." *Proceedings of the National Academy of Sciences* 105(18), 6668–72. DOI: 10.1073/pnas.0709472105.

Dietz, S. (2010). "High impact, low probability? An empirical analysis of risk in the economics of climate change." *Climatic Change* 108(3), 519–41. DOI: 10.1007/s10584–010–9993–4.

Dietz, S. and Asheim, G.B. (2012). "Climate policy under sustainable discounted utilitarianism." *Journal of Environmental Economics and Management* 63(3), 321–35. DOI: 10.1016/j.jeem.2012.01.003.

Dietz, S., Anderson, D., Stern, N., Taylor, C. and Zenghelis, D. (2007). "Right for the right reasons: A final rejoinder on the Stern Review." *World Economics* 8(2), 229–58.

Dietz, S., Hope, C., Stern, N. and Zenghelis, D. (2007). "Reflections on the Stern Review (1): A robust case for strong action to reduce the risks of climate change." *World Economics* 8(1), 121–68.

Diffenbaugh, N.S. (2009). "Influence of modern land cover on the climate of the United States." *Climate Dynamics* 33(7–8), 945–58. DOI: 10.1007/s00382–009–0566-z.

Domingues, C.M., Church, J.A., White, N.J., Gleckler, P.J., Wijffels, S.E., Barker, P.M. and Dunn, J.R. (2008). "Improved estimates of upper-ocean warming and multi-decadal sea-level rise." *Nature* 453(7198), 1090–93. DOI: 10.1038/nature07080.

Donato, D.C., Kauffman, J.B., Murdiyarso, D., Kurnianto, S., Stidham, M. and Kanninen, M. (2011). "Mangroves among the most carbon-rich forests in the tropics." *Nature Geoscience* 4(5), 293–7. DOI: 10.1038/ngeo1123.

Dorrepaal, E., Toet, S., van Logtestijn, R.S.P., Swart, E., van de Weg, M.J., Callaghan, T.V. and Aerts, R. (2009). "Carbon respiration from subsurface peat accelerated by climate warming in the subarctic." *Nature* 460(7255), 616–19. DOI: 10.1038/nature08216.

Druckman, A., Chitnis, M., Sorrell, S. and Jackson, T. (2011). "Missing carbon reductions? Exploring rebound and backfire effects in UK households." *Energy Policy* 39(6), 3572–81. DOI: 10.1016/j.enpol.2011.03.058.

Earles, J.M., Yeh, S. and Skog, K.E. (2012). "Timing of carbon emissions from global forest clearance." *Nature Climate Change* 2. DOI: 10.1038/nclimate1535.

Edenhofer, O., Knopf, B., Barker, T. *et al.* (2010). "The economics of low stabilization: Model comparison of mitigation strategies and costs." *Energy Journal* 31(Special Issue 1), 11–48. DOI: 10.5547/ISSN0195–6574-EJ-Vol. 31-NoSI-2.

Ehrhardt-Martinez, K. and Laitner, J.A. (2010). "Rebound, technology and people: Mitigating the rebound effect with energy-resource management and people-centered initiatives." Presented at the 2010 American Council for an Energy-Efficient Economy Summer Study, The Climate for Efficiency is Now, August 15–20, Pacific Grove, CA. Available at www.aceee.org/proceedings-paper/ss10/panel07/paper18.

Eisenman, I. and Wettlaufer, J.S. (2008). "Nonlinear threshold behavior during the loss of Arctic sea ice." *Proceedings of the National Academy of Sciences* 106(1), 28–32. DOI: 10.1073/pnas.0806887106.

Ek, K. and Söderholm, P. (2010). "Technology learning in the presence of public R&D: The case of European wind power." *Ecological Economics* 69(12), 2356–62. DOI: 10.1016/j.ecolecon.2010.07.002.

Eliseev, A.V., Mokhov, I.I., Arzhanov, M.M., Demchenko, P.F. and Denisov, S.N. (2008). "Interaction of the methane cycle and processes in wetland ecosystems in a climate model of intermediate complexity." *Izvestiya, Atmospheric and Oceanic Physics* 44(2), 139–52. DOI: 10.1134/S0001433808020011.

Elsner, J.B., Kossin, J.P. and Jagger, T.H. (2008). "The increasing intensity of the strong-est tropical cyclones." *Nature* 455(7209), 92–5. DOI: 10.1038/nature07234.

Emanuel, K., Sundararajan, R. and Williams, J. (2008). "Hurricanes and global warming: Results from downscaling IPCC AR4 simulations." *Bulletin of the American Meteoro-logical Society* 89(3), 347–67. DOI: 10.1175/BAMS-89-3-347.

Energy Modeling Forum (2009). "EMF briefing on climate policy scenarios: U.S. domes-tic and international policy architectures." *Energy Economics* 31(Supplement 2), June 4. Available at http://emf.stanford.edu/events/emf_briefing_on_climate_policy_scenar-ios_us_domestic_and_international_policy_architectures.

Epstein, L.G. and Zin, S.E. (1989). "Substitution, risk aversion, and the temporal behav-ior of consumption and asset returns: A theoretical framework." *Econometrica* 57(4), 937–69. DOI: 10.2307/1913778.

Ermert, V., Fink, A.H., Morse, A.P. and Paeth, H. (2011). "The impact of regional climate change on malaria risk due to greenhouse forcing and land-use changes in trop-ical Africa." *Environmental Health Perspectives* 120(1), 77–84. DOI: 10.1289/ehp.1103681.

Evans, D.J. (2005). "The elasticity of marginal utility of consumption: Estimates for 20 OECD countries." *Fiscal Studies* 26(2), 197–224. DOI: 10.1111/j.1475–5890.2005.00010.x.

Fabry, V.J., Seibel, B.A., Feely, R.A. and Orr, J.C. (2008). "Impacts of ocean acidifica-tion on marine fauna and ecosystem processes." *ICES Journal of Marine Science: Journal du Conseil* 65(3), 414–32. DOI: 10.1093/icesjms/fsn048.

Fan, G., Cao, J., Yang, H., Li, L. and Su, M. (2009). *Toward a Low Carbon Economy: China and the World*. Beijing: China Economists 50 Forum and Stockholm Environment Insti-tute. Available at http://gdrights.org/wp-content/uploads/2009/06/ce50midtermreport.pdf.

Fankhauser, S. and Burton, I. (2011). "Spending adaptation money wisely." *Climate Policy* 11, 1037–49. DOI: 10.1080/14693062.2011.582389.

Fankhauser, S. and Schmidt-Traub, G. (2011). "From adaptation to climate-resilient development: The costs of climate-proofing the Millennium Development Goals in Africa." *Climate and Development* 3, 94–113. DOI: 10.1080/17565529.2011.582267.

Farber, D.A. (2011). "Uncertainty." *Georgetown Law Journal* 99(4), 901–59.

Feely, R.A., Doney, S.C. and Cooley, S.R. (2009). "Ocean acidification: Present condi-tions and future changes in a high-CO_2 world." *Oceanography* 22(4), 37–47.

Fine, J., Busch, C. and Gardere, R. (2012). "The upside hedge value of California's global warming policy given uncertain future oil prices." *Energy Policy* 44, 46–51. DOI: 10.1016/j.enpol.2012.01.010.

Fischer, C. and Fox, A.K. (2011). "The role of trade and competitiveness measures in U.S. climate policy." *American Economic Review* 101(3), 258–62. DOI: 10.1257/aer.101.3.258.

Fischer, C. and Newell, R.G. (2007). *Environmental and Technology Policies for Climate Mitigation*. Discussion Paper 04–05, April 2004, revised February 2007. Washington, DC: Resources for the Future. Available at www.rff.org/documents/RFF-DP-04–05-REV.pdf.

Fisher, A.C., Hanemann, W.M., Roberts, M.J. and Schlenker, W. (2010). "The economic impacts of climate change: Evidence from agricultural output and random fluctuations in weather: Comment." Forthcoming in *American Economic Review*. Available at www.wolfram-schlenker.com/agClimateChange.pdf.

Flanner, M.G., Zender, C.S., Randerson, J.T. and Rasch, P.J. (2007). "Present-day climate forcing and response from black carbon in snow." *Journal of Geophysical Research* 112(D11). DOI: 10.1029/2006JD008003.

Florin, N. and Fennell, P. (2010). *Review of Advanced Carbon Capture Technologies*. Work Stream 2, Report 5A of the AVOID Programme (AV/WS2/D1/R05A). London: Grantham Institute at Imperial College. Available at www.metoffice.gov.uk/avoid/files/resources-researchers/AVOID_WS2_D1_05A_20100114.pdf.

Fogarty, J. and McCally, M. (2010). "Health and safety risks of carbon capture and storage." *JAMA: The Journal of the American Medical Association* 303(1), 67–8. DOI: 10.1001/jama.2009.1951.

Fowles, M. (2007). "Black carbon sequestration as an alternative to bioenergy." *Biomass and Bioenergy* 31(6), 426–32. DOI: 10.1016/j.biombioe.2007.01.012.

Frederick, S., Loewenstein, G. and O'Donoghue, T. (2002). "Time discounting and time preference: A critical review." *Journal of Economic Literature* 40(2), 351–401. DOI: 10.1257/002205102320161311.

Frieler, K., Meinshausen, M., Deimling, T.S. von, Andrews, T. and Forster, P. (2011). "Changes in global-mean precipitation in response to warming, greenhouse gas forcing and black carbon." *Geophysical Research Letters* 38(4), L04702. DOI: 10.1029/2010GL045953.

Funke, M. and Paetz, M. (2010). "Environmental policy under model uncertainty: A robust optimal control approach." *Climatic Change* 107(3–4), 225–39. DOI: 10.1007/s10584-010-9943-1.

Gamble, J.L., ed. (2008). *Analyses of the Effects of Global Change on Human Health and Welfare and Human Systems*. Final Report, Synthesis and Assessment Product 4.6. U.S. Climate Change Science Program. Available at www.climatescience.gov/Library/sap/sap4-6/.

Gao, G. (2007). "Carbon emission right allocation under climate change." *Advances in Climate Change Research* 3(Suppl. 0087–05), 87–91.

Gaunt, J.L. and Lehmann, J. (2008). "Energy balance and emissions associated with biochar sequestration and pyrolysis bioenergy production." *Environmental Science & Technology* 42(11), 4152–8. DOI: 10.1021/es071361i.

Gerlagh, R. (2007). "The level and distribution of costs and benefits over generations of an emission stabilization program." *Energy Economics* 29(1), 126–31. DOI: 10.1016/j.eneco.2006.04.004.

Gerlagh, R. (2008). "A climate-change policy induced shift from innovations in carbon-energy production to carbon-energy savings." *Energy Economics* 30, 425–48. DOI: 10.1016/j.eneco.2006.05.024.

Gerst, M.D., Howarth, R.B. and Borsuk, M.E. (2010). "Accounting for the risk of extreme outcomes in an integrated assessment of climate change." *Energy Policy* 38(8), 4540–48. DOI: 10.1016/j.enpol.2010.04.008.

Gerst, M.D., Howarth, R.B. and Borsuk, M.E. (2011). "Representing risk in an integrated assessment model of climate change."

Geweke, J. (2001). "A note on some limitations of CRRA utility." *Economics Letters* 71(3), 341–5. DOI: 10.1016/S0165–1765(01)00391–3.

Ghini, R., Bettiol, W. and Hamada, E. (2011). "Diseases in tropical and plantation crops as affected by climate changes: Current knowledge and perspectives." *Plant Pathology* 60(1), 122–32. DOI: 10.1111/j.1365–3059.2010.02403.x.

Gibbins, J. and Chalmers, H. (2008). "Preparing for global rollout: A 'developed country first' demonstration programme for rapid CCS deployment." *Energy Policy* 36(2), 501–7. DOI: 10.1016/j.enpol.2007.10.021.

Gillett, N.P., Arora, V.K., Zickfeld, K., Marshall, S.J. and Merryfield, W.J. (2011). "Ongoing climate change following a complete cessation of carbon dioxide emissions." *Nature Geoscience* 4(2), 83–7. DOI: 10.1038/ngeo1047.

Gillingham, K., Newell, R.G. and Pizer, W.A. (2008). "Modeling endogenous technological change for climate policy analysis." *Energy Economics* 30(6), 2734–53. DOI: 16/j. eneco.2008.03.001.

Giorgi, F. and Bi, X. (2009). "Time of emergence (TOE) of GHG-forced precipitation change hot-spots." *Geophysical Research Letters* 36(6). DOI: 10.1029/2009GL037593.

Gleadow, R.M., Evans, J.R., McCaffery, S. and Cavagnaro, T.R. (2009). "Growth and nutritive value of cassava (Manihot esculenta Cranz.) are reduced when grown in elevated CO_2." *Plant Biology* 11, 76–82. DOI: 10.1111/j.1438–8677.2009.00238.x.

Gleick, J. (1987). *Chaos: Making a New Science*. London: Cardinal.

Global Commons Institute (2010). *GCI Briefing: "Contraction & Convergence."* Available at www.gci.org.uk/Briefings/ICE.pdf.

Goes, M., Tuana, N. and Keller, K. (2011). "The economics (or lack thereof) of aerosol geoengineering." *Climatic Change* 109(3–4), 719–44. DOI: 10.1007/ s10584–010–9961-z.

Gohar, L.K. and Lowe, J.A. (2009). *Summary of the emissions mitigation scenarios: Part 2*. Work Stream 1, Report 3 of the AVOID Programme (AV/WS1/D1/R03). London: Met Office Hadley Centre. Available at www.metoffice.gov.uk/avoid/files/resources-researchers/AVOID_WS1_D1_03_20090521.pdf.

Goldstein, D.B., Martinez, S. and Roy, R. (2011). "Are there rebound effects from energy efficiency? – An analysis of empirical data, internal consistency, and solutions." *Electricity Policy*, May 4. Available at www.electricitypolicy.com/articles/are-there-rebound-effects-from-energy-efficiency-an-analysis-of-empirical-data-internal-consistency-and-solutions.

Gomez, N., Mitrovica, J.X., Tamisiea, M.E. and Clark, P.U. (2010). "A new projection of sea level change in response to collapse of marine sectors of the Antarctic Ice Sheet." *Geophysical Journal International* 180(2), 623–34. DOI: 10.1111/j.1365–246X. 2009.04419.x.

Good, S.P. and Caylor, K.K. (2011). "Climatological determinants of woody cover in Africa." *Proceedings of the National Academy of Sciences* 108(12), 4902–7. DOI: 10.1073/pnas.1013100108.

Gopalakrishnan, S., Smith, M.D., Slott, J.M. and Murray, A.B. (2011). "The value of disappearing beaches: A hedonic pricing model with endogenous beach width." *Journal of Environmental Economics and Management* 61(3), 297–310. DOI: 10.1016/j. jeem.2010.09.003.

Graus, W., Roglieri, M., Jaworski, P., Alberio, L. and Worrell, E. (2011). "The promise of carbon capture and storage: Evaluating the capture-readiness of new EU fossil fuel power plants." *Climate Policy* 11(1), 789–812. DOI: 10.3763/cpol.2008.0615.

Greaker, M. and Pade, L.-L. (2009). "Optimal carbon dioxide abatement and technological change: Should emission taxes start high in order to spur R&D?" *Climatic Change* 96(3), 335–55. DOI: 10.1007/s10584–009–9643-x.

Greene, D.L. (2012). "Rebound 2007: Analysis of U.S. light-duty vehicle travel statistics." *Energy Policy* 41, 14–28. DOI: 10.1016/j.enpol.2010.03.083.

Gregory, J.M., Jones, C.D., Cadule, P. and Friedlingstein, P. (2009). "Quantifying carbon cycle feedbacks." *Journal of Climate* 22(19), 5232–50. DOI: 10.1175/2009JCLI2949.1.

Grenada (2011). *Views on the Work Programme to Consider Approaches to Address Loss and Damage.* Views and information on elements to be included in the work programme on loss and damage; submission by Grenada on behalf of the Alliance of Small Island States (AOSIS), February 28, 2011. United Nations Framework Convention on Climate Change. Available at http://unfccc.int/files/adaptation/cancun_adaptation_framework/application/pdf/aosis_28_february_2011.pdf.

Grinsted, A., Moore, J.C. and Jevrejeva, S. (2009). "Reconstructing sea level from paleo and projected temperatures 2000 to 2100 AD." *Climate Dynamics* 34(4), 461–72. DOI: 10.1007/s00382–008–0507–2.

Grossmann, I. and Morgan, M.G. (2011). "Tropical cyclones, climate change, and scientific uncertainty: What do we know, what does it mean, and what should be done?" *Climatic Change* 108(3), 543–79. DOI: 10.1007/s10584–011–0020–1.

Gruber, N. (2011). "Warming up, turning sour, losing breath: Ocean biogeochemistry under global change." *Philosophical Transactions of the Royal Society A: Mathematical, Physical and Engineering Sciences* 369(1943), 1980–96. DOI: 10.1098/rsta.2011.0003.

Guillerminet, M.-L. and Tol, R.S.J. (2008). "Decision making under catastrophic risk and learning: The case of the possible collapse of the West Antarctic Ice Sheet." *Climatic Change* 91(1–2), 193–209. DOI: 10.1007/s10584–008–9447–4.

Ha-Duong, M. and Treich, N. (2004). "Risk aversion, intergenerational equity and climate change." *Environmental and Resource Economics* 28(2), 195–207. DOI: 10.1023/B:EARE.0000029915.04325.25.

Haines, A., McMichael, A.J., Smith, K.R. *et al.* (2010). "Public health benefits of strategies to reduce greenhouse-gas emissions: Overview and implications for policy makers." *The Lancet* 374(9707), 2104–14. DOI: 10.1016/S0140–6736(09)61759–1.

Hallegatte, S. (2012). "Economics: The rising costs of hurricanes." *Nature Climate Change* 2(3), 148–9. DOI: 10.1038/nclimate1427.

Hampicke, U. (2011). "Climate change economics and discounted utilitarianism." *Ecological Economics* 72, 45–52. DOI: 10.1016/j.ecolecon.2011.08.028.

Han, W., Meehl, G.A., Rajagopalan, B., *et al.* (2010). "Patterns of Indian Ocean sea-level change in a warming climate." *Nature Geoscience* 3(8), 546–50. DOI: 10.1038/ngeo901.

Hanemann, M., Dale, L., Vicuña, S., Bickett, D. and Dyckman, C. (2006). *The Economic Cost of Climate Change Impact on California Water: A Scenario Analysis.* CEC-500–2006–003. Prepared for the California Energy Commission, Public Interest Energy Research Program. Available at www.energy.ca.gov/2006publications/CEC-500–2006–003/CEC-500–2006–003.PDF.

Hanemann, W.M. (2008). *What is the Economic Cost of Climate Change?* Berkeley, CA: UC Berkeley. Available at http://repositories.cdlib.org/are_ucb/1071/.

Hansen, J., Nazarenko, L., Ruedy, R., *et al.* (2005). "Earth's energy imbalance: Confirmation and implications." *Science* 308(5727), 1431–5. DOI: 10.1126/science.1110252.

Hansen, J., Sato, M., Kharecha, P. *et al.* (2008). "Target atmospheric CO_2: Where should humanity aim?" *The Open Atmospheric Science Journal* 2, 217–31. DOI: 10.2174/1874282300802010217.

Hanson, S., Nicholls, R., Ranger, N., Hallegatte, S., Corfee-Morlot, J., Herweijer, C. and Chateau, J. (2010). "A global ranking of port cities with high exposure to climate extremes." *Climatic Change* 104(1), 89–111. DOI: 10.1007/s10584–010–9977–4.

Hart, A. and Gnanendran, N. (2009). "Cryogenic CO_2 capture in natural gas." *Energy Procedia* 1(1), 697–706. DOI: 10.1016/j.egypro.2009.01.092.

Hart, R. (2008). "The timing of taxes on CO_2 emissions when technological change is endogenous." *Journal of Environmental Economics and Management* 55(2), 194–212. DOI: 10.1016/j.jeem.2007.06.004.

Harvey, L.D.D. (2008). "Mitigating the atmospheric CO_2 increase and ocean acidification by adding limestone powder to upwelling regions." *Journal of Geophysical Research* 113, C04028. DOI: 200810.1029/2007JC004373.

Hashizume, M., Faruque, A.S.G., Terao, T., Yunus, M., Streatfield, K., Yamamoto, T. and Moji, K. (2010). "The Indian Ocean dipole and cholera incidence in Bangladesh: A time-series analysis." *Environmental Health Perspectives* 119(2), 239–44. DOI: 10.1289/ehp. 1002302.

Haszeldine, R.S. (2009). "Carbon capture and storage: How green can black be?" *Science* 325(5948), 1647–52. DOI: 10.1126/science.1172246.

Hatfield, J.L., Boote, K.J., Kimball, B.A. *et al.* (2008). "Chapter 2: Agriculture." In *The Effects of Climate Change on Agriculture, Land Resources, Water Resources, and Biodiversity*. U.S. Climate Change Science Program Synthesis and Assessment Product 4.3. Available at www.climatescience.gov/Library/sap/sap4–3/final-report/default.htm.

Heberger, M., Cooley, H., Herrera, P., Gleick, P.H. and Moore, E. (2009). *The Impacts of Sea-Level Rise on the California Coast*. California Climate Change Center Paper CEC-500–2009–024-F. Pacific Institute. Available at www.pacinst.org/reports/sea_level_rise/report.pdf.

Hegerl, G.C., Crowley, T.J., Hyde, W.T. and Frame, D.J. (2006). "Climate sensitivity constrained by temperature reconstructions over the past seven centuries." *Nature* 440(7087), 1029–32. DOI: 10.1038/nature04679.

Hegg, D.A., Warren, S.G., Grenfell, T.C., Doherty, S.J., Larson, T.V. and Clarke, A.D. (2009). "Source attribution of black carbon in Arctic snow." *Environmental Science & Technology* 43(11), 4016–21. DOI: 10.1021/es803623f.

Heliasz, M., Johansson, T., Lindroth, A. *et al.* (2011). "Quantification of C uptake in sub-arctic birch forest after setback by an extreme insect outbreak." *Geophysical Research Letters* 38(1). DOI: 10.1029/2010GL044733.

Hendriks, I.E., Duarte, C.M. and Álvarez, M. (2010). "Vulnerability of marine biodiversity to ocean acidification: A meta-analysis." *Estuarine, Coastal and Shelf Science* 86(2), 157–64. DOI: 10.1016/j.ecss.2009.11.022.

Henriques, I. and Sadorsky, P. (2008). "Oil prices and the stock prices of alternative energy companies." *Energy Economics* 30(3), 998–1010. DOI: 10.1016/j.eneco.2007.11.001.

Herring, H. and Sorrell, S., eds. (2009). *Energy Efficiency and Sustainable Consumption: The Rebound Effect*. New York: Palgrave Macmillan.

Herzog, H.J. (2011). "Scaling up carbon dioxide capture and storage: From megatons to gigatons." *Energy Economics* 33(4), 597–604. DOI: 10.1016/j.eneco.2010.11.004.

Hill, J., Polasky, S., Nelson, E. *et al.* (2009). "Climate change and health costs of air emissions from biofuels and gasoline." *Proceedings of the National Academy of Sciences of the United States of America* 106(6), 2077–82. DOI: 10.1073/pnas.0812835106.

Hirota, M., Holmgren, M., Van Nes, E.H. and Scheffer, M. (2011). "Global resilience of tropical forest and savanna to critical transitions." *Science* 334(6053), 232–5. DOI: 10.1126/science.1210657.

Hock, R., de Woul, M., Radić, V. and Dyurgerov, M. (2009). "Mountain glaciers and ice caps around Antarctica make a large sea-level rise contribution." *Geophysical Research Letters* 36(7). DOI: 10.1029/2008GL037020.

Hoel, M. and Sterner, T. (2007). "Discounting and relative prices." *Climatic Change* 84(3–4), 265–80. DOI: 10.1007/s10584–007–9255–2.

Hof, A.F., van Vuuren, D.P. and den Elzen, M.G.J. (2010). "A quantitative minimax regret approach to climate change: Does discounting still matter?" *Ecological Economics* 70(1), 43–51. DOI: 10.1016/j.ecolecon.2010.03.023.

Hof, C., Araújo, M.B., Jetz, W. and Rahbek, C. (2011). "Additive threats from pathogens, climate and land-use change for global amphibian diversity." *Nature* 480, 516–19. DOI: 10.1038/nature10650.

Hofmann, M. and Rahmstorf, S. (2009). "Tipping elements in earth systems special feature: On the stability of the Atlantic meridional overturning circulation." *Proceedings of the National Academy of Sciences of the United States of America* 106(49), 20584–9. DOI: 10.1073/pnas.0909146106.

Höhne, N., Taylor, C., Elias, R. *et al.* (2012). "National GHG emissions reduction pledges and 2°C: Comparison of studies." *Climate Policy* 12(3), 356–77. DOI: 10.1080/14693062.2011.637818.

Hope, C. (2006). "The marginal impact of CO_2 from PAGE2002: An integrated assessment model incorporating the IPCC's five reasons for concern." *Integrated Assessment Journal* 6(1), 19–56.

Hope, C. (2008). "Discount rates, equity weights and the social cost of carbon." *Energy Economics* 30(3), 1011–19. DOI: 10.1016/j.eneco.2006.11.006.

Hope, C. (2011). *The Social Cost of CO_2 from the PAGE09 Model.* Available at www.economics-ejournal.org/economics/discussionpapers/2011–39.

Horton, R., Herweijer, C., Rosenzweig, C., Liu, J., Gornitz, V. and Ruane, A.C. (2008). "Sea level rise projections for current generation CGCMs based on the semi-empirical method." *Geophysical Research Letters* 35(2). DOI: 10.1029/2007GL032486.

House, K.Z., Baclig, A.C., Ranjan, M., van Nierop, E.A., Wilcox, J. and Herzog, H.J. (2011). "Economic and energetic analysis of capturing CO_2 from ambient air." *Proceedings of the National Academy of Sciences* 108(51), 20428–33. DOI: 10.1073/pnas.1012253108.

Howarth, R.B. (2003). "Discounting and uncertainty in climate change policy analysis." *Land Economics* 79(3), 369–81. DOI: 10.3368/le.79.3.369.

Howarth, R.B. (2009). "Discounting, uncertainty, and revealed time preference." *Land Economics* 85(1), 24–40. DOI: 10.3368/le.85.1.24.

Howarth, R.B. and Norgaard, R.B. (1992). "Environmental valuation under sustainable development." *The American Economic Review* 82(2), 473–7.

Howitt, R., Medellín-Azuara, J. and MacEwan, D. (2009). *Estimating the Economic Impacts of Agricultural Yield Related Changes for California.* CEC-500–2009–042-F. California Climate Change Center. Available at www.energy.ca.gov/2009publications/CEC-500–2009–042/CEC-500–2009–042-F.PDF.

Huang, C., Barnett, A.G., Wang, X., Vaneckova, P., FitzGerald, G. and Tong, S. (2011). "Projecting future heat-related mortality under climate change scenarios: A systematic review." *Environmental Health Perspectives* 119(12), 1681–90. DOI: 10.1289/ehp.1103456.

Ingham, A., Ma, J. and Ulph, A. (2007). "Climate change, mitigation and adaptation with uncertainty and learning." *Energy Policy* 35(11), 5354–69. DOI: 10.1016/j. enpol.2006.01.031.

Interagency Working Group (2010). *Social Cost of Carbon for Regulatory Impact Analysis Under Executive Order 12866.* Washington, DC. Available at www.whitehouse. gov/sites/default/files/omb/inforeg/for-agencies/Social-Cost-of-Carbon-for-RIA.pdf.

International Energy Agency (2008). *Energy Technology Perspectives 2008: Scenarios & Strategies to 2050.* Paris. Available at www.iea.org/textbase/nppdf/free/2008/etp2008.pdf.

International Energy Agency (2010a). *World Energy Outlook 2010.* Paris: International Energy Agency. Available at www.worldenergyoutlook.org/2010.asp.

International Energy Agency (2010b). *Energy Technology Perspectives 2010: Scenarios & Strategies to 2050.* Paris. Available at www.iea.org/techno/etp/index.asp.

International Energy Agency (2011). "Prospect of limiting the global increase in temperature to 2°C is getting bleaker." May 30. www.iea.org/index_info.asp?id=1959.

International Institute for Applied Systems Analysis (2009). "RCP Database (version 2.0)." www.iiasa.ac.at/web-apps/tnt/RcpDb/dsd?Action=htmlpage&page=about.

International Maritime Organization (2010). *Assessment Framework for Scientific Research Involving Ocean Fertilization Agreed.* Briefing 50/2010. London. Available at www.imo.org/mediacentre/pressbriefings/pages/assessment-framework-for-scientific-research-involving-ocean-fertilization-agreed.aspx.

IPCC (2001). *Climate Change 2001 – Intergovernmental Panel on Climate Change Third Assessment Report.* Cambridge, UK: Cambridge University Press. Available at www. grida.no/publications/other/ipcc_tar/.

IPCC (2007a). *Climate Change 2007: Impacts, Adaptation and Vulnerability. Contribution of Working Group II to the Fourth Assessment Report of the Intergovernmental Panel on Climate Change.* M.L. Parry, O.F. Canziani, J.P. Palutikof, P.J. van der Linden and C.E. Hanson, eds. Cambridge, UK: Cambridge University Press. Available at www.ipcc.ch/publications_and_data/ar4/wg2/en/contents.html.

IPCC (2007b). *Climate Change 2007 – Intergovernmental Panel on Climate Change Fourth Assessment Report.* Cambridge, UK: Cambridge University Press.

IPCC (2007c). *Climate Change 2007 – Intergovernmental Panel on Climate Change Fourth Assessment Report: Synthesis Report.* Geneva. Available at www.ipcc.ch/publications_and_data/ar4/syr/en/contents.html.

IPCC (2007d). *Climate Change 2007: Mitigation of Climate Change. Contribution of Working Group III to the Fourth Assessment Report of the Intergovernmental Panel on Climate Change.* Cambridge, UK: Cambridge University Press.

IPCC (2007e). *Climate Change 2007: The Physical Science Basis. Contribution of Working Group I to the Fourth Assessment Report of the Intergovernmental Panel on Climate Change.* S. Solomon, D. Qin, M. Manning, *et al.*, eds. Cambridge, UK: Cambridge University Press. Available at www.ipcc.ch/publications_and_data/ar4/wg1/en/contents.html.

Jackson, J.E., Yost, M.G., Karr, C. *et al.* (2010). "Public health impacts of climate change in Washington State: Projected mortality risks due to heat events and air pollution." *Climatic Change* 102(1–2), 159–86. DOI: 10.1007/s10584–010–9852–3.

Jacob, D.J. and Winner, D.A. (2009). "Effect of climate change on air quality." *Atmospheric Environment* 43(1), 51–63. DOI: 10.1016/j.atmosenv.2008.09.051.

Jacobson, M.Z. and Ten Hoeve, J.E. (2012). "Effects of urban surfaces and white roofs on global and regional climate." *Journal of Climate* 25(3), 1028–44. DOI: 10.1175/JCLI-D-11–00032.1.

Jenkins, A. and Holland, D. (2007). "Melting of floating ice and sea level rise." *Geophysical Research Letters* 34(16). DOI: 10.1029/2007GL030784.

Jenkins, G., Murphy, J., Sexton, D., Lowe, J., Jones, P. and Kilsby, C. (2010). *U.K. Climate Projections: Briefing report*. Version 2, December 2010. UK Department for Environment, Food and Rural Affairs. Available at http://ukclimateprojections.defra. gov.uk/images/stories/briefing_pdfs/UKCP09_Briefing_summary_intro.pdf.

Jenkins, J., Nordhaus, T. and Shellenberger, M. (2011). *Energy Emergence: Rebound and Backfire as Emergent Phenomena*. Oakland, CA: The Breakthrough Institute. Available at http://thebreakthrough.org/blog/Energy_Emergence.pdf.

Jensen, S. and Traeger, C. (2011). *Growth and Uncertainty in the Integrated Assessment of Climate Change*. Preliminary version. Ragnar Frisch Centre for Economic Research (Oslo) and University of California-Berkeley. Available at www.webmeets.com/files/ papers/AERE/2011/141/NCCS.pdf.

Jevons, W.S. (1865). *The Coal Question: An Inquiry Concerning the Progress of the Nation, and the Probable Exhaustion of our Coal-Mines*. London and Cambridge, UK: Macmillan and Co.

Jevrejeva, S., Moore, J.C. and Grinsted, A. (2010). "How will sea level respond to changes in natural and anthropogenic forcings by 2100?" *Geophysical Research Letters* 37(7), L07703. DOI: 10.1029/2010GL042947.

John, V.O., Allan, R.P. and Soden, B.J. (2009). "How robust are observed and simulated precipitation responses to tropical ocean warming?" *Geophysical Research Letters* 36(14). DOI: 10.1029/2009GL038276.

Jones, C., Lowe, J., Liddicoat, S. and Betts, R. (2009). "Committed terrestrial ecosystem changes due to climate change." *Nature Geoscience* 2(7), 484–7. DOI: 10.1038/ ngeo555.

Joshi, M., Hawkins, E., Sutton, R., Lowe, J. and Frame, D. (2011). "Projections of when temperature change will exceed 2°C above pre-industrial levels." *Nature Climate Change* 1(8), 407–12. DOI: 10.1038/nclimate1261.

Joskow, P.L. (2012). "Creating a smarter U.S. electricity grid." *Journal of Economic Perspectives* 26(1), 29–48. DOI: 10.1257/jep. 26.1.29.

Kanniche, M., Gros-Bonnivard, R., Jaud, P., Valle-Marcos, J., Amann, J.-M. and Bouallou, C. (2010). "Pre-combustion, post-combustion and oxy-combustion in thermal power plant for CO_2 capture." *Applied Thermal Engineering* 30(1), 53–62. DOI: 10.1016/j.applthermaleng.2009.05.005.

Karp, L. and Rezai, A. (2010). *An Overlapping Generations Model of a Renewable Resource with Imperfect Property Rights*. Available at http://are.berkeley.edu/~karp/ OLGOCT2010.pdf.

Karp, L. and Tsur, Y. (2011). "Time perspective and climate change policy." *Journal of Environmental Economics and Management*. DOI: 10.1016/j.jeem.2011.03.004.

Kartha, S. and Erickson, P. (2011). *Comparison of Annex 1 and Non-Annex 1 Pledges under the Cancun Agreements*. SEI Working Paper WP-US-1107. Somerville, MA: Stockholm Environment Institute-U.S. Center. Available at http://sei-us.org/publications/id/393.

Kaser, G., Großhauser, M. and Marzeion, B. (2010). "Contribution potential of glaciers to water availability in different climate regimes." *Proceedings of the National Academy of Sciences of the United States of America* 107(47), 20223–7. DOI: 10.1073/ pnas.1008162107.

Kaufman, N. (2012). "The bias of integrated assessment models that ignore climate catastrophes." *Climatic Change* 110(3), 575–95. DOI: 10.1007/s10584–011–0140–7.

Kaufmann, R.K. (2011). "The role of market fundamentals and speculation in recent price changes for crude oil." *Energy Policy* 39(1), 105–15. DOI: 10.1016/j. enpol.2010.09.018.

Kearney, M., Porter, W.P., Williams, C., Ritchie, S. and Hoffmann, A.A. (2009). "Integrating biophysical models and evolutionary theory to predict climatic impacts on species' ranges: The dengue mosquito Aedes aegypti in Australia." *Functional Ecology* 23(3), 528–38. DOI: 10.1111/j.1365-2435.2008.01538.x.

Keith, D.W. (2009). "Why capture CO_2 from the atmosphere?" *Science* 325(5948), 1654–5. DOI: 10.1126/science.1175680.

Keith, D.W., Ha-Duong, M. and Stolaroff, J.K. (2005). "Climate strategy with CO_2 capture from the air." *Climatic Change* 74(1–3), 17–45. DOI: 10.1007/ s10584–005–9026-x.

Keller, K., Bolker, B.M. and Bradford, D.F. (2004). "Uncertain climate thresholds and optimal economic growth." *Journal of Environmental Economics and Management* 48, 723–41.

Kellie-Smith, O. and Cox, P.M. (2011). "Emergent dynamics of the climate-economy system in the Anthropocene." *Philosophical Transactions of the Royal Society A: Mathematical, Physical and Engineering Sciences* 369(1938), 868–86. DOI: 10.1098/ rsta.2010.0305.

Kemfert, C. and Truong, T. (2007). "Impact assessment of emissions stabilization scenarios with and without induced technological change." *Energy Policy* 35(11), 5337–45. DOI: 10.1016/j.enpol.2006.01.033.

Kemp, A.C., Horton, B.P., Donnelly, J.P., Mann, M.E., Vermeer, M. and Rahmstorf, S. (2011). "Climate related sea-level variations over the past two millennia." *Proceedings of the National Academy of Sciences of the United States of America* published online before print. DOI: 10.1073/pnas.1015619108.

Khan, A.E., Ireson, A., Kovats, S., Mojumder, S.K., Khusru, A., Rahman, A. and Vineis, P. (2011). "Drinking water salinity and maternal health in coastal Bangladesh: Implications of climate change." *Environmental Health Perspectives* 119(9), 1328–32. DOI: 10.1289/ehp. 1002804.

Khvorostyanov, D.V., Ciais, P., Krinner, G., Zimov, S.A., Corradi, C. and Guggenberger, G. (2008). "Vulnerability of permafrost carbon to global warming. Part II: Sensitivity of permafrost carbon stock to global warming." *Tellus B* 60(2), 265–75. DOI: 10.1111/ j.1600–0889.2007.00336.x.

Khvorostyanov, D.V., Krinner, G., Ciais, P., Heimann, M. and Zimov, S.A. (2008). "Vulnerability of permafrost carbon to global warming. Part I: Model description and role of heat generated by organic matter decomposition." *Tellus B* 60(2), 250–64. DOI: 10. 1111/j.1600–0889.2007.00333.x.

Kim, H.M., Webster, P.J. and Curry, J.A. (2009). "Impact of shifting patterns of Pacific Ocean warming on North Atlantic tropical cyclones." *Science* 325(5936), 77–80. DOI: 10.1126/science.1174062.

Kingdom of Saudi Arabia (2011). *Views on Different Elements of the Cancun Agreement Decision 1/CP16*. Information and views on issues that could be addressed at the joint workshop on matters relating to Article 2, paragraph 3, and Article 3, paragraph 14, of the Kyoto Protocol; submission by Saudi Arabia, February 21, 2011. United Nations Framework Convention on Climate Change. Available at http://unfccc.int/files/adaptation/ cancun_adaptation_framework/application/pdf/saudi_arabia_21_february_2011.pdf.

Kinnaman, T.C. (2011). "The economic impact of shale gas extraction: A review of existing studies." *Ecological Economics* 70(7), 1243–9. DOI: 10.1016/j.ecolecon.2011.02.005.

Kinney, P.L. (2008). "Climate change, air quality, and human health." *American Journal of Preventive Medicine* 35(5), 459–67. DOI: 10.1016/j.amepre.2008.08.025.

Kirilenko, A.P. and Sedjo, R.A. (2007). "Climate change impacts on forestry." *Proceedings of the National Academy of Sciences of the United States of America* 104(50), 19697–702. DOI: 10.1073/pnas.0701424104.

Kitous, A., Criqui, P., Bellevrat, E. and Chateau, B. (2010). "Transformation patterns of the worldwide energy system – Scenarios for the century with the POLES model." *Energy Journal* 31(Special Issue 1), 49–82.

Kjellstrom, T., Holmer, I. and Lemke, B. (2009). "Workplace heat stress, health and productivity – an increasing challenge for low and middle-income countries during climate change." *Global Health Action* 2. DOI: 10.3402/gha.v2i0.2047.

Klibanoff, P., Marinacci, M. and Mukerji, S. (2005). "A smooth model of decision making under ambiguity." *Econometrica* 73(6), 1849–92. DOI: 10.1111/j.1468-0262.2005.00640.x.

Kliejunas, J.T., Geils, B.W., Glaeser, J.M., *et al.* (2009). *Climate and Forest Diseases of Western North America: A Literature Review.* PSW-GTR-225. Albany, CA: U.S. Department of Agriculture, Forest Service, Pacific Southwest Research Station. Available at www.treesearch.fs.fed.us/pubs/33904.

Knight, F.H. (1921). *Risk, Uncertainty and Profit.* New York: Harper & Row.

Knittel, C.R. (2012). "Reducing petroleum consumption from transportation." *Journal of Economic Perspectives* 26(1), 93–118. DOI: 10.1257/jep. 26.1.93.

Knowlton, K., Rotkin-Ellman, M., King, G., *et al.* (2009). "The 2006 California Heat wave: Impacts on hospitalizations and emergency department visits." *Environmental Health Perspectives* 117(1), 61–67.

Knutson, T., Sirutis, J., Garner, S., Vecchi, G. and Held, I. (2008). "Simulated reduction in Atlantic hurricane frequency under twenty-first-century warming conditions." *Nature Geoscience* 1(7), 359–64. DOI: 10.1038/ngeo229.

Köhler, J., Wietschel, M., Whitmarsh, L., Keles, D. and Schade, W. (2010). "Infrastructure investment for a transition to hydrogen automobiles." *Technological Forecasting and Social Change* 77(8), 1237–48. DOI: 16/j.techfore.2010.03.010.

Kolstad, E.W. and Johansson, K.A. (2010). "Uncertainties associated with quantifying climate change impacts on human health: a case study for diarrhea." *Environmental Health Perspectives* 119(3), 299–305. DOI: 10.1289/ehp. 1002060.

Kopp, R.E. and Mignone, B.K. (2012). "The U.S. Government's social cost of carbon estimates after their first two years: Pathways for improvement." *Economics: The Open-Access, Open-Assessment E-Journal.* DOI: 10.5018/economics-ejournal. ja.2012–15.

Kopp, R.E., Golub, A., Keohane, N.O. and Onda, C. (2012). "The influence of the specification of climate change damages on the social cost of carbon." *Economics: The Open-Access, Open-Assessment E-Journal.* DOI: 10.5018/economics-ejournal.ja.2012–13.

Körper, J., Spangehl, T., Cubasch, U. and Huebener, H. (2009). "Decomposition of projected regional sea level rise in the North Atlantic and its relation to the AMOC." *Geophysical Research Letters* 36(19). DOI: 10.1029/2009GL039757.

Kotlarski, S., Jacob, D., Podzun, R. and Paul, F. (2009). "Representing glaciers in a regional climate model." *Climate Dynamics* 34(1), 27–46. DOI: 10.1007/s00382-009-0685-6.

Kousky, C., Kopp, R.E. and Cooke, R.M. (2011). "Risk premia and the social cost of carbon: A review." *Economics: The Open-Access, Open-Assessment E-Journal.* DOI: 10.5018/economics-ejournal.ja.2011–21.

Krawchuk, M.A., Moritz, M.A., Parisien, M.-A., Van Dorn, J. and Hayhoe, K. (2009). "Global pyrogeography: The current and future distribution of wildfire." *PLoS ONE* 4(4), e5102. DOI: 10.1371/journal.pone.0005102.

Krey, V. and Clarke, L. (2011). "Role of renewable energy in climate mitigation: A synthesis of recent scenarios." *Climate Policy* 11(4), 1131–58. DOI: 10.1080/14693062.2011.579308.

Kroeker, K.J., Kordas, R.L., Crim, R.N. and Singh, G.G. (2010). "Meta-analysis reveals negative yet variable effects of ocean acidification on marine organisms." *Ecology Letters* 13(11), 1419–34. DOI: 10.1111/j.1461–0248.2010.01518.x.

Kumar, K.K., Kamala, K., Rajagopalan, B. *et al.* (2010). "The once and future pulse of Indian monsoonal climate." *Climate Dynamics* 36(11–12), 2159–70. DOI: 10.1007/s00382–010–0974–0.

Kwok, R. and Rothrock, D.A. (2009). "Decline in Arctic sea ice thickness from submarine and ICESat records: 1958–2008." *Geophysical Research Letters* 36(15). DOI: 10.1029/2009GL039035.

Kwok, R., Cunningham, G.F., Wensnahan, M., Rigor, I., Zwally, H.J. and Yi, D. (2009). "Thinning and volume loss of the Arctic Ocean sea ice cover: 2003–2008." *Journal of Geophysical Research* 114(C7). DOI: 10.1029/2009JC005312.

Kypreos, S. (2007). "A MERGE model with endogenous technological change and the cost of carbon stabilization." *Energy Policy* 35(11), 5327–36. DOI: 10.1016/j.enpol.2006.01.029.

Lange, A. and Treich, N. (2008). "Uncertainty, learning and ambiguity in economic models on climate policy: Some classical results and new directions." *Climatic Change* 89(1–2), 7–21. DOI: 10.1007/s10584–008–9401–5.

Lassalle, G. and Rochard, E. (2009). "Impact of twenty-first century climate change on diadromous fish spread over Europe, North Africa and the Middle East." *Global Change Biology* 15(5), 1072–89. DOI: 10.1111/j.1365–2486.2008.01794.x.

Le, P.V.V., Kumar, P. and Drewry, D.T. (2011). "Implications for the hydrologic cycle under climate change due to the expansion of bioenergy crops in the Midwestern United States." *Proceedings of the National Academy of Sciences* 108(37), 15085–90. DOI: 10.1073/pnas.1107177108.

Leach, A.J. (2009). "The welfare implications of climate change policy." *Journal of Environmental Economics and Management* 57(2), 151–65. DOI: 10.1016/j.jeem.2007.11.006.

Leakey, A.D.B. (2009). "Rising atmospheric carbon dioxide concentration and the future of C4 crops for food and fuel." *Proceedings of the Royal Society B: Biological Sciences* 276(1666), 2333–43. DOI: 10.1098/rspb.2008.1517.

Lee, J., Veloso, F.M., Hounshell, D.A. and Rubin, E.S. (2010). "Forcing technological change: A case of automobile emissions control technology development in the US." *Technovation* 30(4), 249–64. DOI: 10.1016/j.technovation.2009.12.003.

Lehmann, J., Skjemstad, J., Sohi, S. *et al.* (2008). "Australian climate-carbon cycle feedback reduced by soil black carbon." *Nature Geoscience* 1(12), 832–5. DOI: 10.1038/ngeo358.

Leimbach, M., Bauer, N., Baumstark, L., Lüken, M. and Edenhofer, O. (2010). "Technological change and international trade – Insights from REMIND-R." *Energy Journal* 31(Special Issue 1), 109–36.

Lemoine, D. and Traeger, C. (2011). *Tipping Points and Ambiguity in the Economics of Climate Change.* CUDARE, 1111R. University of California, Berkeley. Available at http://escholarship.org/uc/item/9nd591ww.

Lenihan, J.M., Bachelet, D., Neilson, R.P. and Drapek, R. (2008). "Simulated response of conterminous United States ecosystems to climate change at different levels of fire suppression, CO_2 emission rate, and growth response to CO_2." *Global and Planetary Change* 64(1–2), 16–25. DOI: 10.1016/j.gloplacha.2008.01.006.

Lenton, T.M. and Vaughan, N.E. (2009). "The radiative forcing potential of different climate geoengineering options." *Atmospheric Chemistry and Physics* 9(15), 5539–61. DOI: 10.5194/acp-9-5539-2009.

Lenton, T.M., Held, H., Kriegler, E., Hall, J.W., Lucht, W., Rahmstorf, S. and Schellnhuber, H.J. (2008). "Tipping elements in the Earth's climate system." *Proceedings of the National Academy of Sciences of the United States of America* 105(6), 1786–93. DOI: 10.1073/pnas.0705414105.

Leung, L.R. and Qian, Y. (2009). "Atmospheric rivers induced heavy precipitation and flooding in the western U.S. simulated by the WRF regional climate model." *Geophysical Research Letters* 36(3). DOI: 10.1029/2008GL036445.

Levermann, A., Schewe, J., Petoukhov, V. and Held, H. (2009). "Tipping elements in earth systems special feature: Basic mechanism for abrupt monsoon transitions." *Proceedings of the National Academy of Sciences* 106(49), 20572–7. DOI: 10.1073/pnas.0901414106.

Levinson, R. and Akbari, H. (2009). "Potential benefits of cool roofs on commercial buildings: Conserving energy, saving money, and reducing emission of greenhouse gases and air pollutants." *Energy Efficiency* 3(1), 53–109. DOI: 10.1007/s12053–008–9038–2.

Lewis, S.L., Lopez-Gonzalez, G., Sonké, B. *et al.* (2009). "Increasing carbon storage in intact African tropical forests." *Nature* 457(7232), 1003–6. DOI: 10.1038/nature07771.

Li, Y.P., Huang, G.H. and Chen, X. (2011). "An interval-valued minimax-regret analysis approach for the identification of optimal greenhouse-gas abatement strategies under uncertainty." *Energy Policy* 39(7), 4313–24. DOI: 10.1016/j.enpol.2011.04.049.

Liang, Q.-M., Fan, Y. and Wei, Y.-M. (2009). "The effect of energy end-use efficiency improvement on China's energy use and CO_2 emissions: A CGE model-based analysis." *Energy Efficiency* 2(3), 243–62. DOI: 10.1007/s12053–009–9043–0.

Liess, S., Snyder, P.K. and Harding, K.J. (2011). "The effects of boreal forest expansion on the summer Arctic frontal zone." *Climate Dynamics* 38(9–10), 1805–27. DOI: 10.1007/s00382–011–1064–7.

Lin, N., Emanuel, K., Oppenheimer, M. and Vanmarcke, E. (2012). "Physically based assessment of hurricane surge threat under climate change." *Nature Climate Change* 2(6), 462–7. DOI: 10.1038/nclimate1389.

Liu, H. and Gallagher, K.S. (2009). "Driving carbon capture and storage forward in China." *Energy Procedia* 1(1), 3877–84. DOI: 10.1016/j.egypro.2009.02.190.

Liu, L. (2012). "Inferring the rate of pure time preference under uncertainty." *Ecological Economics* 74, 27–33. DOI: 10.1016/j.ecolecon.2011.11.007.

Liu, Y., Key, J.R. and Wang, X. (2009). "Influence of changes in sea ice concentration and cloud cover on recent Arctic surface temperature trends." *Geophysical Research Letters* 36(20). DOI: 10.1029/2009GL040708.

Lobell, D.B., Bänziger, M., Magorokosho, C. and Vivek, B. (2011). "Nonlinear heat effects on African maize as evidenced by historical yield trials." *Nature Climate Change* 1(1), 42–45. DOI: 10.1038/nclimate1043.

Lobell, D.B., Burke, M.B., Tebaldi, C., Mastrandrea, M.D., Falcon, W.P. and Naylor, R.L. (2008). "Prioritizing climate change adaptation needs for food security in 2030." *Science* 319(5863), 607–10. DOI: 10.1126/science.1152339.

Lobell, D.B., Cahill, K.N. and Field, C.B. (2006). "Weather-based yield forecasts developed for 12 California crops." *California Agriculture* 60(4), 211–15.

Lobell, D.B., Cahill, K.N. and Field, C.B. (2007). "Historical effects of temperature and precipitation on California crop yields." *Climatic Change* 81(2), 187–203. DOI: 10.1007/s10584–006–9141–3.

Lobell, D.B., Schlenker, W. and Costa-Roberts, J. (2011). "Climate trends and global crop production since 1980." *Science* 333(6042), 616–20. DOI: 10.1126/science.1204531.

Lobell, D.B., Sibley, A. and Ivan Ortiz-Monasterio, J. (2012). "Extreme heat effects on wheat senescence in India." *Nature Climate Change* 2(3), 186–9. DOI: 10.1038/nclimate1356.

Lomborg, B. (2010). *Smart solutions to climate change : Comparing costs and benefits.* Cambridge, UK, and New York: Cambridge University Press.

Long, S.P., Ainsworth, E.A., Rogers, A. and Ort, D.R. (2004). "Rising atmospheric carbon dioxide: Plants FACE the future." *Annual Review of Plant Biology* 55, 591–628. DOI: 10.1126/science.1114722.

Lontzek, T.S. and Narita, D. (2011). "Risk-averse mitigation decisions in an unpredictable climate system." *The Scandinavian Journal of Economics* 113(4), 937–58. DOI: 10.1111/j.1467–9442.2011.01679.x.

Lorenz, E.N. (1963). "Deterministic non-periodic flow." *Journal of the Atmospheric Sciences* 20, 130–41.

Lowe, J.A., Huntingford, C., Raper, S.C.B., Jones, C.D., Liddicoat, S.K. and Gohar, L.K. (2009). "How difficult is it to recover from dangerous levels of global warming?" *Environmental Research Letters* 4(1), 014012. DOI: 10.1088/1748–9326/4/1/014012.

Lowry, R. (2010). "Is risk itself a climate-related harm?" *Climatic Change* 106(3), 347–58. DOI: 10.1007/s10584–010–9960–0.

Lu, F., Wang, X., Han, B., Ouyang, Z., Duan, X., Zheng, H. and Miao, H. (2009). "Soil carbon sequestrations by nitrogen fertilizer application, straw return and no-tillage in China's cropland." *Global Change Biology* 15(2), 281–305. DOI: 10.1111/j.1365–2486.2008.01743.x.

Lu, J. (2009). "The dynamics of the Indian Ocean sea surface temperature forcing of Sahel drought." *Climate Dynamics* 33(4), 445–60. DOI: 10.1007/s00382–009–0596–6.

Luedeling, E., Girvetz, E.H., Semenov, M.A. and Brown, P.H. (2011). "Climate change affects winter chill for temperate fruit and nut trees." *PLoS ONE* 6(5), e20155. DOI: 10.1371/journal.pone.0020155.

Luo, Q. (2011). "Temperature thresholds and crop production: A review." *Climatic Change* 109(3–4), 583–98. DOI: 10.1007/s10584–011–0028–6.

Luyssaert, S., Schulze, E.-D., Börner, A. *et al.* (2008). "Old-growth forests as global carbon sinks." *Nature* 455(7210), 213–15. DOI: 10.1038/nature07276.

Maddison, D. and Rehdanz, K. (2011). "The impact of climate on life satisfaction." *Ecological Economics* 70(12), 2437–45. DOI: 10.1016/j.ecolecon.2011.07.027.

Magne, B., Kypreos, S. and Turton, H. (2010). "Technology options for low stabilization pathways with MERGE." *Energy Journal* 31(Special Issue 1), 83–108.

Mahlstein, I., Portmann, R.W., Daniel, J.S., Solomon, S. and Knutti, R. (2012). "Perceptible changes in regional precipitation in a future climate." *Geophysical Research Letters* 39(5). DOI: 10.1029/2011GL050738.

Maisonnave, H., Pycroft, J., Saveyn, B. and Ciscar, J.-C. (2012). "Does climate policy make the EU economy more resilient to oil price rises? A CGE analysis." *Energy Policy* 47, 172–9. DOI: 10.1016/j.enpol.2012.04.053.

Malhi, Y., Aragão, L.E.O.C., Galbraith, D. *et al.* (2009). "Exploring the likelihood and mechanism of a climate-change-induced dieback of the Amazon rainforest." *Proceedings of the National Academy of Sciences of the United States of America* (PNAS Early Edition). DOI: 10.1073/pnas.0804619106.

Malhi, Y., Roberts, J.T., Betts, R.A., Killeen, T.J., Li, W. and Nobre, C.A. (2008). "Climate change, deforestation, and the fate of the Amazon." *Science* 319(5860), 169–72. DOI: 10.1126/science.1146961.

Mani, N.J., Suhas, E. and Goswami, B.N. (2009). "Can global warming make Indian monsoon weather less predictable?" *Geophysical Research Letters* 36(8). DOI: 10.1029/2009GL037989.

Mann, M.E. and Emanuel, K.A. (2006). "Atlantic hurricane trends linked to climate change." *Eos, Transactions American Geophysical Union* 87(24). DOI: 10.1029/2006EO240001.

Mann, M.E., Woodruff, J.D., Donnelly, J.P. and Zhang, Z. (2009). "Atlantic hurricanes and climate over the past 1,500 years." *Nature* 460(7257), 880–83. DOI: 10.1038/nature08219.

Margulis, S., Bucher, A., Cordeli, D. *et al.* (2008). *The Economics of Adaptation to Climate Change: Methodology Report.* Washington, DC: The World Bank. Available at http://siteresources.worldbank.org/INTCC/Resources/MethodologyReport0209.pdf.

Markandya, A., Armstrong, B.G., Hales, S., *et al.* (2009). "Public health benefits of strategies to reduce greenhouse-gas emissions: Low-carbon electricity generation." *The Lancet* 374(9706), 2006–15. DOI: 10.1016/S0140–6736(09)61715–3.

Marten, A.L. (2011). "Transient temperature response modeling in IAMs: The effects of over simplification on the SCC." *Economics: The Open-Access, Open-Assessment E-Journal.* DOI: 10.5018/economics-ejournal.ja.2011–18.

Maslanik, J., Stroeve, J., Fowler, C. and Emery, W. (2011). "Distribution and trends in Arctic sea ice age through spring 2011." *Geophysical Research Letters* 38(13), L13502. DOI: 10.1029/2011GL047735.

Mathis, J.T., Cross, J.N. and Bates, N.R. (2011). "The role of ocean acidification in systemic carbonate mineral suppression in the Bering Sea." *Geophysical Research Letters* 38(19). DOI: 10.1029/2011GL048884.

Mathis, J.T., Pickart, R.S., Byrne, R.H. *et al.* (2012). "Storm-induced upwelling of high p CO_2 waters onto the continental shelf of the western Arctic Ocean and implications for carbonate mineral saturation states." *Geophysical Research Letters* 39(7). DOI: 10.1029/2012GL051574.

Matthews, H.D. and Caldeira, K. (2008). "Stabilizing climate requires near-zero emissions." *Geophysical Research Letters* 35(L04705). DOI: 200810.1029/2007GL032388.

Mazzi, E.A. and Dowlatabadi, H. (2007). "Air quality impacts of climate mitigation: UK policy and passenger vehicle choice." *Environmental Science & Technology* 41(2), 387–92. DOI: 10.1021/es060517w.

McConnell, J.R., Edwards, R., Kok, G.L. *et al.* (2007). "20th-century industrial black carbon emissions altered Arctic climate forcing." *Science* 317(5843), 1381–4. DOI: 10.1126/science.1144856.

McCusker, K.E., Battisti, D.S. and Bitz, C.M. (2012). "The climate response to stratospheric sulfate injections and implications for addressing climate emergencies." *Journal of Climate* 25(9), 3096–3116. DOI: 10.1175/JCLI-D-11–00183.1.

McKinsey & Company (2009). *Pathways to a Low-Carbon Economy: Version 2 of the Global Greenhouse Gas Abatement Cost Curve.* Available at www.mckinsey.com/clientservice/ccsi/pathways_low_carbon_economy.asp.

McMahon, S.M., Parker, G.G. and Miller, D.R. (2010). "Evidence for a recent increase in forest growth." *Proceedings of the National Academy of Sciences of the United States of America* 107(8), 3611–15. DOI: 10.1073/pnas.0912376107.

McMichael, A.J. (2012). "Insights from past millennia into climatic impacts on human health and survival." *Proceedings of the National Academy of Sciences* 109(13), 4730–37. DOI: 10.1073/pnas.1120177109.

Meehl, G.A., Arblaster, J.M. and Collins, W.D. (2008). "Effects of black carbon aerosols on the Indian monsoon." *Journal of Climate* 21(12), 2869–82. DOI: 10.1175/2007JCLI1777.1.

Mehra, R. and Prescott, E.C. (1985). "The equity premium: A puzzle." *Journal of Monetary Economics* 15(2), 145–61. DOI: 10.1016/0304–3932(85)90061–3.

Mendelsohn, R., Emanuel, K., Chonabayashi, S. and Bakkensen, L. (2012). "The impact of climate change on global tropical cyclone damage." *Nature Climate Change* 2(3), 205–9. DOI: 10.1038/nclimate1357.

Mendelsohn, R., Nordhaus, W.D. and Shaw, D. (1994). "The impact of global warming on agriculture: A Ricardian analysis." *The American Economic Review* 84(4), 753–71.

Menon, S., Akbari, H., Mahanama, S., Sednev, I. and Levinson, R. (2010). "Radiative forcing and temperature response to changes in urban albedos and associated CO_2 offsets." *Environmental Research Letters* 5(1), 014005. DOI: 10.1088/1748–9326/5/1/014005.

Mez, L. (2012). "Nuclear energy – any solution for sustainability and climate protection?" *Energy Policy* 48, 56–63. DOI: 10.1016/j.enpol.2012.04.047.

Michetti, M. and Rosa, R. (2012). "Afforestation and timber management compliance strategies in climate policy: A computable general equilibrium analysis." *Ecological Economics* 77, 139–48. DOI: 10.1016/j.ecolecon.2012.02.020.

Milinski, M., Sommerfeld, R.D., Krambeck, H.-J., Reed, F.A. and Marotzke, J. (2008). "The collective-risk social dilemma and the prevention of simulated dangerous climate change." *Proceedings of the National Academy of Sciences* 105(7), 2291–4. DOI: 10.1073/pnas.0709546105.

Millner, A., Dietz, S. and Heal, G. (2010). *Ambiguity and Climate Policy*. NBER Working Paper 16050.

Mills, E. (2007). "Synergisms between climate change mitigation and adaptation: An insurance perspective." *Mitigation and Adaptation Strategies for Global Change* 12(5), 809–42. DOI: 10.1007/s11027–007–9101-x.

Mills, E. (2009). "A global review of insurance industry responses to climate change." *The Geneva Papers on Risk and Insurance Issues and Practice* 34(3), 323–59. DOI: 10.1057/gpp. 2009.14.

Min, S.-K., Zhang, X., Zwiers, F.W., Friederichs, P. and Hense, A. (2008). "Signal detectability in extreme precipitation changes assessed from twentieth century climate simulations." *Climate Dynamics* 32(1), 95–111. DOI: 10.1007/s00382–008–0376–8.

Min, S.-K., Zhang, X., Zwiers, F.W. and Hegerl, G.C. (2011). "Human contribution to more-intense precipitation extremes." *Nature* 470(7334), 378–81. DOI: 10.1038/nature09763.

Mitrovica, J.X., Gomez, N. and Clark, P.U. (2009). "The sea-level fingerprint of West Antarctic collapse." *Science* 323(5915), 753. DOI: 10.1126/science.1166510.

Moffet, R.C. and Prather, K.A. (2009). "In-situ measurements of the mixing state and optical properties of soot with implications for radiative forcing estimates." *Proceedings of the National Academy of Sciences of the United States of America* 106(29), 11872–7. DOI: 10.1073/pnas.0900040106.

Moore, J.C., Jevrejeva, S. and Grinsted, A. (2010). "Efficacy of geoengineering to limit 21st century sea-level rise." *Proceedings of the National Academy of Sciences of the United States of America* 107(36), 15699–703. DOI: 10.1073/pnas.1008153107.

Morgan, P., Heyerdahl, E.K. and Gibson, C.E. (2008). "Multi-season climate synchro-nized forest fires throughout the 20th century, Northern Rockies, USA." *Ecology* 89(3), 717–28. DOI: 10.1890/06–2049.1.

Moridis, G.J. and Reagan, M.T. (2009). "Interrelationship of dissociating oceanic hydrates and global climate: Methane hydrate response to rising water temperatures." Supplement 1: Awards Ceremony Speeches and Abstracts of the 19th Annual V.M. Goldschmidt Conference, A905. DOI: 10.1016/j.gca.2009.05.011.

Mousavi, M.E., Irish, J.L., Frey, A.E., Olivera, F. and Edge, B.L. (2010). "Global warming and hurricanes: The potential impact of hurricane intensification and sea level rise on coastal flooding." *Climatic Change* 104(3–4), 575–97. DOI: 10.1007/s10584–009–9790–0.

Muller, N.Z., Mendelsohn, R. and Nordhaus, W. (2011). "Environmental accounting for pollution in the United States economy." *American Economic Review* 101(5), 1649–75. DOI: 10.1257/aer.101.5.1649.

Munday, P.L., Dixson, D.L., Donelson, J.M., Jones, G.P., Pratchett, M.S., Devitsina, G.V. and Døving, K.B. (2009). "Ocean acidification impairs olfactory discrimination and homing ability of a marine fish." *Proceedings of the National Academy of Sciences.* DOI: 10.1073/pnas.0809996106.

Murphy, J.M., Sexton, D.M.H., Barnett, D.N., Jones, G.S., Webb, M.J., Collins, M. and Stainforth, D.A. (2004). "Quantification of modelling uncertainties in a large ensemble of climate change simulations." *Nature* 430(7001), 768–72. DOI: 10.1038/nature02771.

Murphy, R. and Jaccard, M. (2011). "Energy efficiency and the cost of GHG abatement: A comparison of bottom-up and hybrid models for the US." *Energy Policy* 39(11), 7146–55. DOI: 10.1016/j.enpol.2011.08.033.

Myhre, G. (2009). "Consistency between satellite-derived and modeled estimates of the direct aerosol effect." *Science* 325(5937), 187–90. DOI: 10.1126/science.1174461.

Nakicenovic, N., Alcamo, J., Davis, G. *et al.* (2000). *Special Report on Emissions Scen-arios.* The Hague: Intergovernmental Panel on Climate Change. Available at www.grida.no/publications/other/ipcc_sr/?src=/climate/ipcc/emission.

Narain, S. and Riddle, M. (2007). "Greenhouse justice: An entitlement framework for managing the global atmospheric commons." In J.K. Boyce and E.A. Stanton, eds. *Reclaiming Nature: Environmental Justice and Ecological Restoration.* London: Anthem Press, pp. 401–14.

Narain, U., Margulis, S. and Essam, T. (2011). "Estimating costs of adaptation to climate change." *Climate Policy* 11(3), 1001–19. DOI: 10.1080/14693062.2011.582387.

National Institute of Oceanography (2009). "LOHAFEX provides surprising insights on plankton ecology that dampen hopes of using the southern ocean to sequester atmos-pheric CO_2." Joint press release with the Council of Scientific & Industrial Research, New Delhi, and the Alfred Wegener Institute for Polar and Marine Research in the Helmholtz Association, Germany. Goa, India.

Negishi, T. (1972). *General Equilibrium Theory and International Trade.* Amsterdam and London: North-Holland Publishing Company.

Nelson, J.A. (2011). "Ethics and the economist: What climate change demands of us." *Ecological Economics.*

Newbold, S.C. and Daigneault, A. (2009). "Climate response uncertainty and the benefits of greenhouse gas emissions reductions." *Environmental and Resource Economics* 44(3), 351–77. DOI: 10.1007/s10640–009–9290–8.

Ng, P. and Zhao, X. (2011). "No matter how it is measured, income declines with global warming." *Ecological Economics* 70(5), 963–70. DOI: 10.1016/j.ecolecon.2010.12.012.

Ng, Y.-K. (2010). "Consumption tradeoff vs. catastrophes avoidance: Implications of some recent results in happiness studies on the economics of climate change." *Climatic Change* 105(1–2), 109–27. DOI: 10.1007/s10584–010–9880-z.

Nicholls, R.J. and Cazenave, A. (2010). "Sea-level rise and its impact on coastal zones." *Science* 328(5985), 1517–1520. DOI: 10.1126/science.1185782.

Nicholls, R.J., Hanson, S., Herweijer, C. *et al.* (2008). *Ranking Port Cities with High Exposure and Vulnerability to Climate Extremes: Exposure Estimates*. Paris: Organisation for Economic Cooperation and Development. Available at http://dx.doi.org/10.1787/011766488208.

Nicholls, R.J., Marinova, N., Lowe, J.A. *et al.* (2011). "Sea-level rise and its possible impacts given a 'beyond 4 C world' in the twenty-first century." *Philosophical Transactions of the Royal Society A: Mathematical, Physical and Engineering Sciences* 369(1934), 161–81. DOI: 10.1098/rsta.2010.0291.

Nigam, S. and Guan, B. (2010). "Atlantic tropical cyclones in the twentieth century: Natural variability and secular change in cyclone count." *Climate Dynamics* 36(11–12), 2279–93. DOI: 10.1007/s00382–010–0908-x.

NOAA Earth System Research Laboratory (2010). *The NOAA Annual Greenhouse Gas Index (AGGI)*. Boulder, CO: National Oceanic and Atmospheric Administration. Available at www.esrl.noaa.gov/gmd/aggi/.

NOAA Earth System Research Laboratory (2012). *Trends in Atmospheric Carbon Dioxide*. Boulder, CO: National Oceanic & Atmospheric Administration. Available at www.esrl.noaa.gov/gmd/ccgg/trends/.

Norby, R.J., DeLucia, E.H., Gielen, B. *et al.* (2005). "Forest response to elevated CO_2 is conserved across a broad range of productivity." *Proceedings of the National Academy of Sciences of the United States of America* 102(50), 18052–6. DOI: 10.1073/pnas.0509478102.

Nordhaus, W.D. (2007). "A review of The Stern Review on the Economics of Climate Change." *Journal of Economic Literature* 45(3), 17. DOI: 10.1257/jel.45.3.686.

Nordhaus, W.D. (2007). *Accompanying Notes and Documentation on Development of DICE-2007 Model: Notes on DICE-2007.v8 of September 21, 2007*. New Haven, CT: Yale University. Available at http://nordhaus.econ.yale.edu/Accom_Notes_100507.pdf.

Nordhaus, W.D. (2008). *A Question of Balance: Economic Modeling of Global Warming*. New Haven, CT: Yale University Press.

Nordhaus, W.D. (2009). *An Analysis of the Dismal Theorem*. Cowles Foundation Discussion Paper No. 1686. New Haven, CT: Cowles Foundation for Research in Economics, Yale University. Available at http://cowles.econ.yale.edu/P/cd/d16b/d1686.pdf.

Nordhaus, W.D. and Boyer, J. (1999). "Roll the DICE again: The economics of global warming." Yale University Working Paper.

Nordhaus, W.D. and Boyer, J. (2000). *Warming the World: Economic Models of Global Warming*. Cambridge, MA: MIT Press.

Nye, J.A., Link, J.S., Hare, J.A. and Overholtz, W.J. (2009). "Changing spatial distribution of fish stocks in relation to climate and population size on the Northeast United States continental shelf." *Marine Ecology Progress Series* 393, 111–29.

O'Donnell, J.A., Harden, J.W., McGuire, A.D. and Romanovsky, V.E. (2010). "Exploring the sensitivity of soil carbon dynamics to climate change, fire disturbance and permafrost thaw in a black spruce ecosystem." *Biogeosciences Discussions* 7(6), 8853–93.

Ohlson, M., Dahlberg, B., Okland, T., Brown, K.J. and Halvorsen, R. (2009). "The charcoal carbon pool in boreal forest soils." *Nature Geoscience* 2(10), 692–5. DOI: 10.1038/ngeo617.

Olajire, A.A. (2010). "CO_2 capture and separation technologies for end-of-pipe applications: A review." *Energy* 35(6), 2610–28. DOI: 10.1016/j.energy.2010.02.030.

Olmstead, A.L. and Rhode, P.W. (2010). "Adapting North American wheat production to climatic challenges, 1839–2009." *Proceedings of the National Academy of Sciences* 108(2), 480–85. DOI: 10.1073/pnas.1008279108.

Oppenheimer, M., O'Neill, B.C. and Webster, M. (2008). "Negative learning." *Climatic Change* 89(1–2), 155–72. DOI: 10.1007/s10584–008–9405–1.

Orr, F.M. (2009). "Onshore geologic storage of CO_2." *Science* 325(5948), 1656–8. DOI: 10.1126/science.1175677.

Ostro, B.D., Roth, L.A., Green, R.S. and Basu, R. (2009). "Estimating the mortality effect of the July 2006 California heat wave." *Environmental Research* 109, 614–19. DOI: 10.1016/j.envres.2009.03.010.

Overpeck, J.T. and Weiss, J.L. (2009). "Projections of future sea level becoming more dire." *Proceedings of the National Academy of Sciences of the United States of America* 106(51), 21461–2. DOI: 10.1073/pnas.0912878107.

Oxfam International (2007). *Adapting to Climate Change: What's Needed in Poor Countries, and Who Should Pay.* Oxfam Briefing Paper 104. Available at www.oxfam.org/en/policy/briefingpapers/bp104_climate_change_0705.

Pagani, M., Liu, Z., LaRiviere, J. and Ravelo, A.C. (2009). "High Earth-system climate sensitivity determined from Pliocene carbon dioxide concentrations." *Nature Geoscience* 3(1), 27–30. DOI: 10.1038/ngeo724.

Pan, Y., Birdsey, R.A., Fang, J. *et al.* (2011). "A large and persistent carbon sink in the world's forests." *Science* 333(6045), 988–93. DOI: 10.1126/science.1201609.

Pandolfi, J.M., Connolly, S.R., Marshall, D.J. and Cohen, A.L. (2011). "Projecting coral reef futures under global warming and ocean acidification." *Science* 333(6041), 418–22. DOI: 10.1126/science.1204794.

Pardaens, A.K., Lowe, J.A., Brown, S., Nicholls, R.J. and de Gusmão, D. de (2011). "Sea-level rise and impacts projections under a future scenario with large greenhouse gas emission reductions." *Geophysical Research Letters* 38(12), L12604. DOI: 10.1029/2011GL047678.

Parry, M., Arnell, N., Berry, P. *et al.* (2009). *Assessing the Costs of Adaptation to Climate Change: A Review of the UNFCCC and Other Recent Estimates.* London: International Institute for Environment and Development (UK) and the Grantham Institute for Climate Change, Imperial College London. Available at http://pubs.iied.org/pubs/pdfs/11501IIED.pdf.

Pathak, H. and Wassmann, R. (2008). "Quantitative evaluation of climatic variability and risks for wheat yield in India." *Climatic Change* 93(1–2), 157–75. DOI: 10.1007/s10584–008–9463–4.

Peduzzi, P., Chatenoux, B., Dao, H. *et al.* (2012). "Global trends in tropical cyclone risk." *Nature Climate Change* 2(4), 289–94. DOI: 10.1038/nclimate1410.

Pendergrass, A.G. and Hartmann, D.L. (2012). "Global-mean precipitation and black carbon in AR4 simulations." *Geophysical Research Letters* 39(1), L01703. DOI: 10.1029/2011GL050067.

Perez, R., Zweibel, K. and Hoff, T.E. (2011). "Solar power generation in the U.S.: Too expensive, or a bargain?" *Energy Policy* 39(11), 7290–97. DOI: 10.1016/j. enpol.2011.08.052.

Peters, O. (2011). "The time resolution of the St Petersburg paradox." *Philosophical Transactions of the Royal Society A: Mathematical, Physical and Engineering Sciences* 369(1956), 4913–31. DOI: 10.1098/rsta.2011.0065.

Pezzey, J.C.V. and Jotzo, F. (2012). "Tax-versus-trading and efficient revenue recycling as issues for greenhouse gas abatement." *Journal of Environmental Economics and Management* 64(2), 230–36. DOI: 10.1016/j.jeem.2012.02.006.

Phillips, O.L., Aragão, L.E.O.C., Lewis, S.L., *et al.* (2009). "Drought sensitivity of the Amazon rainforest." *Science* 323(5919), 1344–7. DOI: 10.1126/science.1164033.

Phillips, O.L., Lewis, S.L., Baker, T.R., Chao, K.-J. and Higuchi, N. (2008). "The changing Amazon forest." *Philosophical Transactions of the Royal Society B: Biological Sciences* 363(1498), 1819–27. DOI: 10.1098/rstb.2007.0033.

Pielke Jr., R.A. (2009). "An idealized assessment of the economics of air capture of carbon dioxide in mitigation policy." *Environmental Science & Policy* 12(3), 216–25. DOI: 10.1016/j.envsci.2009.01.002.

Pindyck, R.S. (2011). "Fat tails, thin tails, and climate change policy." *Review of Environmental Economics and Policy* 5(2), 258–74. DOI: 10.1093/reep/rer005.

Pindyck, R.S. (2012). "Uncertain outcomes and climate change policy." *Journal of Environmental Economics and Management* 63(3), 289–303. DOI: 10.1016/j.jeem.2011.12.001.

Pollard, R.T., Salter, I., Sanders, R.J. *et al.* (2009). "Southern Ocean deep-water carbon export enhanced by natural iron fertilization." *Nature* 457(7229), 577–80. DOI: 10.1038/nature07716.

Pongratz, J., Reick, C.H., Raddatz, T., Caldeira, K. and Claussen, M. (2011). "Past land use decisions have increased mitigation potential of reforestation." *Geophysical Research Letters* 38(15). DOI: 10.1029/2011GL047848.

Popp, D. and Newell, R.G. (2009). *Where Does Energy R&D Come From? Examining Crowding Out from Environmentally-Friendly R&D.* NBER Working Paper No. 15423. Cambridge, MA: National Bureau of Economic Research. Available at www. nber.org/papers/w15423.

Porter, M.E. and van der Linde, C. (1995). "Toward a new conception of the environment-competitiveness relationship." *The Journal of Economic Perspectives* 9(4), 97–118.

Portmann, R.W., Solomon, S. and Hegerl, G.C. (2009). "Spatial and seasonal patterns in climate change, temperatures, and precipitation across the United States." *Proceedings of the National Academy of Sciences of the United States of America* 106(18), 7324–9. DOI: 10.1073/pnas.0808533106.

Portney, P.R. and Weyant, J.P. (1999). *Discounting and Intergenerational Equity.* Washington, DC: Resources for the Future.

Price, S.F., Payne, A.J., Howat, I.M. and Smith, B.E. (2011). "Committed sea-level rise for the next century from Greenland ice sheet dynamics during the past decade." *Proceedings of the National Academy of Sciences* 108(22), 8978–83. DOI: 10.1073/ pnas.1017313108.

Pritchard, H.D., Arthern, R.J., Vaughan, D.G. and Edwards, L.A. (2009). "Extensive dynamic thinning on the margins of the Greenland and Antarctic ice sheets." *Nature* 461(7266), 971–5. DOI: 10.1038/nature08471.

Pycroft, J., Vergano, L., Hope, C., Paci, D. and Ciscar, J.C. (2011). "A tale of tails: Uncertainty and the social cost of carbon dioxide." *Economics: The Open-Access, Open-Assessment E-Journal.* DOI: 10.5018/economics-ejournal.ja.2011-22.

Rabin, M. (2000). "Risk aversion and expected-utility theory: A calibration theorem." *Econometrica* 68(5), 1281–92. DOI: 10.1111/1468–0262.00158.

Rabin, M. and Thaler, R.H. (2001). "Anomalies: Risk aversion." *The Journal of Economic Perspectives* 15(1), 219–32. DOI: 10.1257/jep. 15.1.219.

Rahmstorf, S. (2007). "A semi-empirical approach to projecting future sea-level rise." *Science* 315(5810), 368–70. DOI: 10.1126/science.1135456.

Ramana, M.V., Ramanathan, V., Feng, Y., Yoon, S.-C., Kim, S.-W., Carmichael, G.R. and Schauer, J.J. (2010). "Warming influenced by the ratio of black carbon to sulphate and the black-carbon source." *Nature Geoscience* 3(8), 542–5. DOI: 10.1038/ngeo918.

Ramanathan, V. and Carmichael, G. (2008). "Global and regional climate changes due to black carbon." *Nature Geoscience* 1(4), 221–7. DOI: 10.1038/ngeo156.

Ramsey, F.P. (1928). "A mathematical theory of saving." *The Economic Journal* 138(152), 543–59.

Randerson, J.T., Liu, H., Flanner, M.G., *et al.* (2006). "The impact of boreal forest fire on climate warming." *Science* 314(5802), 1130–32. DOI: 10.1126/science.1132075.

Rasch, P.J., Crutzen, P.J. and Coleman, D.B. (2008). "Exploring the geoengineering of climate using stratospheric sulfate aerosols: The role of particle size." *Geophysical Research Letters* 35(L02809). DOI: 10.1029/2007GL032179.

Reilly, J.M., Graham, J. and Hrubovcak, J. (2001). *Agriculture: The Potential Consequences of Climate Variability and Change for the United States.* U.S. National Assessment of the Potential Consequences of Climate Variability and Change, U.S. Global Change Research Program. New York: Cambridge University Press.

Repo, M.E., Susiluoto, S., Lind, S.E. *et al.* (2009). "Large N₂O emissions from cryoturbated peat soil in tundra." *Nature Geoscience* 2(3), 189–92. DOI: 10.1038/ngeo434.

Rezai, A., Foley, D.K. and Taylor, L. (2011). "Global warming and economic externalities." *Economic Theory* 49(2), 329–51. DOI: 10.1007/s00199–010–0592–4.

Richardson, K., Steffen, W., Schellnhuber, H.J. *et al.* (2009). *Synthesis Report: Climate Change: Global Risks, Challenges & Decisions.* Synthesis report for Climate Congress held March 3–5, 2009, in Copenhagen. Copenhagen: University of Copenhagen. Available at http://climatecongress.ku.dk/pdf/synthesisreport.

Ries, J.B., Cohen, A.L. and McCorkle, D.C. (2009). "Marine calcifiers exhibit mixed responses to CO_2-induced ocean acidification." *Geology* 37(12), 1131–4. DOI: 10.1130/G30210A.1.

Rijnsdorp, A.D., Peck, M.A., Engelhard, G.H., Möllmann, C. and Pinnegar, J.K. (2009). "Resolving the effect of climate change on fish populations." *ICES Journal of Marine Science: Journal du Conseil* 66(7), 1570–83. DOI: 10.1093/icesjms/fsp056.

Roberts, K.G., Gloy, B.A., Joseph, S., Scott, N.R. and Lehmann, J. (2010). "Life cycle assessment of biochar systems: Estimating the energetic, economic, and climate change potential." *Environmental Science & Technology* 44(2), 827–33. DOI: 10.1021/es902266r.

Robock, A., Oman, L. and Stenchikov, G.L. (2008). "Regional climate responses to geoengineering with tropical and Arctic SO_2 injections." *Journal of Geophysical Research* 113(D16101). DOI: 200810.1029/2008JD010050.

Rochelle, G.T. (2009). "Amine scrubbing for CO_2 capture." *Science* 325(5948), 1652–1654. DOI: 10.1126/science.1176731.

Roe, G. (2009). "Feedbacks, timescales, and seeing red." *Annual Review of Earth and Planetary Sciences* 37(1), 93–115. DOI: 10.1146/annurev.earth.061008.134734.

Roe, G.H. and Armour, K.C. (2011). "How sensitive is climate sensitivity?" *Geophysical Research Letters* 38(14), L14708. DOI: 10.1029/2011GL047913.

Roe, G.H. and Baker, M.B. (2007). "Why is climate sensitivity so unpredictable?" *Science* 318(5850), 629–32. DOI: 10.1126/science.1144735.

Roe, G.H. and Baker, M.B. (2011). "Comment on 'Another look at climate sensitivity' by Zaliapin and Ghil (2010)." *Nonlinear Processes in Geophysics* 18(1), 125–7. DOI: 10.5194/npg-18–125–2011.

Rogelj, J., Hare, W., Lowe, J., *et al.* (2011). "Emission pathways consistent with a 2°C global temperature limit." *Nature Climate Change* 1(8), 413–18. DOI: 10.1038/nclimate1258.

Rohling, E.J., Grant, K., Bolshaw, M., Roberts, A.P., Siddall, M., Hemleben, C. and Kucera, M. (2009). "Antarctic temperature and global sea level closely coupled over the past five glacial cycles." *Nature Geoscience* 2(7), 500–504. DOI: 10.1038/ngeo557.

Rohling, E.J., Grant, K., Hemleben, C., Siddall, M., Hoogakker, B.A.A., Bolshaw, M. and Kucera, M. (2008). "High rates of sea-level rise during the last interglacial period." *Nature Geoscience* 1(1), 38–42. DOI: 10.1038/ngeo.2007.28.

Rosenfeld, D., Lohmann, U., Raga, G.B. *et al.* (2008). "Flood or drought: How do aerosols affect precipitation?" *Science* 321(5894), 1309–13. DOI: 10.1126/science.1160606.

Rosenzweig, C., Karoly, D., Vicarelli, M. *et al.* (2008). "Attributing physical and biological impacts to anthropogenic climate change." *Nature* 453(7193), 353–7. DOI: 10.1038/nature06937.

Roughgarden, T. and Schneider, S.H. (1999). "Climate change policy: Quantifying uncertainties for damages and optimal carbon taxes." *Energy Policy* 27(7), 415–29. DOI: 10.1016/S0301–4215(99)00030–0.

Rout, U.K., Akimoto, K., Sano, F. and Tomoda, T. (2010). "Introduction of subsidisation in nascent climate-friendly learning technologies and evaluation of its effectiveness." *Energy Policy* 38(1), 520–32. DOI: 10.1016/j.enpol.2009.10.003.

Royer, D.L., Berner, R.A. and Park, J. (2007). "Climate sensitivity constrained by CO_2 concentrations over the past 420 million years." *Nature* 446(7135), 530–32. DOI: 10.1038/nature05699.

Rozenberg, J., Hallegatte, S., Vogt-Schilb, A., Sassi, O., Guivarch, C., Waisman, H. and Hourcade, J.-C. (2010). "Climate policies as a hedge against the uncertainty on future oil supply." *Climatic Change* 101(3–4), 663–8. DOI: 10.1007/s10584–010–9868–8.

Rübbelke, D.T.G. (2011). "International support of climate change policies in developing countries: Strategic, moral and fairness aspects." *Ecological Economics* 70(8), 1470–80. DOI: 16/j.ecolecon.2011.03.007.

Runde, J. (1998). "Clarifying Frank Knight's discussion of the meaning of risk and uncertainty." *Cambridge Journal of Economics* 22(5), 539–46. DOI: 10.1093/cje/22.5.539.

Samuelson, P.A. (1937). "A note on measurement of utility." *The Review of Economic Studies* 4(2), 155–61. DOI: 10.2307/2967612.

Sanderson, M.G., Hemming, D.L. and Betts, R.A. (2011). "Regional temperature and precipitation changes under high-end (≥4°C) global warming." *Philosophical Transactions of the Royal Society A: Mathematical, Physical and Engineering Sciences* 369(1934), 85–98. DOI: 10.1098/rsta.2010.0283.

Saul, U. and Seidel, C. (2011). "Does leadership promote cooperation in climate change mitigation policy?" *Climate Policy* 11(2), 901–21. DOI: 10.3763/cpol.2009.0004.

Schlenker, W. and Lobell, D.B. (2010). "Robust negative impacts of climate change on African agriculture." *Environmental Research Letters* 5(1), 014010. DOI: 10.1088/1748–9326/5/1/014010.

Schlenker, W. and Roberts, M.J. (2009). "Nonlinear temperature effects indicate severe damages to U.S. crop yields under climate change." *Proceedings of the National*

Academy of Sciences of the United States of America 106(37), 15594–8. DOI: 10.1073/pnas.0906865106.

Schlenker, W., Hanemann, W.M. and Fisher, A.C. (2005). "Will U.S. agriculture really benefit from global warming? Accounting for irrigation in the hedonic approach." *The American Economic Review* 88(1), 113–25. DOI: 10.1257/0002828053828455.

Schlenker, W., Hanemann, W.M. and Fisher, A.C. (2006). "The impact of global warming on U.S. agriculture: An econometric analysis of optimal growing conditions." *The Review of Economics and Statistics* 88(1), 113–25. DOI: 10.1162/rest.2006.88.1.113.

Schlenker, W., Hanemann, W.M. and Fisher, A.C. (2007). "Water availability, degree days, and the potential impact of climate change on irrigated agriculture in California." *Climatic Change* 81(1), 19–38. DOI: 10.1007/s10584–005–9008-z.

Schlesinger, W.H. (2010). "On fertilizer-induced soil carbon sequestration in China's croplands." *Global Change Biology* 16(2), 849–50. DOI: 10.1111/j.1365–2486.2009.01958.x.

Schmittner, A., Urban, N.M., Shakun, J.D. *et al.* (2011). "Climate sensitivity estimated from temperature reconstructions of the last glacial maximum." *Science* 334(6061), 1385–8. DOI: 10.1126/science.1203513.

Schneider, L. (2009). "Assessing the additionality of CDM projects: Practical experiences and lessons learned." *Climate Policy* 9(3), 242–54. DOI: 10.3763/cpol.2008.0533.

Schuur, E.A.G., Vogel, J.G., Crummer, K.G., Lee, H., Sickman, J.O. and Osterkamp, T.E. (2009). "The effect of permafrost thaw on old carbon release and net carbon exchange from tundra." *Nature* 459(7246), 556–9. DOI: 10.1038/nature08031.

Scrieciu, S.Ş., Barker, T. and Ackerman, F. (2011). "Pushing the boundaries of climate economics: Critical issues to consider in climate policy analysis." *Ecological Economics*. DOI: 10.1016/j.ecolecon.2011.10.016.

Seierstad, I.A. and Bader, J. (2008). "Impact of a projected future Arctic sea ice reduction on extratropical storminess and the NAO." *Climate Dynamics* 33(7–8), 937–43. DOI: 10.1007/s00382–008–0463-x.

Seppälä, R., Buck, A. and Katila, P. (2009). *Adaptation of Forests and People to Climate Change – A Global Assessment Report.* IUFRO World Series Vol. 22. Helsinki: International Union of Forest Research Organizations. Available at www.iufro.org/download/file/4485/4496/Full_Report.pdf.

Serreze, M.C. (2011). "Climate change: Rethinking the sea-ice tipping point." *Nature* 471(7336), 47–8. DOI: 10.1038/471047a.

Shaffer, G. (2010). "Long-term effectiveness and consequences of carbon dioxide sequestration." *Nature Geoscience* 3(7), 464–7. DOI: 10.1038/ngeo896.

Shakhova, N., Semiletov, I., Salyuk, A. and Kosmach, D. (2008). "Anomalies of methane in the atmosphere over the East Siberian shelf: Is there any sign of methane leakage from shallow shelf hydrates?" *Geophysical Research Abstracts* 10, EGU2008–A–01526.

Shakhova, N., Semiletov, I., Salyuk, A., Yusupov, V., Kosmach, D. and Gustafsson, O. (2010). "Extensive methane venting to the atmosphere from sediments of the East Siberian Arctic Shelf." *Science* 327(5970), 1246–50. DOI: 10.1126/science.1182221.

Sheffield, P.E. and Landrigan, P.J. (2011). "Global climate change and children's health: Threats and strategies for prevention." *Environmental Health Perspectives* 119(3), 291–8. DOI: 10.1289/ehp. 1002233.

Shepherd, A., Wingham, D., Wallis, D., Giles, K., Laxon, S. and Sundal, A.V. (2010). "Recent loss of floating ice and the consequent sea level contribution." *Geophysical Research Letters* 37(L13503). DOI: 201010.1029/2010GL042496.

Shepherd, J., Caldeira, K., Cox, P. *et al.* (2009). *Geoengineering the Climate: Science, Governance and Uncertainty.* London: The Royal Society. Available at http://royalsociety.org/geoengineering-the-climate/.

Sherwood, S.C. and Huber, M. (2010). "An adaptability limit to climate change due to heat stress." *Proceedings of the National Academy of Sciences of the United States of America* 107(21), 9552–5. DOI: 10.1073/pnas.0913352107.

Shindell, D. and Faluvegi, G. (2009). "Climate response to regional radiative forcing during the twentieth century." *Nature Geoscience* 2(4), 294–300. DOI: 10.1038/ngeo473.

Shindell, D., Kuylenstierna, J.C.I., Vignati, E. *et al.* (2012). "Simultaneously mitigating near-term climate change and improving human health and food security." *Science* 335(6065), 183–9. DOI: 10.1126/science.1210026.

Simmonds, I. and Keay, K. (2009). "Extraordinary September Arctic sea ice reductions and their relationships with storm behavior over 1979–2008." *Geophysical Research Letters* 36(19). DOI: 10.1029/2009GL039810.

Slangen, A., Katsman, C., van de Wal, R., Vermeersen, L. and Riva, R. (2012). "Towards regional projections of twenty-first century sea-level change based on IPCC SRES scenarios." *Climate Dynamics* 38(5), 1191–1209. DOI: 10.1007/s00382–011–1057–6.

Smith, J. (1997). "Setting priorities for adapting to climate change." *Global Environmental Change* 7(3), 251–64. DOI: 10.1016/S0959–3780(97)00001–0.

Smith, J.B., Dickinson, T., Donahue, J.D.B., Burton, I., Haites, E., Klein, R.J.T. and Patwardhan, A. (2011). "Development and climate change adaptation funding: Coordination and integration." *Climate Policy* 11(3), 987. DOI: 10.1080/14693062.2011.582385.

Smith, J.B., Schneider, S.H., Oppenheimer, M. *et al.* (2009). "Assessing dangerous climate change through an update of the Intergovernmental Panel on Climate Change (IPCC) 'reasons for concern'." *Proceedings of the National Academy of Sciences of the United States of America* 106(11), 4133–7. DOI: 10.1073/pnas.0812355106.

Smith, P., Martino, D., Cai, Z. *et al.* (2007). "Policy and technological constraints to implementation of greenhouse gas mitigation options in agriculture." *Agriculture, Ecosystems & Environment* 118(1–4), 6–28. DOI: 10.1016/j.agee.2006.06.006.

Solomon, S., Daniel, J.S., Neely, R.R., Vernier, J.-P., Dutton, E.G. and Thomason, L.W. (2011). "The persistently variable 'background' stratospheric aerosol layer and global climate change." *Science* 333(6044), 866–70. DOI: 10.1126/science.1206027.

Solomon, S., Plattner, G.-K., Knutti, R. and Friedlingstein, P. (2009). "Irreversible climate change due to carbon dioxide emissions." *Proceedings of the National Academy of Sciences of the United States of America* 106(6), 1704–9. DOI: 10.1073/pnas.0812721106.

Sorooshian, A., Feingold, G., Lebsock, M.D., Jiang, H. and Stephens, G.L. (2009). "On the precipitation susceptibility of clouds to aerosol perturbations." *Geophysical Research Letters* 36(13). DOI: 10.1029/2009GL038993.

Sorrell, S. (2007). *The Rebound Effect: An Assessment of the Evidence for Economy-wide Energy Savings from Improved Energy Efficiency.* Report produced by the Sussex Energy Group for the Technology and Policy Assessment function of the UK Energy Research Centre. London. Available at www.ukerc.ac.uk/support/tiki-index.php?page=ReboundEffect.

Sorrell, S. (2009). "Jevons' Paradox revisited: The evidence for backfire from improved energy efficiency." *Energy Policy* 37(4), 1456–69. DOI: 10.1016/j.enpol.2008.12.003.

Spiegelhalter, D.J. and Riesch, H. (2011). "Don't know, can't know: embracing deeper uncertainties when analysing risks." *Philosophical Transactions of the Royal Society A: Mathematical, Physical and Engineering Sciences* 369(1956), 4730–50. DOI: 10.1098/rsta.2011.0163.

Stanton, E.A. (2011). "Negishi welfare weights in integrated assessment models: The mathematics of global inequality." *Climatic Change* 107(3–4), 417–32. DOI: 10.1007/s10584–010–9967–6.

Stanton, E.A. and Ackerman, F. (2009). "Climate and development economics: Balancing science, politics, and equity." *Natural Resources Forum* 33(4), 262–73. DOI: 10.1111/j.1477–8947.2009.01251.x.

Stanton, E.A. and Ackerman, F. (2010). *Emission Reduction, Interstate Equity, and the Price of Carbon.* Economics for Equity and the Environment report. Somerville, MA: Stockholm Environment Institute-U.S. Center. Available at http://sei-us.org/publications/id/327.

Stanton, E.A., Ackerman, F. and Kartha, S. (2009). "Inside the integrated assessment models: Four issues in climate economics." *Climate and Development* 1(2), 166–84. DOI: 10.3763/cdev.2009.0015.

Stanton, E.A., Davis, M. and Fencl, A. (2010). *Costing Climate Impacts and Adaptation: A Canadian Study on Coastal Zones.* Report commissioned by the National Round Table on the Environment and the Economy, Canada. Somerville, MA: Stockholm Environment Institute-U.S. Center. Available at http://sei-us.org/publications/id/409.

Steig, E.J., Schneider, D.P., Rutherford, S.D., Mann, M.E., Comiso, J.C. and Shindell, D.T. (2009). "Warming of the Antarctic ice-sheet surface since the 1957 International Geophysical Year." *Nature* 460(7256), 459–62. DOI: 10.1038/nature08286.

Steinhurst, W. and Sabodash, V. (2011). *The Jevons Paradox and Energy Efficiency: A Brief Overview of its Origins and Relevance to Utility Energy Efficiency Programs.* Prepared for the Southern Environmental Law Center. Cambridge, MA: Synapse Energy Economics Inc. Available at www.synapse-energy.com/Downloads/Synapse-Paper.2011–02.33.Jevons-Paradox-and-Energy-Efficiency.11–006.pdf.

Stern, N. (2006). *The Economics of Climate Change: The Stern Review.* Cambridge, UK: Cambridge University Press.

Stern, N. (2008). "The economics of climate change." *American Economic Review* 98(2), 1–37. DOI: 10.1257/aer.98.2.1.

Stern, N. (2009). *A Blueprint for a Safer Planet.* New York: Random House.

Sterner, T. and Persson, U.M. (2008). "An even sterner review: Introducing relative prices into the discounting debate." *Review of Environmental Economics and Policy* 2(1), 61–76. DOI: 10.1093/reep/rem024.

Stevens, B. and Feingold, G. (2009). "Untangling aerosol effects on clouds and precipitation in a buffered system." *Nature* 461(7264), 607–13. DOI: 10.1038/nature08281.

Strauss, B.H., Ziemlinski, R., Weiss, J.L. and Overpeck, J.T. (2012). "Tidally adjusted estimates of topographic vulnerability to sea level rise and flooding for the contiguous United States." *Environmental Research Letters* 7(1), 014033. DOI: 10.1088/1748–9326/7/1/014033.

Stroeve, J., Holland, M.M., Meier, W., Scambos, T. and Serreze, M. (2007). "Arctic sea ice decline: Faster than forecast." *Geophysical Research Letters* 34(9). DOI: 10.1029/2007GL029703.

Stroeve, J.C., Serreze, M.C., Holland, M.M., Kay, J.E., Malanik, J. and Barrett, A.P. (2011). "The Arctic's rapidly shrinking sea ice cover: a research synthesis." *Climatic Change* 110(3–4), 1005–27. DOI: 10.1007/s10584–011–0101–1.

Strong, A.L., Cullen, J.J. and Chisholm, S.W. (2009). "Ocean fertilization: Science, policy, and commerce." *Oceanography* 22(3), 236–61.

Su, Q. (2012). "A quantile regression analysis of the rebound effect: Evidence from the 2009 National Household Transportation Survey in the United States." *Energy Policy* 45, 368–77. DOI: 10.1016/j.enpol.2012.02.045.

Sumaila, U.R., Cheung, W.W.L., Lam, V.W.Y., Pauly, D. and Herrick, S. (2011). "Climate change impacts on the biophysics and economics of world fisheries." *Nature Climate Change* 1(9), 449–56. DOI: 10.1038/nclimate1301.

Summers, L. and Zeckhauser, R. (2008). "Policymaking for posterity." *Journal of Risk and Uncertainty* 37(2–3), 115–40. DOI: 10.1007/s11166–008–9052-y.

Swaine, M.D. and Grace, J. (2007). "Lianas may be favoured by low rainfall: Evidence from Ghana." *Plant Ecology* 192(2), 271–6. DOI: 10.1007/s11258–007–9319–4.

Szulczewski, M.L., MacMinn, C.W., Herzog, H.J. and Juanes, R. (2012). "Lifetime of carbon capture and storage as a climate-change mitigation technology." *Proceedings of the National Academy of Sciences* 109(14), 5185–9. DOI: 10.1073/pnas.1115347109.

Tagaris, E., Liao, K.-J., DeLucia, A.J., Deck, L., Amar, P. and Russell, A.G. (2009). "Potential impact of climate change on air pollution-related human health effects." *Environmental Science and Technology* 43(13), 4979–88.

Tarnocai, C., Canadell, J.G., Schuur, E.A.G., Kuhry, P., Mazhitova, G. and Zimov, S. (2009). "Soil organic carbon pools in the northern circumpolar permafrost region." *Global Biogeochemical Cycles* 23(2), GB2023. DOI: 10.1029/2008GB003327.

Taschetto, A.S., Ummenhofer, C.C., Sen Gupta, A. and England, M.H. (2009). "Effect of anomalous warming in the central Pacific on the Australian monsoon." *Geophysical Research Letters* 36(12). DOI: 10.1029/2009GL038416.

TEEB (2008). *The Economics of Ecosystems & Biodiversity: An Interim Report.* Bonn: European Commission and Federal Environment Ministry, Germany. Available at www.teebweb.org/LinkClick.aspx?fileticket=u2fMSQoWJf0%3d&tabid=1278&language=en-US.

Tewksbury, J.J., Huey, R.B. and Deutsch, C.A. (2008). "Putting the heat on tropical animals." *Science* 320(5881), 1296–7. DOI: 10.1126/science.1159328.

The World Bank (2006). "Clean energy and development: Towards an investment framework."

The World Bank (2010). *Economics of Adaptation to Climate Change: Synthesis Report.* Washington, DC. Available at http://beta.worldbank.org/sites/default/files/documents/EACCSynthesisReport.pdf.

The World Bank and United Nations (2010). *Natural Hazards, UnNatural Disasters: The Economics of Effective Prevention.* Washington, DC. Available at www.gfdrr.org/gfdrr/NHUD-home.

Thomas, S. (2012). "What will the Fukushima disaster change?" *Energy Policy* 45, 12–17. DOI: 10.1016/j.enpol.2012.02.010.

Thornton, P.E., Doney, S.C., Lindsay, K., *et al.* (2009). "Carbon-nitrogen interactions regulate climate-carbon cycle feedbacks: Results from an atmosphere-ocean general circulation model." *Biogeosciences* 6(10), 2099–2120. DOI: 10.5194/bg-6–2099–2009.

Tillett, T. (2011). "Climate change and children's health: Protecting and preparing our youngest." *Environmental Health Perspectives* 119(3), a132. DOI: 10.1289/ehp. 119-a132b.

Tilmes, S., Müller, R. and Salawitch, R. (2008). "The sensitivity of polar ozone depletion to proposed geoengineering schemes." *Science* 320(5880), 1201–4. DOI: 10.1126/science.1153966.

Tol, R.S.J. (2002). "Estimates of the damage costs of climate change, Part II. Dynamic estimates." *Environmental and Resource Economics* 21(2), 135–60. DOI: 10.1023/A:1014539414591.

Tol, R.S.J. (2003). "Is the uncertainty about climate change too large for expected cost–benefit analysis?" *Climatic Change* 56(3), 265–89. DOI: 10.1023/A:1021753906949.

Tol, R.S.J. and Yohe, G.W. (2006). "A review of the Stern Review." *World Economics* 7(4), 233–50.

Traeger, C.P. (2011). "Sustainability, limited substitutability, and non-constant social discount rates." *Journal of Environmental Economics and Management* 62(2), 215–28. DOI: 10.1016/j.jeem.2011.02.001.

Tsao, J.Y., Saunders, H.D., Creighton, J.R., Coltrin, M.E. and Simmons, J.A. (2010). "Solid-state lighting: An energy-economics perspective." *Journal of Physics D: Applied Physics* 43(35), 354001. DOI: 10.1088/0022-3727/43/35/354001.

Tubiello, F.N., Amthor, J.S., Boote, K.J. *et al.* (2007). "Crop response to elevated CO_2 and world food supply: A comment on 'Food for Thought ...' by Long *et al.*, Science 312:1918–1921, 2006." *European Journal of Agronomy* 26(3), 215–23. DOI: 10.1016/j.eja.2006.10.002.

Turley, C., Eby, M., Ridgwell, A.J. *et al.* (2010). "The societal challenge of ocean acidification." *Marine Pollution Bulletin* 60, 787–92. DOI: 10.1016/j.marpolbul.2010.05.006.

Turner, A.G. and Slingo, J.M. (2009). "Uncertainties in future projections of extreme precipitation in the Indian monsoon region." *Atmospheric Science Letters* 10(3), 152–8. DOI: 10.1002/asl.223.

Tyrrell, T. (2011). "Anthropogenic modification of the oceans." *Philosophical Transactions of the Royal Society A: Mathematical, Physical and Engineering Sciences* 369(1938), 887–908. DOI: 10.1098/rsta.2010.0334.

United Nations (1992). *United Nations Framework Convention on Climate Change.* Available at http://unfccc.int/essential_background/convention/items/2627.php.

United Nations Development Programme (2007). *Fighting Climate Change: Human Solidarity in a Divided World.* Human Development Report 2007/2008. New York: Palgrave Macmillan. Available at http://hdr.undp.org/en/reports/global/hdr2007-2008/.

United Nations Environment Programme (2010). *The Emissions Gap Report: Are the Copenhagen Accord Pledges Sufficient to Limit Global Warming to 2°C or 1.5°C?* Available at www.unep.org/publications/ebooks/emissionsgapreport/.

United Nations Environment Programme and World Meteorological Organization (2011). *Integrated Assessment of Black Carbon and Tropospheric Ozone: Summary for Decision Makers.* Bonn, Germany. Available at www.unep.org/dewa/Portals/67/pdf/Black-Carbon_SDM.pdf.

United Nations Framework Convention on Climate Change (2007). *Investment and Financial Flows to Address Climate Change.* Available at www.undp.org.tr/publicationsDocuments/Investment%20and%20Financial%20Flows%20to%20Address%20Climate%20Change.pdf.

United Nations Framework Convention on Climate Change (2008). *Investment and Financial Flows to Address Climate Change: An Update.* FCCC/TP/2008/7. Available at http://unfccc.int/resource/docs/2008/tp/07.pdf.

UN-REDD Programme (n.d.). *About REDD+.* United Nations Collaborative Programme on Reducing Emissions from Deforestation and Forest Degradation in Developing Countries. Available at www.un-redd.org/AboutREDD/tabid/582/Default.aspx [accessed February 24, 2011].

Usher, W. and Strachan, N. (2012). "Critical mid-term uncertainties in long-term decarbonisation pathways." *Energy Policy* 41, 433–44. DOI: 10.1016/j.enpol.2011.11.004.

Vafeidis, A.T., Nicholls, R.J., McFadden, L. *et al.* (2008). "A new global coastal database for impact and vulnerability analysis to sea-level rise." *Journal of Coastal Research* 244, 917–24. DOI: 10.2112/06–0725.1.

Van Den Broeke, M., Bamber, J., Ettema, J. *et al.* (2009). "Partitioning recent Greenland mass loss." *Science* 326(5955), 984–6. DOI: 10.1126/science.1178176.

van Groenigen, K.J., Osenberg, C.W. and Hungate, B.A. (2011). "Increased soil emissions of potent greenhouse gases under increased atmospheric CO_2." *Nature* 475(7355), 214–16. DOI: 10.1038/nature10176.

van Mantgem, P.J., Stephenson, N.L., Byrne, J.C. *et al.* (2009). "Widespread increase of tree mortality rates in the Western United States." *Science* 323(5913), 521–4. DOI: 10.1126/science.1165000.

van Vuuren, D.P., Isaac, M., den Elzen, M.G.J., Stehfest, E. and van Vliet, J. (2010). "Low stabilization scenarios and implications for major world regions from an integrated assessment perspective." *Energy Journal* 31(Special Issue 1), 165–92.

Vaughan, N.E. and Lenton, T.M. (2011). "A review of climate geoengineering proposals." *Climatic Change* 109(3–4), 745–90. DOI: 10.1007/s10584–011–0027–7.

Vaughan, N.E., Lenton, T.M. and Shepherd, J.G. (2009). "Climate change mitigation: Trade-offs between delay and strength of action required." *Climatic Change* 96(1–2), 29–43. DOI: 10.1007/s10584–009–9573–7.

Vavrus, S., Waliser, D., Schweiger, A. and Francis, J. (2008). "Simulations of 20th and 21st century Arctic cloud amount in the global climate models assessed in the IPCC AR4." *Climate Dynamics* 33(7–8), 1099–1115. DOI: 10.1007/s00382–008–0475–6.

Velicogna, I. (2009). "Increasing rates of ice mass loss from the Greenland and Antarctic ice sheets revealed by GRACE." *Geophysical Research Letters* 36(19). DOI: 10.1029/2009GL040222.

Vermeer, M. and Rahmstorf, S. (2009). "Global sea level linked to global temperature." *Proceedings of the National Academy of Sciences* 106(51), 21527–21532. DOI: 10.1073/pnas.0907765106.

Veron, J.E.N., Hoegh-Guldberg, O., Lenton, T.M. *et al.* (2009). "The coral reef crisis: The critical importance of <350 ppm CO_2." *Marine Pollution Bulletin* 58(10), 1428–36. DOI: 10.1016/j.marpolbul.2009.09.009.

Vielle, M. and Viguier, L. (2007). "On the climate change effects of high oil prices." *Energy Policy* 35(2), 844–9. DOI: 10.1016/j.enpol.2006.03.022.

Volodin, E.M. (2008). "Methane cycle in the INM RAS climate model." *Izvestiya, Atmospheric and Oceanic Physics* 44(2), 153–9. DOI: 10.1134/S0001433808020023.

Vona, F. and Patriarca, F. (2011). "Income inequality and the development of environmental technologies." *Ecological Economics* 70(11), 2201–13. DOI: 10.1016/j.ecolecon.2011.06.027.

Wallack, J.S. and Ramanathan, V. (2009). "The other climate changers." *Foreign Affairs* 5(88), 105–13.

Walther, G.R. (2010). "Community and ecosystem responses to recent climate change." *Philosophical Transactions of the Royal Society B: Biological Sciences* 365(1549), 2019–24. DOI: 10.1098/rstb.2010.0021.

Wang, C. and Lee, S.-K. (2008). "Global warming and United States landfalling hurricanes." *Geophysical Research Letters* 35(2). DOI: 10.1029/2007GL032396.

Wang, C. and Lee, S.-K. (2009). "Reply to comment by Joseph J. Barsugli on 'Global warming and United States landfalling hurricanes'." *Geophysical Research Letters* 36(1). DOI: 10.1029/2008GL035111.

Wang, C., Kim, D., Ekman, A.M.L., Barth, M.C. and Rasch, P.J. (2009). "Impact of anthropogenic aerosols on Indian summer monsoon." *Geophysical Research Letters* 36(L21704). DOI: 10.1029/2009GL040114.

Wang, J., Wang, E., Luo, Q. and Kirby, M. (2009). "Modelling the sensitivity of wheat growth and water balance to climate change in Southeast Australia." *Climatic Change* 96(1–2), 79–96. DOI: 10.1007/s10584–009–9599-x.

Wang, R., Wu, L. and Wang, C. (2011). "Typhoon track changes associated with global warming." *Journal of Climate* 24(14), 3748–52. DOI: 10.1175/JCLI-D-11–00074.1.

Warren, R. (2011). "The role of interactions in a world implementing adaptation and mitigation solutions to climate change." *Philosophical Transactions of the Royal Society A: Mathematical, Physical and Engineering Sciences* 369(1934), 217–41. DOI: 10.1098/rsta.2010.0271.

Warren, R., Arnell, N., Berry, P. *et al.* (2009). *Review of Literature Subsequent to IPCC AR4.* Work Stream 1, Deliverable 2, Report 1 of the AVOID Programme (AV/WS1/ D2/R01). London: Tyndall Centre and Met Office Hadley Centre. Available at www. metoffice.gov.uk/avoid/files/resources-researchers/AVOID_WS1_D2_01_20090725. pdf.

Warren, R., Price, J., Fischlin, A., Nava Santos, S. and Midgley, G. (2010). "Increasing impacts of climate change upon ecosystems with increasing global mean temperature rise." *Climatic Change* 106(2), 141–77. DOI: 10.1007/s10584–010–9923–5.

Watkiss, P. and Downing, T.E. (2008). "The social cost of carbon: Valuation estimates and their use in UK policy." *Integrated Assessment Journal* 8(1), 85–105.

Webster, M., Jakobovits, L. and Norton, J. (2008). "Learning about climate change and implications for near-term policy." *Climatic Change* 89(1–2), 67–85. DOI: 10.1007/ s10584–008–9406–0.

Weiss, J.L., Overpeck, J.T. and Strauss, B. (2011). "Implications of recent sea level rise science for low-elevation areas in coastal cities of the conterminous U.S.A." *Climatic Change* 105(3–4), 635–45. DOI: 10.1007/s10584–011–0024-x.

Weiss, M., Junginger, M., Patel, M.K. and Blok, K. (2010). "A review of experience curve analyses for energy demand technologies." *Technological Forecasting and Social Change* 77(3), 411–28. DOI: 10.1016/j.techfore.2009.10.009.

Weitzman, M.L. (1998). "Why the far-distant future should be discounted at its lowest possible rate." *Journal of Environmental Economics and Management* 36(3), 201–8. DOI: 10.1006/jeem.1998.1052.

Weitzman, M.L. (2007a). "A review of the Stern Review on the Economics of Climate Change." *Journal of Economic Literature* 45(3), 703–24. DOI: 10.1257/jel.45.3.703.

Weitzman, M.L. (2007b). "Subjective expectations and asset-return puzzles." *American Economic Review* 97(4), 1102–30. DOI: 10.1257/aer.97.4.1102.

Weitzman, M.L. (2009). "On modeling and interpreting the economics of catastrophic climate change." *The Review of Economics and Statistics* 91(1), 1–19. DOI: 10.1162/ rest.91.1.1.

Weitzman, M.L. (2010a). *GHG Targets as Insurance Against Catastrophic Climate Damages.* NBER Working Paper No. 16136. Cambridge, MA: National Bureau of Economic Research. Available at www.nber.org/papers/w16136.

Weitzman, M.L. (2010b). "Risk-adjusted gamma discounting." *Journal of Environmental Economics and Management* 60(1), 1–13. DOI: 10.1016/j.jeem.2010.03.002.

Weitzman, M.L. (2011). "Revisiting fat-tailed uncertainty in the economics of climate change." *Review of Environmental Economics and Policy* Symposium on Fat Tails (forthcoming).

Wenger, S.J., Isaak, D.J., Luce, C.H. *et al.* (2011). "Flow regime, temperature, and biotic interactions drive differential declines of trout species under climate change." *Proceedings of the National Academy of Sciences* 108(34), 14175–80. DOI: 10.1073/pnas.1103097108.

Westerling, A.L., Hidalgo, H.G., Cayan, D.R. and Swetnam, T.W. (2006). "Warming and earlier spring increase Western U.S. forest wildfire activity." *Science* 313(5789), 940–43. DOI: 10.1126/science.1128834.

Weyant, J.P., de la Chesnaye, F.C. and Blanford, G.J. (2006). "Overview of EMF-21: Multigas mitigation and climate policy." *The Energy Journal* (special issue: EMF 21 Multi-Greenhouse Gas Mitigation and Climate Policy, published by the Energy Modeling Forum), 3–32.

WGBU [German Advisory Council on Global Change] (2009). *Solving the Climate Dilemma: The Budget Approach.* Special Report. Berlin. Available at www.wbgu.de/fileadmin/templates/dateien/veroeffentlichungen/sondergutachten/sn2009/wbgu_sn2009_en.pdf.

Wigley, T.M.L. (2005). "The climate change commitment." *Science* 307(5716), 1766–9. DOI: 10.1126/science.1103934.

Wilby, R.L. and Dessai, S. (2010). "Robust adaptation to climate change." *Weather* 65(7), 180–85. DOI: 10.1002/wea.543.

Wilkinson, C. and Souter, D., eds. (2008). *Status of Caribbean Coral Reefs After Bleaching and Hurricanes in 2005.* Townsville, Australia: Global Coral Reef Monitoring Network and Reef and Rainforest Research Centre. Available at http://coris.noaa.gov/activities/caribbean_rpt/SCRBH2005_rpt.pdf.

Williams, J.H., DeBenedictis, A., Ghanadan, R. *et al.* (2011). "The technology path to deep greenhouse gas emissions cuts by 2050: The pivotal role of electricity." *Science* 335(6064), 53–9. DOI: 10.1126/science.1208365.

Williams, K.D., Ingram, W.J. and Gregory, J.M. (2008). "Time variation of effective climate sensitivity in GCMs." *Journal of Climate* 21(19), 5076–90. DOI: 10.1175/2008JCLI2371.1.

Wilson, S.G. and Fischetti, T.R. (2010). *Coastline Population Trends in the United States: 1960 to 2008.* P25–1139. U.S. Census Bureau. Available at www.census.gov/prod/2010pubs/p25-1139.pdf.

Wood, P.J. (2011). "Climate change and game theory." *Annals of the New York Academy of Sciences* 1219(1), 153–70. DOI: 10.1111/j.1749–6632.2010.05891.x.

World Resources Institute (2000). "Map: Population distribution within 100 km of coastlines." *Earth Trends: The Environmental Information Portal.* Available at http://earthtrends.wri.org/text/population-health/map-196.html.

World Resources Institute (2012). "Climate Analysis Indicators Tool." *CAIT 8.0.* http://cait.wri.org/.

Wright, S.J., Muller-Landau, H.C. and Schipper, J. (2009). "The future of tropical species on a warmer planet." *Conservation Biology* 23(6), 1418–26. DOI: 10.1111/j.1523–1739.2009.01337.x.

Wu, L. and Wang, B. (2008). "What has changed the proportion of intense hurricanes in the last 30 years?" *Journal of Climate* 21(6), 1432–9. DOI: 10.1175/2007JCLI1715.1.

Wu, S.-Y., Najjar, R. and Siewert, J. (2008). "Potential impacts of sea-level rise on the Mid- and Upper-Atlantic Region of the United States." *Climatic Change* 95(1–2), 121–38. DOI: 10.1007/s10584–008–9522-x.

Xiong, W., Conway, D., Lin, E. and Holman, I. (2009). "Potential impacts of climate change and climate variability on China's rice yield and production." *Climate Research* 40(1), 23–35. DOI: 10.3354/cr00802.

Xiong, W., Lin, E., Ju, H. and Xu, Y. (2007). "Climate change and critical thresholds in China's food security." *Climatic Change* 81(2), 205–21. DOI: 10.1007/s10584-006-9123-5.

Xu, B., Cao, J., Hansen, J. *et al.* (2009). "Black soot and the survival of Tibetan glaciers." *Proceedings of the National Academy of Sciences* 106(52), 22114–18. DOI: 10.1073/pnas.0910444106.

Yacoub, S., Kotit, S. and Yacoub, M.H. (2011). "Disease appearance and evolution against a background of climate change and reduced resources." *Philosophical Transactions of the Royal Society A: Mathematical, Physical and Engineering Sciences* 369(1942), 1719–29. DOI: 10.1098/rsta.2011.0013.

Yin, J., Schlesinger, M.E. and Stouffer, R.J. (2009). "Model projections of rapid sea-level rise on the northeast coast of the United States." *Nature Geoscience* 2(4), 262–6. DOI: 10.1038/ngeo462.

Yohe, G.W. (2006). "Some thoughts on the damage estimates presented in the Stern Review." *Integrated Assessment Journal* 6(3), 65–72.

Yohe, G.W. and Tol, R.S.J. (2007). *Precaution and a Dismal Theorem: Implications for Climate Policy and Climate Research.* Working Paper FNU-145. Hamburg: Hamburg University and Centre for Marine and Atmospheric Science. Available at https://www.fnu.zmaw.de/fileadmin/fnu-files/publication/working-papers/dismaltheoremwp.pdf.

Yu, J. and Wang, Y. (2009). "Response of tropical cyclone potential intensity over the north Indian Ocean to global warming." *Geophysical Research Letters* 36(3). DOI: 10.1029/2008GL036742.

Zaehle, S., Friedlingstein, P. and Friend, A.D. (2010). "Terrestrial nitrogen feedbacks may accelerate future climate change." *Geophysical Research Letters* 37(1). DOI: 10.1029/2009GL041345.

Zaliapin, I. and Ghil, M. (2010). "Another look at climate sensitivity." *Nonlinear Processes in Geophysics* 17(2), 113–22. DOI: 10.5194/npg-17-113-2010.

Zarzycki, C.M. and Bond, T.C. (2010). "How much can the vertical distribution of black carbon affect its global direct radiative forcing?" *Geophysical Research Letters* 37(20). DOI: 10.1029/2010GL044555.

Zeng, N. and Yoon, J. (2009). "Expansion of the world's deserts due to vegetation-albedo feedback under global warming." *Geophysical Research Letters* 36(L17401). DOI: 10.1029/2009GL039699.

Zhang, R. and Delworth, T.L. (2009). "A new method for attributing climate variations over the Atlantic Hurricane Basin's main development region." *Geophysical Research Letters* 36(6). DOI: 10.1029/2009GL037260.

Zickfeld, K., Levermann, A., Morgan, M.G., Kuhlbrodt, T., Rahmstorf, S. and Keith, D.W. (2007). "Expert judgements on the response of the Atlantic meridional overturning circulation to climate change." *Climatic Change* 82(3–4), 235–65. DOI: 10.1007/s10584-007-9246-3.

Ziska, L., Knowlton, K., Rogers, C. *et al.* (2011). "Recent warming by latitude associated with increased length of ragweed pollen season in central North America." *Proceedings of the National Academy of Sciences* 108(10), 4248–51. DOI: 10.1073/pnas.1014107108.

Index

Page numbers in *italics* denote tables.

Taylor & Francis

eBooks

FOR LIBRARIES

ORDER YOUR FREE 30 DAY INSTITUTIONAL TRIAL TODAY!

Over 23,000 eBook titles in the Humanities, Social Sciences, STM and Law from some of the world's leading imprints.

Choose from a range of subject packages or create your own!

Benefits for **you**

▶ Free MARC records

▶ COUNTER-compliant usage statistics

▶ Flexible purchase and pricing options

Benefits for your **user**

▶ Off-site, anytime access via Athens or referring URL

▶ Print or copy pages or chapters

▶ Full content search

▶ Bookmark, highlight and annotate text

▶ Access to thousands of pages of quality research at the click of a button

For more information, pricing enquiries or to order a free trial, contact your local online sales team.

UK and Rest of World: **online.sales@tandf.co.uk**

US, Canada and Latin America: **e-reference@taylorandfrancis.com**

www.ebooksubscriptions.com

ALPSP Award for BEST eBOOK PUBLISHER 2009 Finalist

Taylor & Francis eBooks
Taylor & Francis Group

A flexible and dynamic resource for teaching, learning and research.